AN
UNLIKELY CHEMISTRY

S. Krishnaswamy is a well-known documentary and television film-maker. He is a recipient of many coveted awards, including the Padma Shri by the Government of India; Life Time Achievement Award from the US International Film and Video Festival, Los Angeles; Honor Summus Award from the Watumull Foundation, Hawaii, among many other awards. He co-authored the book *Indian Film* with Erik Barnouw.

In Praise of the Author

'The uniqueness of my old friend Krishnaswamy's effort is that from day one he had an objective before him. He did not go into film-making for money-making; he made those films which were historically important, culturally significant, leaving a message for the nation.'

—*I.K. Gujral, former prime minister*

'Krishnaswamy's *Indus Valley to Indira Gandhi* was the first ever well-documented movie (on history) made in a fashion in which all of us could see and benefit from it. That was a great service rendered and I think that kind of a thinking "out of the box" and before the time comes, are the kind of things India has always been proud of.'

—*Defence Minister Nirmala Sitharaman*

'I would say Krishnaswamy and his family are modern yogis. I will not hesitate in calling him a "yogi" because Swami Vivekananda wanted such people who are devoted to their nation, their culture—with that passion—that is the mark of a yogi.'

—*Swami Atmaghanananda, Ramakrishna Math*

'It is said that if you want to create history, write something worth reading or do something worth writing about. Krishnaswamy has done both... I recommend that his documentaries be prescribed for students for them to know the greatness of this country.'

—*Justice Ramasubramaniam, Judge, Madras High Court*

'In Mahabharata, there is a verse: "Where there is Dharma, there is Sri Krishna; Where there is Krishna, there is victory". I would like to say, "Where there is Dharma, there is Krishnaswamy; Where there is Krishnaswamy, there is victory".'

—*Swami Abhiramananda, Ramakrishna Mission*

'One of the things about the work of Krishnaswamy is that he is not superficial. He took on an astonishing variety of topics, big issues spanning the economic, social, political, cultural, aesthetic and literary dimensions... I salute the independence and integrity of this man of creative distinction.'

—*N. Ram, Chairman,* The Hindu *Group of Publications and former Editor-in-Chief,* The Hindu

AN
UNLIKELY
CHEMISTRY
Autobiography of a Couple

S. KRISHNASWAMY

RUPA

Published by
Rupa Publications India Pvt. Ltd 2018
7/16, Ansari Road, Daryaganj
New Delhi 110002

Sales Centres:

Allahabad Bengaluru Chennai
Hyderabad Jaipur Kathmandu
Kolkata Mumbai

Copyright © S. Krishnaswamy 2018

The views and opinions expressed in this book are the author's own and the facts are as reported by him which have been verified to the extent possible, and the publishers are not in any way liable for the same.

While every effort has been made to trace copyright holders and obtain permission, this has not been possible in all cases; any omissions brought to our attention will be remedied in future editions.

All rights reserved.
No part of this publication may be reproduced, transmitted, or stored in a retrieval system, in any form or by any means, electronic, mechanical, photocopying, recording or otherwise, without the prior permission of the publisher.

ISBN: 978-81-291-4915-2

First impression 2018

10 9 8 7 6 5 4 3 2 1

The moral right of the author has been asserted.

Printed by Parksons Graphics Pvt. Ltd.

This book is sold subject to the condition that it shall not, by way of trade or otherwise, be lent, resold, hired out, or otherwise circulated, without the publisher's prior consent, in any form of binding or cover other than that in which it is published.

In the revered memory of
Meenakshi Subrahmanyam
and
Mangalam Balachandran

Contents

Foreword   *ix*

1. Curtain Raiser   1
2. Before We Met   10
3. Mother's Choice   101
4. The Myth of My Film on Indira Gandhi   126
5. A Non-Political Woman's Political Biography   157
6. An Ambivalent Transition   174
7. Y2K   227
8. Sojourns in Search   252
9. If the Angel Returned   280

Annexures   299

Acknowledgements   353

Foreword

At first glance, the award-winning pioneer documentary-film-maker S. Krishnaswamy's book does not readily fit into any familiar genre. It then, gradually, unfolds as a narrative mosaic, which is at once the biography of a young scientist, who despite her brilliant academic record had to give up her passion for research in Ayurveda because of extraneous reasons; the narration of some socio-political events of the last half a century; analytical essays on mass media and politics; a profound philosophical analysis of the Indian psyche; besides an essay on love and relationships. Indeed, it is a tribute to the author that such an amalgam has been crafted to be so very readable.

Krishnaswamy says in the book that as a teenager he learnt magic tricks to entertain children and that he practises the hobby even today, whenever there are children around. His book is also a magic box from which he pulls out a rainbow of emotions, patriotism, art, world view, history and humour—all based on life, wedded to truth.

The author quotes Valmiki's shloka that his Ramayana is as much Sita's story as that of Rama; and in that tradition, Krishnaswamy has chosen to call his book Mohana's biography, while it is also his autobiography. Yes! It is a biography of Mohana, the author's spouse, whose progress as a scientist was hindered by political policies when she was on the threshold of international acclaim. After she won the Hari Om Ashram's

National Award for research in Ayurveda; after her visit to China as a guest of the Institute of Medicinal Plant Development (IMPLAD) in Beijing; and after such other recognitions, her interest migrated to media and she collaborated with her husband, giving up her passionate pursuit of research in Ayurveda.

And then to the author's own story: he recalls that the screening of a skewed, satirical American documentary on India, when he was a student of Mass Media at Columbia University, New York, in 1960, strongly motivated him to make films on the tapestry of India's rich heritage; and this passion became his avocation.

A decade after his return to India, amidst many obstacles—financial and emotional—the author made his marathon four-hour film which traced 5,000 years of history and heritage titled, *Indus Valley to Indira Gandhi*, spanning the millennia. It became the first Indian film acquired by a Hollywood company, Warner Brothers. Ironically, it also became a subject of controversy as it was grossly misunderstood as a film on Indira Gandhi and the Emergency she had declared, just as the film was getting released. L.K. Advani, who soon became the minister for information and broadcasting, when the Janata Party was voted to power, admired the film a lot, albeit he hated its title.

As a documentary-film-maker, the author narrates with sensitivity his interactions with heads of state and icons of religion and gives eyewitness accounts of dramatic events.

As co-author of the pioneering book on Indian films, published by Columbia University Press and later by Oxford University Press, he light-heartedly recounts his interactions with some major stars and veterans of Indian cinema.

His narration of court cases the Krishnaswamy couple faced against their interpretation of history in a TV serial (due to the politics of regional parties) throw light on many facets of the history of Tamil Nadu in the twentieth century. The couple came out in flying colours in all judgments of the high court, upholding their interpretation of history.

The book vividly unfolds the experience of the Krishnaswamys in their effort to make a series of films on the impact of ancient Indian culture in Southeast Asia. This chapter is inspiring, while revealing an aspect of Indian heritage not adequately explored by historians. The dedication and devotion to the cause of making these films, the many trials and tribulations during the production, including their getting caught in a major earthquake while filming in Indonesia, adds to the adventurous interludes of the book.

The book illustrates with examples of how the TV serials created by the Krishnaswamys are born from a genuine concern for society and its values, proving that excellence has its own rewards of popularity, without catering to the lower denominators of the tastes of an audience.

In terms of personal relationships, the book reveals Krishnaswamy's reverence for his mother, without losing his independent views, and his admiration for his father who swam against the colonial current, making films promoting the freedom struggle in the 1930s and 1940s as vivid images at one level, while at another, the mutual respect and love between him and his wife show their tender humane faces in their journey of life together.

About a hundred photographs and a few collages, add to the kaleidoscopic nature of the book, creating an interesting mosaic for reading.

How the couple—attracted over the decades by the unique spiritual path of Swami Vivekananda—became ardent initiated disciples of the revered Swami Gautamananda, Adhyaksha of the Ramakrishna Math, is narrated with experiential fervour.

The concluding chapters of the book are as political as they are deeply personal. Having remained academic and politically non-aligned for decades, the Krishnaswamys began to identify the Bharatiya Janata Party (BJP) as the emerging hope for India from the 1990s. The author also fervently hopes that India becomes the torchbearer of a new order of the world.

Krishnaswamy's academic paper read at the Washington Institute for Values, USA, on 'Culture as Political Phenomena', reproduced in the Annexure of the book, highlights the philosophical profile of the author. There are also valuable articles on Ayurveda by Mohana and how she has continued her interest in the science of Ayurveda even after her moving away from formal research.

One may or may not agree with everything in the wide spectrum of the author's views, but I have no hesitation in saying that this book is 'essential reading' to understand modern India.

M.S. Swaminathan
Chennai, 2017

Curtain Raiser

I am writing the biography of the person dearest to me—my wife. History is not merely about kings and their wars. We should know the story of people at large—not necessarily only those of politicians or film stars. How else can we relate to the lives of people influenced by the socio-political milieu, beyond their control?

I should introduce Mohana and me briefly, before you begin to explore this book. Apart from being wife and husband for forty-eight years at the time of writing this, we have also been working together for about thirty years—she as the producer, and I as the writer-director of a few hundred documentary films, and over a dozen TV serials, some of which have got us national and international awards and recognition. Perhaps, an extract from her speech about me, when the President of India conferred on me the Padma Shri award in May 2009, would throw some light. Several of our friends joined and hosted a dinner to celebrate this, and a dozen celebrities felicitated me for the honour. Rather unusually, the organizers invited Mohana also to speak about me. I take the liberty of quoting from the video footage of that speech, to introduce who we both are.

> I hated history as a subject in school, and considered studying it as a whole waste of time. My concentration on science was such that I got the university gold medal in chemistry in the BSc exams and the university second

Mohana and Krishnaswamy

rank in MSc (biochemistry). When I was completing my PhD as a scientist, in 1976, Babu—as we call my husband at home—was completing his marathon film *Indus Valley to Indira Gandhi*. I began to slowly develop an interest in history. Then I continued my postdoctoral research in Ayurveda at a central government laboratory. International journals published my twenty-odd research papers and I was invited to deliver guest lectures in China and the US.

At that time, in the early 1980s, three things happened

simultaneously. The first was the government policy of reservations, which hindered my progress as a scientist, with many roadblocks to serious research, the details of which are beyond the scope of this evening's meeting. The second was my own enthusiasm for arts, having learnt classical dance and Hindustani music, with intrinsic involvement in Hindi literature, which had made me a part-time participant in the activities of my husband's company—Krishnaswamy Associates. The third was my family situation—my husband was polygamous; his first wife was 'documentary films', and the second was 'Indian history and heritage'; I got the third place. Instead of fighting with the other two with jealousy, I began to make friends with them. Yes! Babu's enthusiasm for history as well as media was just contagious, to say the least. I gradually became a friend of both history and media. Hence, when circumstances due to national policy made me drift away from science, the driving seat of Krishnaswamy Associates, as head of the company, came to me on a platter.

Hypothetically, if my husband was making commercially oriented, escapist feature films, conflicting with sensitive social interest, I would have rejected this offer and preferred to remain a homemaker, when I had to give up science for reasons beyond my control. On the other hand, if my husband was a get-rich-quick businessman, offering me even the throne of an empire, I am sure I would have quietly walked away from the scene. But here is a man who quenched my intellectual and creative thirst, strong in his convictions that his work should be a fresh breeze to enrich culture, enliven society and enlighten people. I began to tread his path.

I respect and admire Krishnaswamy not because

he is my husband, but because: he is an idealist who has succeeded in his uncompromising ways, with integrity and social responsibility; he is a man with gender sensitivity, who respects women; 'means' are as important to him as 'ends'. Commenting on his *Indus Valley to Indira Gandhi*, Professor James Beverege of UNESCO said, 'It is very boldly conceived and most ably executed. But the miracle is that the producer survived it.' The 'miracle' is valid for almost everything that Babu has done, and I stand witness to that reality. I salute him for his vision, his values, and his versatility. I am not talking to blow our own trumpets. I mean to highlight the fact that one can achieve reasonable material success without ever compromising one's basic values.

In forty-eight years of matrimony (perhaps more appropriately described as grihasthasrama—a Sanskrit term which extends beyond what is implied by its English equivalent), we have had our share of love, passion, quarrel, perceptual agreement and differences on issues related to family, profession, as well as macro-level ideas about our country and the world at large gradually graduating in our mental make-up (though not in a ritually recognized fashion) to vanaprastha– a Sanskrit term which is often erroneously understood as 'running away' to the forests.

My theme in this book is how a woman who was very near her goal (with international recognition from her peers) of being a committed 'scientist' changed track and became a media person—not out of her own volition, but due to the sociopolitical ethos of India in the twentieth century, related to a history that goes back millennia. Any real story is of value to the next generation. So is this. It is a story of deprivation and disillusionment to start with, and the story of a struggle leading to success—not only in professional terms, but often in emotional terms of coming to grips with our relationship that sometimes soured with a 'need to understand', which is an understatement. For, 'research in biochemistry' was not just a career for her, but a 'spiritual quest'. God gave her the strength to continue her quest for truth, though not in her originally chosen path as a scientist. But God is a tough taskmaster. It did not happen overnight.

No two human beings reach a 'perfect understanding' of each other. We are no exception. Marriage gives you the opportunity for such understanding to a great extent, but it is for the couple to grab the opportunity and succeed in building a genuine relationship. After all, if you truly 'know' just one person, you would actually know God! The most difficult thing is to know 'oneself'. Next only to knowing oneself is to know any one other person. Why not your spouse?

On my part, when I tried to reach such an understanding, she did not reciprocate. In all fairness, on many occasions, when she tried to understand, I did not cooperate. But neither of us gave up. She has been generous to say that I have contributed more to the success of the relationship. If there is any truth in that, it is perhaps because I am ten years older, and I often treat her as an innocent child, but never undermining her innate brilliance. Both my mother and her mother contributed to bridging any emotional strains in the first decade of our marriage. Mohana can never forget my mother affectionately telling her, 'My son doesn't only love you. He respects you.'

Kavyam Ramayanam kritsnam sitayah charitam mahat,
paulastya vadam iti aivam chakara charita vratah
—Valmiki Ramayana

Valmiki says that 'he has named Sita's sublime epic legend as Ramayana, besides narrating the slaying of Ravana'. Thus, in Maharishi Valmiki's own words, the Ramayana is also known as

'Sitayah Charitam Mahat'—the noble story of Sita. As Sita's story is intertwined with that of Rama, my narrative here is as much my autobiography as the biography of my wife.

Four Days after Free India's First Birthday

Mohana was born in Ranchi (then in Bihar, now the capital of the state of Jharkhand) as the tenth and youngest child of Mangalam and her husband, S. Balachandra Iyer, on 19 August 1948—four days after India celebrated the first anniversary of independence from the British Empire. Her eldest brother, Mani, and eldest sister, Janaki, were more than two decades older than her.

Mohana's father was born in 1899 at Siddhamalli village near Kumbakonam in Tanjore (now Thanjavur) district of Tamil Nadu (then Madras Presidency). His father, a Vedic scholar, passed away when he was very young. His mother, with his cooperative uncles, educated Balachandran; but as ill luck would have it, she too died when he was twelve and still in school. By then, he had got a merit

Mohana in school

scholarship and with affectionate uncles and aunts to support him, he pursued college education, securing his BA degree. He married Mangalam, Mohana's mother, when he was still a student at St Joseph's College, Tiruchy. He was nineteen and she was eleven. Soon after graduation, he became a government accountant and after serving for some time in Bangalore (now Bengaluru) and Madras (now Chennai), he was promoted and posted in Ranchi.

With six brothers and three sisters—all elder to her—Mohana was indeed pampered not only by her parents, but also by all her siblings. Mangalam (who became a grandmother within a year after Mohana was born) was so possessive of this child that she organized tuition for her at home, without sending her to school till she directly joined Class V. Educated in the Hindi heartland, she picked up not only conversational Hindi, but also developed a keen interest in Hindi literature. She shared this interest with two of her three sisters.

In the meantime, Balachandran got promoted and transferred to Hyderabad. Mohana was admitted to a Marwari school, where she learnt Hindi and a little Marathi, while picking up conversational Telugu and a smattering of Urdu. She became a teachers' pet as she always got the first or second rank in any subject. Concurrently, she joined a local dance school and began to learn Bharatanatyam. Exuberant, innocent, friendly and an extrovert, with an affectionate family and friends, she had no concept of what 'sorrow' or even 'worry' could be, save what she saw in the 'tragedies' of popular Hindi cinema. Although she was interested in dancing and singing, her dream was to become a medical doctor or a pure scientist. Her desire to pursue science and medicine was not influenced by idea of pursuing a career may be financially lucrative and profitable, but by an intrinsic love to serve fellow human beings as a doctor or be a scientist to formulate medicines that may cure thousands of sick people. One thing in which she had no interest at all was 'politics' in the widest sense of the term. She was not aware in the least that individual lives, aspirations and dreams can be redirected, trivialized, if not shattered by socio-political policies in vogue. She chose to follow an alternate path that was available to her because the man she married happened to be in media, and she was anyway interested in the arts as a hobby.

Seven Years after the Salt March

I share my date of birth—29 July—with one of India's great industrialists, J.R.D. Tata, although I was born in 1938, several years later than him. India was in the midst of a unique struggle—the only non-violent war in world history—led by a saintly politician, a Mahatma by name M.K. Gandhi, who believed that 'Means are as important as ends'. Seven years before I was born, his march to the salt pan to pick up a handful of salt became a milestone in history.

Among the millions under the spell of the Mahatma was my father, K. Subrahmanyam, a young lawyer-turned-film-maker. He used the nascent medium in his hand to inculcate the spirit of nationalism and the freedom struggle in his Tamil audience; to fight obscurantist notions

Meenakshi Subrahmanyam

of inequality such as caste; to empower a new generation of women and propagate such other ideals that were dear to his icon—the Mahatma. The world was preoccupied with the worst war in human history. Let's hope there won't be anything worse in future, which lead to another Hiroshima and Nagasaki.

K. Subrahmanyam

I was born the seventh child (and third son) to Meenakshi, a musician and lyricist in Sanskrit and Tamil, who had at the age of eight received mantra deeksha (spiritual initiation) as a srividya upaasaka from a saintly visitor to her grandparents' home. She grew up as an ardent devotee of Chandrasekarendra Saraswati, Sankaracharya of Kanchi. I was born when my father was at the pinnacle of success in his career, creativity and mass popularity. I have sometimes wondered whether I have a psychic relationship with my father's film *Thyagabhoomi*, which was under production when I was in my mother's womb. Haven't we heard of such a relationship between twins?

We move on to the story.

Before We Met

Born on 20 April 1904, in Papanasam near Kumbakonam in Thanjavur district, my father was the eldest son of a prominent advocate, C.S. Krishnaswamy Iyer. His mother, Vengalakshmi, passed away soon after her second son, Viswanathan, was born. 'CSK', as my grandfather was known, never married again, playing the role of father and mother to raise his two sons. Subrahmanyam grew up as a multifaceted talented young man and joined the Government Arts College, Kumbakonam to pursue his BA degree.[1] My mother, Meenakshi, was born to S. Natesa Iyer, a journalist who worked for the *Free Press Journal* in Bombay (now Mumbai) and was associated with Annie Besant in Chennai. My grandmother, also named Meenakshi, delivered a child when she was hardly fourteen and passed away three days after the delivery. Her parents Rao Bahadur K.S. Venkatrama Iyer and Visalakshi named their grandchild Meenakshi treating her as the replacement of their daughter, Meenakshi; and brought her up without her

---

[1]There are two biographies of my father: Valampuri Somanathan's book தமிழ்ப்பட உலகின் தந்தை டைரக்டர் கே. சுப்ரமணியம் in Tamil (Father of the Tamil Film World), and Professor M.R. Rangarajan's *Director K. Subrahmanyam—A Biography* in English. I have also made a biographical documentary in English with extracts from his important films titled *He Swam Against the Colonial Current—Director K. Subrahmanyam*, produced for the Public Service Broadcasting Trust, New Delhi. Krishnaswamy Associates has made a Tamil documentary *Tirai Ulaga Thanthai* with extracts from his films, which is available on *www.indianimprints.com*.

knowing for a long time that she was their grandchild and not their daughter.

My mother was born on 11 September 1911. When she was about eight years of age, Rao Bahadur and his wife started looking for a marital alliance. CSK was also looking for a bride for his elder son, Subrahmanyam, who was a student at the Kumbakonam College.

Rao Bahadur visited the college as a chief guest for an occasion, got to know the youngster, and made up his mind to make him his grandson-in-law. My father was sixteen and my mother was nine years old when their marriage was celebrated on a grand scale in Nagapattinam, a small port town with its history going back centuries.

It was within two years of the Jallianwala Bagh massacre, and Mahatma Gandhi was launching his first non-cooperation movement across the country. Subrahmanyam became a member of the Indian National Congress—a membership he retained till 1947, when soon after independence Mahatma Gandhi advised the dissolution of the Indian National Congress stating that it had served its objective and that new political parties should get space to come to power in the newly independent nation.

Back to the 1920s! Subrahmanyam studied law and enrolled as an advocate assisting his grandfather-in-law, Venkatrama Iyer. Although he was a successful lawyer, his interest was in the arts, in particular in the new medium of cinema. Venkatrama Iyer advanced finance to a company called Associated Pictures appointing Mumbai-trained Raja Sandow as director of the silent movies the company produced. Subrahmanyam wrote a couple of stories for these films on contemporary themes as against the convention of that period to make films of folklore or mythology. Although this company was initially successful, it closed down along with hundreds of such companies when silent cinema became talkies in India.

In 1934, Subrahmanyam was called upon by a new film producer to direct a feature film for him. And he never looked back. He established his own production company. His company made several commercially successful films. Many of them were popular, and known for their social significance, reflecting nationalist aspirations far ahead of their time. The high watermark of his creativity as a film-maker, *Thyagabhoomi*, was banned by the British a few weeks after its release, since it provoked enormous nationalist aspirations among its audience although the thrust of the story was more on women's empowerment. My father had also founded a film production studio in partnership with some friends, which he sold later. It was renamed Gemini Studio, which produced some major blockbusters of Indian cinema.

I am referring to Subrahmanyam by name when I deal with his professional accomplishments, political views, contributions to the arts, and social commitment to cinema. When I talk about him as a person, I take the role of his son. Psychologists believe that a man holds his father as a role model, if not as an omnipotent force when the father protects the child. As the child grows up to be a young man, the omnipotent image suffers and the son may begin to see the human side of his father including his strengths and weaknesses, capacity and incapacity. In my case, however, I began to adore my father as a hero more after I reached the age of twenty and beyond, than during my boyhood, because I developed the faculty to understand what a great human being he was.

At the height of success and fame, in 1937, my father built a palatial house at Santhome High Road, Chennai, within a short distance from the historic Santhome Cathedral. With 10,000 square feet of built area, the house was in a corner of about 2 acres of land, with a flower garden and fountain in front of the house, a lawn that could accommodate five hundred guests for tea on one side, and a kitchen garden-cum-banana plantation in the rear. In houses of that vintage, there were no attached bathrooms. A set of bathrooms were all placed at the rear of the house. There was a spacious kitchen attached to the dining hall which could accommodate about sixty people at a time. There were fifty-sixty people at lunch or dinner including family members and guests almost every day. During mealtimes, everybody squatted on a wooden plank on the floor. Apart from a bedroom for my parents, there were two dormitory kind of rooms which all of us children shared. There were separate visitors' rooms for my mother and father in addition to the common living/drawing room. I was born in my mother's room in this bungalow. It was common for women to deliver babies at home without getting admitted into a nursing home. Nurses and midwives besides the gynaecologist were all present and I met D'Silva, the nurse who handled me first when I was born, described me as a 'fat little fellow'. She was one of my mother's best friends, spending all her spare time with her.

Mendelism

After studying the nursery classes in the St Thomas Convent School which was round the corner from our home, I had to be shifted since boys were not allowed in that school beyond Class I. It was a time when schools canvassed with parents to admit their children in their school. A few years earlier, my father's friend, Mr Sharma, and his German wife had started a new school called Children Garden School on Edward Elliot Road (now, Dr Radhakrishnan Salai). They persuaded my father to send me to their school. I remember studying there for two years: Class II and Class IV. There was a system called 'double promotion' by which children who got the first two ranks could skip one grade and go to the next. So I never studied Class III. When I finished my Class IV, the headmaster of the Besant Theosophical School in Adyar made a courtesy call on my father. My father had been his student in Papanasam and the grand old man wanted to have the distinction of teaching his student's child. And so for my Class V, I was shifted to Besant Theosophical School (which functioned in a campus adjacent to the Theosophical Society—where the Krishnamurti Foundation School functions now).

I was one of the few students in the school who lived outside the Adyar area and we were all picked up by a school vehicle and dropped back in our homes in the evening. Our classes started at 7 a.m. For the summer vacation after Class V, I visited my mother's grandmother in Nagapattinam.

My brother Ramanan (Ramanu), who was three years elder to me was in school there, since my parents felt that at least one child should stay with the old lady (great grand mother). There were several things that attracted me to Nagapattinam including the fact that I had my brother to play with. Like all grandmothers, my great-grandmother was an expert in spoiling the two of us. I liked the idea of riding a bullock cart to the school when my father had nine cars in his compound varying in size from a

The author and his elder brother Ramanan c.a. 1942

Baby Austin to a bus, not counting the vehicles given to his office staff. But there was a certain charm in our cart driver, Venkatapathy, taking us around the small town and so I decided to stay back. Although my mother strongly resisted this first, she yielded to my tears and I spent the next six years there—the first four years with my brother and the following two years just with my great-grandmother after Ramanan joined college in Chennai.

Our whole family had a very unusual habit. We called our mother by her pet name, 'Patta', while we called our great-grandmother 'Amma'. Within months of my joining the National High School, Nagapattinam, India's independence was declared and the nation was given the status of a dominion of the British Commonwealth. Three years later, India would become a republic, but continuing as a member of the Commonwealth the word 'British' was dropped.

Unlike the common women of that era, Visalakshi, my great-grandmother was an erudite scholar in Tamil and Sanskrit. She had a habit of reading some chapters of the Valmiki Ramayana every day along with its Tamil translation. She performed her pooja for one hour every morning and read the Ramayana at night. She was gradually losing her eyesight and felt very sad that she was unable to read. She was delighted when I volunteered to read for her. And so for the next two years, I read Valmiki with the Tamil translation aloud to her, besides other scriptures. She had a library of about a hundred books, from which she would choose what I should read in a given week. My tuition teacher, Ramamurthy Iyer, would start the day teaching the school lessons at 7 a.m. and I concluded my day by reading scriptures for my great-grandmother between 7 p.m. and 8 p.m. I developed an interest, which I thought I would not be able to pursue after I shift to college in Chennai. I wanted to learn rudimentary chanting of the Vedas. Amma was delighted. She called in a priest. I learnt to recite some of the basic hymns, such as *Purusha Suktam* and *Sri Suktam*. Before that the upanayanam (sacred thread) celebration was conducted when both Ramanan and I were initiated. Ramanan was fifteen and I was twelve. While my father performed the role of the guru to initiate my brother, my eldest sister Lalitha's husband, Krishnamurti, performed the role of the guru for me. In those six years, when I visited my parents only for the two holiday seasons—in summer and during Christmas—I began to see the gradual decline in the level of prosperity at home in Chennai.

Venkatrama Iyer was not only famous as a criminal lawyer but also as the chairman of the Nagapattinam Municipality contributing significantly to the small town to such an extent that although he died a year before I was born, the teachers in the National High School would introduce me as 'the greatgrandson of the municipal chairman who brought piped water supply to the town'.

In the first decade of the twentieth century, Rao Bahadur had a grouse against his wife, Visalakshi, that she gave him only a daughter. It was a popular superstition that a man without a son would end up in hell even if he had harmed none in his lifetime. It was common for men—tormented by the thought of torture in hell—to take a second wife to have a son. Venkatrama Iyer married Parvathavardini, who was thirty years younger, and built a house for her in the midst of his agricultural farm, which was a one-hour ride by bullock cart from Nagapattinam. Parvathavardini alias Kunjammal (affectionately called Chinnamma), however, was not blessed with any child at all. Visalakshi had accepted life with stoic tolerance.

In the last few years of his life, Rao Bahadur decided to adopt a boy and asked my father whether he would give his son in adoption. At that point in time, my eldest brother was the only son of my parents while they had three daughters. Although my father's relatives staunchly opposed the idea, my parents jointly agreed to accept the old man's request and their son, Balakrishnan (Balu for short), aged about five, was adopted by the old couple and naturally inherited Rao Bahadur's wealth after he passed away in 1937. All of us children loved and respected the two great-grandmothers.

As a student in Nagapattinam, once in a couple of weeks I visited the village in our own bullock cart to spend time with Chinnamma and also visit my brother Balu's farmhouse located near her house, which was managed by an agent on his behalf. I came to know the different varieties of paddy and their cultivation methods, got friendly with the farm labourers and supervized the bookkeeping, on behalf of Balu.

Every year when my father visited us for a couple of days, there was joy in the village although he was not the legal landlord. When my brother Ramanan and I had our upanayanam celebrations and got formally initiated with the Gayatri Mantra, my father took us to the village the very next day and organized a grand common lunch for us with the Dalit (in old parlance Harijan or untouchable) workers. He was a practising Gandhian. During our visit to Chennai after the upanayanam, he introduced us to a venerable old man, Kanagalingam. Staunch followers of the poet Subramania Bharati would remember him. Bharati believed in the value of Brahminism, but he refused to recognize that a Brahmin was one born in a Brahmin family. Like Swami Vivekananda, Bharati believed that varna was based on a man's quality. Kanagalingam was born a Dalit. The poet had performed brahmopadesam and given him the sacred thread.

Gradually, my grandmother's health was failing. In 1953, I joined Vivekananda College in Chennai. The education pattern at that time was eleven years in school before joining college, two years in the intermediate class in college, and two years more for getting a bachelor's degree.

Lamarckism

There were many threads in my thought process as a teenager—the ritual orthodoxy of my mother, the rudimentary Vedic training under my great-grandmother's supervision, the broad Gandhian and humanitarian approach of my father. I admired my father for his world vision, societal contribution and the extraordinary affection that he showered on anybody who came in contact with him. But I was tormented by the fact that he had not been fair to my mother. How could such a great man develop an interest in another woman? The other woman in his life was S.D. Subbalakshmi, a film star introduced by him, who became an icon for the Tamil filmgoer from 1934 for over a decade. The issue bothered me as a teenager.

But when my mother had forgiven him, I realized that it was not anybody's right to raise questions. I avoided being judgemental. S.D. Subbalakshmi (SDS) or Uffa, as my siblings

The author's father (performing a role in one of his films) with his second wife S.D. Subbalakshmi

and I called her, tried her best to endear herself to all of us, children, with remarkable success. My mother apparently spent several years in tears when we were little kids. But she learnt not to merely tolerate but accept the reality. In later years, I had clashes with my mother at the level of ideas without affecting our love for each other at any time. The differences were limited to her orthodoxy.

Visalakshi passed away in Nagapattinam within a few months of my shifting to Chennai to join college. Although biologically she was my mother's grandmother, my mother had never seen her own mother, and we treated Visalakshi as a grandmother.

I realized that my father's financial status was going down badly for a variety of reasons. Even in the first decade after independence, the Congress party was losing several stalwarts who had fought for freedom. My father was hand-picked by the Soviet Union to visit the USSR in 1951. He was among the half a dozen film personalities from West Bengal, Mumbai and Chennai who were invited. Having belonged to the socialist group within the Congress party, he was deeply impressed by the progress of the Soviet Union. Bending towards the left without becoming a member of the Communist Party, he was one of the founders of the Indo-Soviet Cultural Society of which he was the vice president at the national level. The film industry had been undergoing a transformation in the post Second World War era. A pioneer like him could not adjust to new changes which were largely influenced by the influx of unaccounted money into film-making. Having grown up as a nationalist, it was not in his DNA to adopt any means other than those 100 per cent legal and fair. The following extract from *Indian Film*[2] explains the economic changes which impacted the Indian film industry.

---

[2]*Indian Film* is a book co-authored by the author and Prof. Erik Barnouw.

The year 1940 brought to India a spurt in industrial activity. Iron and steel production was expanding. Indian factories, in spite of the war boycott by the [Indian] National Congress, were making field guns, machine guns, bombs, depth charges, and ammunition for British and Allied forces in various parts of the world. Increased employment put extra money in circulation. The motion picture theatres were crowded. A drift from rural areas to city factories augmented the boom. Meanwhile, the industrial growth also brought shortages and a black market in essential items such as steel, cement, cotton, foods (similar to that of First World War). Anticipation of rising prices brought speculation. When rice prices shot up, fortunes were made by the rice speculators. Thus, the bulging funds in circulation included not only the wages of industrial workers but also various kinds of illicit profit. The new money that became available to the film industry included black market money.

A problem for the black marketeer was that his profits could not be openly reinvested. Therefore, offers made to film stars in the early 1940s included a device that was apparently new to the film world. The star would receive a one-film contract calling for payment of ₹20,000. In actuality, he would receive ₹50,000, but the additional ₹30,000 would be in cash, without any written record. To the star this extra sum, this payment 'in black', was, of course, tax-free—the star's delight—and coincided neatly with the investor's interest in off-the-record investment.

Not surprisingly, the 'black payment' system soon spread, though on a smaller scale, to other key figures such as music directors—considered, after the stars, as the most important elements in box-office success. To receive part of one's salary 'in black' was a badge of distinction. The rumour that this or that star received 75 per cent of his salary 'in black' and only 25 per cent 'in white' came to be heard frequently in trade circles, and contributed to the star's prestige and bargaining power.

As the industry became more and more fragmented into small production units, which more often than not dissolved after one production, to be replaced by others, the film industry became an increasingly attractive investment opportunity for black marketeers.

A year after my father's visit to the Soviet Union, the Motion Picture Producers' Association of America invited about a dozen Indian film personalities to Hollywood. My father was the only person from Tamil Nadu and also the only person from the previous year's delegation to the USSR, who was included in this one to America. His trips to both the Soviet Union and to America happened when I was in school. The Directors' Guild of America gave him an award for his contribution to Indian cinema, while Walt Disney honoured him with a 'Key of Friendship'—a beautiful memento designed by Disney himself.[3]

---

[3] My father told his friends at the South Indian Film Chamber of Commerce (SIFCC), which he had co-founded fifteen years earlier, that the international honours he had received as an individual film-maker were to be treated as meant for the South Indian film industry. During his visit to the Soviet Union, the immensely popular comedy pair of Tamil cinema N.S. Krishnan and T.A. Madhuram had also been members of the same delegation. The Russians made a two-hour documentary film on the visit of that Indian delegation. The Russians gifted the 'rights' of that documentary for the territory of South India jointly to my father and Krishnan. They, in turn, donated those rights to the SIFCC. The film was commercially released and the proceeds (as per the donors' wishes) became a part of the film chamber's seed money to buy a plot of land to construct their own building. My father also gifted to the chamber the priceless mementos he had received in Hollywood so as to be displayed in the chamber. Several

Addressing a large students' gathering, my father said, 'Unlike Asia and Europe, America is like a baby-in-arms. Indeed, they have grown rich. Try and give expensive toys in the hands of a little child without supervision, and you may well find them broken in no time. American society is likely to break down. And unfortunately, that may affect human civilization as a whole.'

All this had an indelible impact on my teenage mind. My mental roller-coaster ride started. Once I entered college, my favourite author was Bertrand Russell. I saw immense logic in the philosophical argument that 'God' was a figment of our imagination; that faith in God was born out of man's insecurity. From reciting Vedic hymns and reading the Ramayana every day, I was gradually transformed into an agnostic. In particular, three titles of Bertrand Russell made a great impact on me— *Conquest of Happiness, In Praise of Idleness,* and *Why I Am Not a Christian?*

For about twenty years, I had made a habit of giving a copy of *A Conquest of Happiness* as my standard gift to anybody who was getting married, or was celebrating a birthday. In later years, however, several of Russell's original concepts had been either borrowed or had influenced other writers and were indirectly penetrating society in large measure. In my opinion, the first prize will go to *In Praise of Idleness*. I can never forget his description of Jesus Christ as a young man in modern times carrying his manuscript titled *The Bible* to try and get it published and how it is rejected by one publisher after another. One of them says, 'Abridge it, young man, and cut short chapters like

---

years later, when I wanted to take a look at the Russian film as well as the award of the Directors' Guild of America and Walt Disney's Key of Friendship given to my father, the office bearers of the SIFCC could not trace any of them. Six decades later, a new set of office bearers honoured my father's memory by installing his bronze bust in the foyer of its building.

Genesis. Who has got time to read all these?' Perhaps, Russell's most famous book is *Why I Am Not a Christian?*, but I could not appreciate its details because I was not that familiar with Christian literature. Suffice it to say that by the time I spent two years in Vivekananda College, in spite of the fact that it was run by the Ramakrishna Mission, the major influence on me was agnosticism. This influence of Bertrand Russell was reinforced by several Marxist friends, who visited my father, including stalwarts of the Communist Party like P. Ramamurthi (PR as he was popularly known).

Many years later, PR told me, 'Well, I had almost convinced your father that he should join our party. But the stumbling block was his faith in God.' C. Subramaniam (CS), then union minister (duly christened in later decades as the Father of India's Green Revolution), instantly intervened saying, 'Indeed! God saved your father.' Although they were political rivals, PR and CS were great friends—and that was possible in the political culture of that era.

My father dreamt of India's ideal society as being a combination of the economic austerity and redistribution of wealth followed by the USSR on the one hand, with the social and political free institutions of Western democracy on the other—but rooted in the Indian ethos of spirituality.

At this juncture, I moved from Vivekananda College to Presidency College, Chennai, one of the oldest colleges of India to pursue my undergraduate degree in physics.

In 1956, the Madras Film Society organized a seminar on South Indian cinema. Besides getting film industry leaders to participate in the seminar, they asked the students' union of two colleges to send representatives to speak. I represented our union. Several leading producers, directors and actors participated in the event. The image of the film industry had taken a bad beating in the years since independence. Most films of the 1950s had retrograde values in general with male chauvinist titles like *Kanavanae Kan Kanda Deivam* (Husband Is The Living God) glorifying the enslaved status of women. This was in sharp contrast to the idealism of the films of the 1930s and 1940s by people like my father and B.N. Reddy. My father tapped me on my shoulder and said, 'Look, you and I are scheduled to talk in the same session. The organizers were not aware that Presidency College would send you to represent their union.' For a moment, I thought I would withdraw from speaking and go away under some pretence, but I realized that it would be cowardly to run away.

I was too preoccupied gathering my thoughts to speak and manage the situation of disagreeing with some of my father's comments. There was an element of bravado combined with nervousness. I started analysing how post-independence Tamil cinema was insipid, ephemeral, and gender insensitive. A rather harsh statement that I made remains etched in my memory. I said, 'As long as the audience is attracted to film stars in the

Swami Chinmayananda visits Krishnaswamy Associates in 1987, to preview some documentaries

manner of watching animals in the zoo with curiosity, it is okay! But if the admiration grows beyond that, making them political icons, it would be a socially catastrophic situation. I hope such gloom doesn't descend on Tamil Nadu.' (I would make a more sober statement today.)

Within a few months of joining Presidency College, my father's secretary, Padmanabhan alias Pappan, insisted that I should accompany him to Swami Chinmayananda's discourses on the Bhagavad Gita. Rather reluctantly, but as a measure of pleasing Pappan, I accompanied him. This became the period of my second transformation. Chinmayananda was a great orator and guru, who could explain the most difficult concepts of Vedanta and the Bhagavad Gita in simple terms. Without my raising questions, he very often answered the doubts of an agnostic. Although I began hearing him reluctantly, I found myself hypnotized by this remarkable swamiji. Perhaps, the phase when I questioned the existence of God was important to later understand life in depth and not remain a dumb and blind believer. I sought private audience with the swamiji a few times and in response to my mother's invitation, he also visited us at home to bless the family.

Within six months of my arrival in Chennai to join college, we had to vacate the palatial house in which I was born. While on the one side my father was not as shrewd a businessman as he was a creative person, on the other, some of his so-called close friends and relatives defrauded him by chicanery. My father was abroad when all of us had to vacate the house. He knew that it was happening but he was helpless. He gave instructions mainly to my two elder brothers.

We found a rented house in Gandhi Nagar, Adyar, which was an independent bungalow, hardly 20 per cent in size of what we were used to living in at Santhome. To ensure that my mother's spirit was not sagging, all of us children tried our best

Gang of six in a car journey across India

to brave the situation. By that time, my two elder sisters, Lalitha and Bama, were married. My mother had lost one child much before I was born and so we were four sons and two daughters who shifted to the new small house. I recall how my brother Ramanu and I were the last two to leave the old compound in a Baby Austin Tourer car with my brother driving. Narrating it without melodrama, as we came out of the gate, we saw a few relatives heckling at us. Such irksome moments can trigger very negative reactions, but fortunately for us, they merely triggered the challenge to succeed. A major principle in life was getting formed in my mind—'Forgive, but never forget.' I learnt over the years that if you don't forgive, you carry the negative baggage and it hurts. At the same time, if you forget, you would not know how to face such a situation again. Remembering is a part of the learning process and forgiving is a part of the cleansing process.

Even as I was studying BSc Physics, I enrolled in a course leading to a diploma of the British Institute of Radio Engineers, London. Soon after getting my BSc degree, to gain practical experience, my father sent me to an audio recording studio as an apprentice, for six months. I had the ambition to study abroad. Despite the financial strain, my father offered to send Ramanu to the USSR and me to America for further studies. I jumped and accepted the proposal, while my brother didn't.

A gentleman working in Gemini Studios offered unsolicited advice to my father suggesting that the RCA Institute in downtown Manhattan was probably the best place I should go to as he was an alumnus of that institute. It was an era in which information about courses abroad was not so easily available. I got admission in the RCA Institute. Although the application to obtain foreign exchange to study abroad was to be submitted to the Reserve Bank of India (RBI), Chennai, some papers had to be referred to Delhi. The trains to Delhi were fully booked for a few weeks, and so my brothers took a snap decision that they would accompany me to Delhi by driving all the way. We left the very next day, equipped with road maps. Balu and Ramanu along with Pappan joined me in a small Fiat. Hearing about this marathon round trip of about 4,000 km, M.G. Ramachandran (the matinee idol, MGR) graciously offered to lend his personal driver. As we were ready to leave, T.K. Balachandran (film actor who later turned a producer) joined us on this journey of Bharat darshan.

The six of us crammed ourselves into that small car for such a long journey. We travelled about 400 km a day, had no advance planning, spent nights in small hotels and reached Delhi in four days. At a different level, it was an extraordinarily revealing experience. Filthy and poor habitations (unfit even for cattle) in which people were living in most northern parts of India shocked me. We made brief stops for sightseeing of monuments and landscapes. There were only a few hours of work in Delhi with regard to my foreign exchange application. It had become more or less an excuse for the youthful group to take a holiday across the country.

We drove further to Haridwar and Rishikesh. We had a darshan of Swami Sivananda at Rishikesh, and a customary dip in the Ganga. For me, the lasting images that fortnight were those of the emaciated men and women virtually struggling for existence against the elements of nature. The ground reality of our country was in sharp contrast to the high levels of metaphysical thinking reflected in our ancient literature. Without exaggeration, sometimes I shed tears.

From left: (sitting) Ramanu, Swami Sivananda and Pappan; (standing) the author (in glasses) and the driver

As an Alien

On 29 July 1960, my twenty-second birthday, I received my first passport. Within a few days thereafter, I got the US students' visa, the RBI permit for foreign exchange and my Air India ticket for Chennai–New York via Mumbai with stopovers of about a week each in Paris and London. I had never visited Mumbai or Calcutta (now Kolkata). Virtually, the first metro city larger than Chennai, which I saw was Paris.

Malcolm Adiseshiah was the deputy director general of UNESCO. I knew him from my boyhood, as he was my father's friend. His wife, Elizabeth, showered affection on me. The Adiseshiahs felt that they should introduce me to the West under their 'parental' guidance. The first thing they gave me was a culture shock by taking me to a striptease show in a restaurant. Elizabeth said, 'You will be exposed to all this when you are away from home in New York. It is better that you get introduced when two guardians are with you.' Malcolm was an internationally reputed economist and educationist.

I visited Notre Dame Cathedral and the Chartres Cathedral and was deeply moved by their inspiring aesthetics epitomizing the European Renaissance. 'I get the same spiritually elevating experience here which I receive in Tirupathi or Thanjavur,' I wrote to my mother from the Cathedral—something which she remembered all her life.

After a week in Paris, I landed in London. One week later when I reported at Heathrow for my flight to New York, after checking in—in that era without computers, bookings were done manually—the airline counter officials realized that the flight was overbooked. Eighteen passengers with confirmed tickets had no seats. I was on that list, but my luggage had been loaded in the aircraft, although I did not get my boarding pass. The angry passengers used abusive language against the Air India traffic staff. I expressed sympathy for the counter staff since they were facing the heat for somebody else's fault in the system, and requested to explain what alternative arrangements they were making. Air India started sending the stranded passengers by different airlines across the Atlantic such as TWA and British Airways. In appreciation of my cooperating with the airline staff, they gave me a first class seat in Alitalia against my economy ticket. My first experience of flying was from Chennai to Mumbai by a propeller aircraft called Skymaster; I got a Boeing 707 from Mumbai to Paris and Paris to London. That was one of the first jet aircraft acquired by Air India. And then I experienced flying first class for the long haul.

I stayed for two days in International House facing the river next to the riverside church. Cherukapalli Nehru, a geologist from Andhra Pradesh, suggested that it would be more economical if I shared a small apartment with a fellow student. We both looked around and fixed up one at 120th Street diagonally opposite Columbia University. The landlady, Francisca Thorn, was very considerate at a time when most other landladies preferred only white men to occupy their rooms. We got two adjacent rooms in her apartment. But she permitted us the liberal use of her kitchen, so we could cook Indian dishes twice or thrice a week.

I walked a lot across Manhattan, for two reasons: first, as the best way to understand the new city; second, to conserve the valuable foreign exchange by not spending on transport. I did what a normal tourist would do. I went to the top of the Empire State Building; I took a circle tour boat around the island. I attended shows at the Radio City Music Hall and more conventional theatre in Broadway. Then came the crucial day, when I had to join the RCA Institute. It was a good institute by reputation. But it was for people trained at the level of a polytechnic. My fellow students there had mostly completed their high school and I was the only graduate. After attending classes for four days, I met the director and despite many other people telling otherwise, I found him a friendly middle-aged person. I showed my bachelor's degree and said, 'Please forgive me, sir, after attending a few classes, I think I am overqualified to be a student here.'

He sympathized with me and asked, 'Do you plan to go back?'

'No. I will look for an alternative course to take me on to a master's degree,' I said.

He said, 'Best of luck! Go and try and don't worry about the tuition fees you sent from India. I will organize full refund.' I perceived a genuinely liberal, generous face of America. I visited New York University, the City University as well as Columbia University. I found the media curriculum at Columbia University most fascinating. It dealt with both theoretical and practical aspects of media from the psychology of communication to the aesthetics and technology of film-making, besides world history of media, covering also advertising and public relations. There was a strong segment on the societal impact of media and the responsibility of media persons.

The deadline to apply for admission was about seventy-two hours away. And I was told that the process would take at least ten days. A lady at the admissions office saw the disappointment on my face and gave a tip: 'If you manage to meet the head of the department, there is perhaps a chance.' I dashed to the department and managed to meet him.

An Anchor

That meeting with Professor Erik Barnouw changed several things for me. He very sincerely asked me, 'Why did you come to New York to learn technology and then change to creative communications?'

I explained my background and present plight. I was armed

with something else too. In my spare time in India, after my graduation, I had written a forty-page article titled 'A Thesis on Expression'. It dealt with human communications and mass media outlining the relationship between visuals, music and words, and I handed it to him, introducing myself also as the son of one of India's film pioneers. He took my article and made me wait for fifteen minutes for him to browse through it.

He called me back and said, 'I can admit you without delay on one condition. I have discretionary authority to take anybody as a "Special Student". You will enjoy all the privileges and classes as any regular student but this does not lead you to a formal degree of the university. Will that be okay for you?'

I instantly replied, 'Yes! I plan to be a self-employed professional. I may not need a degree, generally required only to apply for a job.'

He set the ball rolling. The admissions office, however, pointed out that the visa stamp on my passport mentioned the RCA Institute as the place of study. It was important that I get it changed. So I rushed to the immigration authorities. I met an officer, who rudely asked, 'If you fellows come to this country to become doctors, you can't change your school to become engineers. No!'

I convinced him by showing him the syllabus of the RCA Institute and

Professor Erik Barnouw

Columbia University—both mentioning 'TV', implying these two were the same. He was satisfied, although there was an ocean of a difference between the two. He casually put the stamp on it and changed the entry and returned the passport to me. I rushed back to the university and paid my fees for admission in a photo finish. Of course, it was possible to pay the fees because the RCA Institute had refunded the money to me.

As a 'Special Student', besides attending courses in which I had enrolled, such as TV and documentary production, history of cinema, script writing, and psychology of communications, I had the privilege of being able to attend even classes unrelated to the courses for which I was enrolled, and so I attended classes in ancient Greek theatre, which had influenced modern theatre in Europe. My colleagues in the class, in the main course, ranged from those who were of my age to those in their forties, fifties and a few in the sixties. It is common in American society that people work for some time after taking an undergraduate degree, and then join a master's degree course in the subject of their choice. That was very new to me since in India there was an age bar beyond which you could not join a class.

Three of my colleagues became my special friends: Bob Lowe, who taught modern art in the university, was attending our class to understand the relationship between painting and cinema; and then there were Barbara Tillman, a Jewish girl, and Marie Hayes, a devout Catholic—both about five years elder to me. During the first semester, there were unforgettable incidents that seem more like fiction than reality from this distance in time.

Bob Lowe wanted to shift his residence from the village in downtown Manhattan to a building closer to Columbia University. We both wandered around looking for packers and movers to shift his furniture and artiefacts. Bob found the process was too expensive. As we were walking near a used-cars showroom, I noticed a very spacious van with its price displayed as $99. I told Bob, 'Look, why don't you buy this?' He said, 'Are you crazy? It will go to the junk yard in another week's time.' I said, 'I am serious. Buy this vehicle, use it for 4–5 days for shifting your materials, and then junk it. It would still be only a fraction of the cost that the packers and movers are demanding.' Bob took the vehicle for a trial, struck a deal with the showroom and we came out with the car. We did several rounds of moving his furniture, and it was the last consignment of goods we were transporting around two o'clock one night. We had loaded all the belongings into the car. Bob got into the driving seat and I was about to get in by his side, when two policemen stopped us, refusing to let the car go. Neither of us had carried our ID cards. Bob was in an artiste's outfit with colours strewn from his paint brush all over. I was in a tracksuit. The cops did a thorough inspection of the materials loaded into the vehicle and after some cross-examination, they let us go but insisted that we present ourselves at the police station by nine o'clock in the morning—some seven hours from the time they stopped us. Bob dropped me to my apartment and went home. I got up around nine o'clock and as per habit switched on the TV for the morning news. Was I shocked! The building from which we were shifting was the main visual related to the headlines. There was a murder at midnight in one of those apartments, and the police were looking for suspects. I got frightened and informed Bob immediately. We both rushed to the police station and presented our credentials. Fortunately by that time the police had a clue. Later that day, they arrested the suspect.

During my college days in Chennai, Professor Jayasekar, a young highly talented magician, had become a good friend of mine. I learnt a bit from him and magic became my hobby. My interest never went beyond exploring small tricks to entertain children, and card magic to keep adults wondering. Bob had very pretty twin daughters who were about five years old and I endeared myself to them with my little tricks.

Another significant event with Bob concerned my irreverence towards and mockery of modern art. Years later, I changed my attitude and began to appreciate some kinds of abstract art. But as a student at that age, I just laughed at it as meaningless brushstrokes. Picasso, in particular, and modern art, in general, were topics of controversy debated with strong feelings on both sides. There were those who believed that the so-called 'modern art' was just a deception with neither meaning nor beauty. Equally strong was the view that traditional realistic artworks like landscapes, portraits, etc., were dumb and that the genius of an artiste blossomed truly in the modern art form. Bob belonged to the latter group, passionately advocating abstract art. We had debated modern art off and on in class and outside. Of course, the classic defence of the modern art form is that it does not have to have a verbal meaning.

It should be remembered that this was the age of the manual typewriter. As students, we were all preparing our term papers by typing them ourselves. Towards the end of my years in New York, I acquired a portable electric typewriter. One morning on a holiday, I was typing a script for a short film. I found I had run out of carbon paper to keep a copy for myself as the original would go to the professor. I suspended typing and walked up to the nearby stationery shop and bought carbon paper in half a dozen colours. I don't quite remember why I needed all those colours. When I started typing again, by mistake I crumpled a new red carbon sheet, instead of the old one to be thrown. The copy developed very interesting thin lines created by the crumpled paper. Fascinated by this art form, I crumpled one sheet from each of the colour carbon papers and rolled them all through the typewriter to create a mosaic of multicoloured lines in one sheet of paper. I carefully drew a border like a frame and titled the work as 'Rhythm of Silence'. I followed it with some more originals with the same technique titled 'Colours of Melody' and 'Shades of Harmony'. Proudly in possession of the three creations of fun, I walked up to Bob's apartment, which was only a few blocks away. With a very serious face I told him, 'You know, Bob, I have created three pieces of modern art.'

An obviously elated Bob said, 'I knew this was coming. Let me take a look.' I gave one piece at a time as he fixed them on his easel with drawing pins, stood a few feet away, turned on the focus light on them and spent about five minutes staring at them. Turning to me dramatically, he broke his silence. 'You have created three classics in your first attempt. I rarely come across such brilliance.' I thought it was his sarcasm in return for my attempt to make fun of the art form. And then it slowly dawned on me that he was quite serious. He went on to say, 'Only a Hindu could have drawn this.' I was so damn embarrassed that I wanted to confess and apologize. But he gave me no opportunity. He called aloud to his wife, 'Esther! Please come here and see what Babu has done?'

Esther arrived with a cup of coffee for me and began analysing my paintings. She also praised them to my embarrassment. I did not reveal the secret in her presence since she was not as close to me as Bob. I waited for an opportune time to apologize for the prank. But before Esther left the room, the doorbell rang and there came three art students of Bob.

After the introductions, Bob asked each of them to absorb the essence of my three works of art and interpret them. What followed during the next twenty minutes was a combination of profound interpretations ranging from Karl Marx to Sigmund Freud. I couldn't explain and apologize in the presence of his students.

I was reminded of the many jokes on modern art. Yet, at another level, it dawned on me that we do not always communicate what we intend to. What we write, paint, sculpt or sing gets a distinct identity of its own which may or may not be what we sought to convey—as the meanings are in the minds of those who perceive them.

Two days later, I made bold to confess that I was really not serious and I apologized profusely for my attempt at making fun of his art form. Bob hastened his reply. 'You don't need to apologize. We all discover new techniques of artisteic expression only in this manner. I know that you have adopted some unique technique.' Embarrassed, I explained to him the carbon paper accident, and said I did it only in the spirit of a prank. Bob wouldn't agree. 'Your prank is the expression of your inner spirit and I stand by all the appreciation that I poured on your works of art.' I didn't argue further as my conscience was clear that I had told him the truth.

Snowstorm in a Bathtub

In the film production class, usually one 16mm film camera (to make student films) was allotted to two students to share. Barbara Tillman and I were allotted one camera for shooting films to be submitted at the end of the term. One fine morning, as I got up from bed I saw a heavenly sight through the window. Yes! It was the first time ever I saw snowfall. It was most inviting. I hurriedly put on my overcoat and went out. After loitering for ten minutes, I felt I needed a camera. But our common camera of the university was at that time with Barbara. I rang her up and told her how excited I was to see snow and requested if she could spare the camera. She said, 'Sure, you can have it today. But I am not ready for the day yet. Would you pick it up from my apartment in an hour?'

Her apartment was a twenty-minute walk from mine. After enjoying the snowfall in the streets for another hour, I rang the doorbell at her building entrance. 'Who is it?' asked her voice on the intercom at the front door of the apartment building.

'Hi Barbara! Can I pick up the camera?'

'Oh Babu! I am so sorry to make you wait. You can come inside and wait in the lobby. Come up to my apartment after about twenty minutes.'

'That's okay,' I said.

She continued apologetically, 'I just had a shower; haven't got dressed yet; so give me a little time.'

Twenty minutes later, I took the elevator to her floor and rang the doorbell. 'Is that Babu?'

'Yeah.'

'Sorry, Babu! You have to give me five more minutes since I am almost naked. I'll wear something decent and open the door for you.'

'Okay!'

When the door opened, I walked in and started laughing.

'What are you laughing about?'

'Can't you guess?'

'No, I can't.'

'Nothing really! I was just wondering that if you took so long to put on this bikini, how much time would you need to really get dressed up?'

'Naughty fellow!' She gave me the camera and continued, 'Later in the day, I will join you in your shoot.'

'That's great! But you will freeze if you come out like this. Take three hours to put on an overcoat.'

After spending a few hours outdoors, I realized that something was going wrong. I stood in the middle of almost deserted roads. Public transport had come to a halt. Parked cars all around were buried in heavy snow. I walked back to my apartment to take a break and switched on the TV. All the channels blared that New York was hit by the worst snowstorm in forty years. Until I saw the TV warning I was under the impression that snowfall at any time would be like this. I didn't realize that frostbite was affecting me. My skin started peeling like that of a snake and was dropping like autumn leaves. It was not painful, but itchy and very uncomfortable. The next morning, I went to the university infirmary. It was my first exposure to corporate American medical practice. Out of the medical insurance the students paid for, the insurance company paid for our treatment. I was put through several tests to check my skin condition. While I expected a doctor to give a prescription and a cream, they hurriedly took me in as an 'inpatient' and allotted a bed in the students' ward. Among the specialists to interview me was a psychiatrist, to determine if I suffered from neurodermatitis, due to mental depression. In two days, the tests revealed that I was normal by all standards.

On receiving the reports, Wiseman, the chief physician, asked, 'Is it true that you Indians have the exotic habit of some kind of an oil bath?'

'Yes, doctor. I normally take an oil bath once a week.'

'Have you continued that after arriving in New York?'

'No.'

'Well, you should take an oil bath daily for the next one week.'

I did not realize that that was the beginning of a whole comic scene.

'What kind of oil do you use?'

'Sesame oil. I tried the sesame oil some Chinese shops here sell. It has a foul smell. It is not the same kind as we get in India.'

'Don't worry, I will solve the problem.'

An hour later, the hospital matron told me that they planned to use peanut oil which was available in plenty in the supermarket. I overheard a nurse and the matron conversing behind a curtain.

'Look at these exotic Indians. He probably belongs to a

maharaja's family to take a bath in oil.'

About thirty minutes later, a few attendants brought about a dozen oil cans of a gallon each. They were organizing oil to fill up the bathtub for me to get into. I called the matron and said, 'Sister! This is not the kind of oil bath I normally take. We only smear oil on ourselves before taking a shower.' She could not change the doctor's instructions and suggested that I talk to the doctor directly, if any procedures were to be changed. I explained my point of view to Wiseman on the phone. But he said, 'Rubbing oil on the skin would further affect the skin.' We arrived at a compromise. I filled the bathtub with water of the temperature I liked and a gallon of oil was poured into that. I had to stay in the tub for twenty minutes, twice a day; the oil was changed every time. After a week of this treatment, I returned to normal and profusely thanked Wiseman.

The matron was very kind. But the nurse cursed herself for having to help a nigger. I overheard the matron arguing with the youngster, who never changed her attitude. I took it as an opportunity to experience centuries of discrimination the African–Americans had faced.

Although it was a general ward for students, I had an independent room with an attached bathroom. I had many visitors including some fellow students, and Swami Budhananda from the Vedanta Society, besides K. Balaraman, the New York correspondent of *The Hindu*.

My landlady, Francisca Thorn, sat by my side one day and told me why she was taking a special interest in me. She had even been cleaning my room and taking my clothes to the laundry, extending almost the kind of pampering that I enjoyed back home. Francisca had lost her son ten years earlier. If he had survived, he would have been of my age and gait.

Barbara visited me and chatted at length about her childhood, giving me an insight into the trauma she had faced.

Born to Jewish parents in 1933, she was in a concentration camp during the Second World War. When she was ten, she witnessed her parents being shot dead. Soon after the war, she came to America as a child refugee and now, fifteen years later, she was standing on her own feet because of the generosity of the American government. Somewhere in her heart she longed an egalitarian society—perhaps guided by the principles of Karl Marx. She hated Germans and loved sections of the American society which rejected all religions. But she remained a Jew in her inner spirit. Each of my obstacles including the hospital stay became a classroom to understand the world, history, the nature of human beings and all their sufferings.

Beyond Film Studies

Marie Hayes had joined the communications course to strengthen her teaching skills. A few years elder to me, she was passionate about three things: first, her mother; second, the

The author directing a student film in New York

children she was teaching in a school; and third, her unshaken commitment to the Second Coming of Christ, which she fervently hoped would happen in her lifetime. Having lost her father, she had decided to remain a spinster in order to take care of her elderly mother. My first encounter with her was within a few weeks of the beginning of our first semester. It was Professor George Stoney's class. He had gained fame as a documentary-film-maker and one of his celebrated films very sensitively portrayed a woman's pain and pleasure combined in adding a new member to the human family. It had been filmed with the consent of a hospital and the woman whose delivery was to be filmed. The kind of films that we watched varied from news footage from the first and second world wars, classics of Eisenstein and Pudovkin from Russia, George Grearson's monumental British documentary classics and the inimitable works of Robert Flaherty, including his classics *Nanook of the North* and *Moana*.

Stoney gave two exercises to us. First, he expected each student to write a film script; second, he wanted each one of us to make a short film, but not based on the script submitted. The logic was that you can conceive a script which will demand larger resources to produce than the limited film-making facilities in the university. The second project was to make a short film within the constraints and still impress. He considered both to be equally important. I made a film on the problems of old age in America. I was distressed to see those hundreds of desperately lonely faces. I found them by the riverside; sitting on park benches; and elsewhere. They were not necessarily poor people in economic terms. I befriended one such lady, who was about seventy-five. One could see the glow in her eyes when I gave her an offer to appear in a short film. During the interviews she told me that she had a daughter and a son, who called her once in a few weeks on the telephone. 'The main purpose of the calls is to find out if I am alive.' She got a Mother's Day greeting card every year as a ritual. She had a small studio apartment in a prosperous locality not far from the university. She made a matter-of-fact statement, without emotion, that her children were waiting for her end, to sell the property and take their shares. When I made a ten-minute film about her by the riverside park and a few visuals of her apartment—her own statements being the main voice track—I hardly imagined that there would be many similar scenes in India half a century later. The project did not need our getting a script clearance from our professor. Stoney liked it a great deal and showed my film to students of his other classes as well. Erik Barnouw said that he was deeply moved by the young foreigner from a different culture, portraying one of the major social problems of America with sensitivity, after spending only a few months in that country. Sharma, an Indian documentary-film-maker who was working in the United Nations (UN), saw this film and showed it to his colleagues in the film department.

The other project to be done simultaneously was my writing a script for a thirty-minute film. I chose to write a piece of fiction.

Remember, that was an era when you hardly found an Indian student in American campuses. Well, we were a few who got together for a weekend chat although we had varied interests, studying different subjects. Within the confines of the mass media and journalism departments, I was the only Indian face. There was a lot of curiosity about India—some genuine and some very superficial. Keeping that audience in mind, I wrote a short film script based on religious concepts. It reflected how social degradation had made the Hindu religion a bundle of superstitions and rituals, while on a higher plane, there were no conflicts between contemporary science and Hindu metaphysics. It was a period in which the church ridiculed Darwin's theory, resulting in a major conflict between science and theology.

My script was one of the few selected by Stoney and distributed to the whole class as one of the few considered important to be discussed by the whole class. Two students vehemently opposed my script. One of them was Marie Hayes. She condemned the script as sacrilege and as an affront to the Christian faith. Stoney calmed her down, saying, 'Look, the class should understand one thing. We are discussing a script not for evaluating the idea it conveys, not for opposing or defending anybody's beliefs and opinions. We are here to learn and practise the art of film script writing. Let us confine the discussion to that.'

My script dealt with my idea of how a child observes the world and how what may be considered as ordinary sights—on the roadside, in the park or in somebody's home—convey meanings to the child and help mould his personality. We can look at the universe as a classroom.

I apologized profusely to Marie for unintentionally hurting her sentiments. Concurrent with learning film-making, I had several sessions with Marie to understand Christian theology, with Barbara to understand Judaism, with Bob to understand the styles of modern art; and with another friend, who was under police 'surveillance', for his possible involvement in the communist movement. A year's education in New York was not only all about cinema, TV and communication.

An Australian Breeze?

At this point, it is essential to go in flashback to Chennai about seven months, before I left for New York.

Several eminent people from abroad who visited Chennai visited my father to get a flavour of South Indian culture. He was the president of the Indo-Soviet Cultural Society and vice president of the World Peace Council, which was considered a leftist intellectual organization. In the 1940s, he had founded Nrithyodaya, a dance school for the underprivileged.

The author presents a memento to Malcolm Adiseshiah at the twenty-first anniversary of Krishnaswamy Associates in 1984; the chief guest, Nedunchezhiyan, senior minister of Tamil Nadu, looks on

Among those who visited my father in 1959 were Ivan Smith and his wife. An Australian citizen, Ivan Smith was an undersecretary in the UN at its headquarters. To broaden our view, my father used to send one of his sons or daughters to take such distinguished visitors from abroad around the city for sightseeing or to keep company for a dance or music performance. I became the informal tourist guide for the Smiths, taking them to the museum, a couple of temples and to the ancient monuments at Mahabalipuram, spending several hours with them over a couple of days. I found them to be excellent listeners and talked at length about the Bhagavad Gita, the Ramayana, the Mahabharata and the fundamentals of Hindu metaphysics. When my father expressed his plan of sending me to New York for study, Smith spontaneously remarked, 'It's a wonderful idea! You support him for the first few months.' Then, he turned to me, 'I will give you part-time employment in the UN to take care of your expenses for the rest of the year.' He reconfirmed to my father that he was serious and that it was not a casual statement. Within a week of my arrival in New York, I met him in his office and he invited me home for dinner. His wife reminded him of his commitment And he confirmed that he had not forgotten. I was elated to get a letter from a lower official in the UN Secretariat, that I was given 'Trainee' status as a tourist guide to the UN building, subject to my getting permission from the US immigration authorities. Armed with this letter, I promptly went to the immigration office. All this was within the first five or six weeks of my joining Columbia. An immigration officer told me that a student visa holder was 'not entitled to work here even part-time during the first six months of his stay in the United States.'

Another officer clarified that since I had a letter from an official of the UN, perhaps there were some provisions to allow me to work, if the letter from the UN was differently worded. I returned with confidence that I could work it out by meeting Ivan.

And now, my first personal experience of how events in a remote part of the world can affect an individual unfolded before me. It was a period of conflict in Congo. UN Secretary General Dag Hammarskjöld hand-picked Ivan to visit Congo and coordinate with the UN Peacekeeping Forces there. Ivan Smith had left for Congo at very short notice and nobody knew how long it would take him to return.

World Packed in a Suitcase

The fifteenth UN General Assembly was very special, as it was addressed by several world leaders including Khrushchev, Macmillan, Eisenhower, Jawaharlal Nehru, Marshal Tito, and Nasser. Due to security reasons, for most of the time the visitors' galleries were closed because of the VVIPs' presence. Despite that, because of Ivan Smith's introduction, I had a temporary pass to the gallery. It was a session that got headlines every day around the globe. When I informed Professor Barnouw that I had this entry pass, he said, 'You are a "Special Student" here, which means you are in America to receive education in the widest sense of the term. You can skip class whenever you like, if you are attracted to a particular session of the General Assembly.' I did not use my entry pass daily but spent a few hours once in a couple of days. On one such day, I became eyewitness to an extraordinary event. Khrushchev removed his shoe and banged it on the desk. The whole world was stunned.

Nikita Khrushchev, the then head of USSR council of ministers, had dramatically chosen to sail in a ship across the Atlantic instead of flying. He stayed on board the Soviet ship and attended the UN General Assembly session, never checking into a hotel in Manhattan. The cold war was at its peak. The US government refused him a visa to travel anywhere except within Manhattan Island to attend the UN session. Even as Khrushchev was crossing the Atlantic, the Soviet Union launched the world's first man-made satellite: Sputnik. The timing was perfect for him to remain in the headlines.

I was desperately in need of that part-time UN job, which I didn't get. The money I had taken with me was almost exhausted. My brothers had obtained a foreign exchange permit from the RBI to remit some US dollars every month to me for my expenses, since we could not take for granted the job promised by Ivan Smith. Soon after I shifted from the RCA Institute to Columbia University, I wrote to the Reserve Bank informing them of this change for their records, as an honest (or naive) citizen of India. An exalted RBI clerk promptly cancelled my foreign exchange permit, treating my change of institution as a violation. My family, particularly my mother, was very perturbed. I was running out of cash. My professor and my American as well as the few Indian friends I had were not only sympathetic but also very cooperative.

Francisca Thorn, my landlady, said that she was fascinated by the saris that Indian women wore. She said if only my family could send a couple of saris for her, she would deem it as equal to two months' rent. Within a fortnight, I got a parcel from home with half a dozen saris for her to choose from. She helped me to sell the other four.

After the first semester, there was a relief. The pioneer documentarian Robert Flaherty's wife, who had collaborated with her husband in making his iconic films, was one of my teachers. Erik Barnouw, Mrs Flaherty, George Stoney and other faculty members were unanimous in giving me very high grades in their assessments. Erik Barnouw circulated my term paper 'Is American Media Free?' to all his students and to those in the journalism department. American TV was chained by corporate business and carpetbaggers. No programme could be telecast without the sponsors' nod. Very often, the sponsors supported the most stupid or insipid programmes. Any show that portrayed poverty in America, or life in the Harlem etc., found no sponsors. There was no public broadcasting service in that era and in my paper I argued the need for one such.

Despite this seemingly anti-American stance of my term paper, most liberal and truly independent as the academics of the university were, considered this as a very fair assessment and one of them openly said, 'It is remarkable that a foreign student from a different cultural background is able to assess our media culture so accurately within a short span of time.'

All this landed me in being recruited by the New York State Education Department with the recommendation of the university as a trainee in Educational Television Production. The WPIX was a station dedicated to educational programmes and I was now a 'Production Associate' of a weekly serial of twenty-six episodes titled *World Neighbors*.

The UN General Assembly session was over and the demand for additional temporary staff had ceased. With the result, even though Ivan Smith was back in New York, there was no job for me. But funds from home through friends travelling to America, along with a stipend from the education department (for which no change in visa status was required) helped me to carry on for the next several months.

It looked as though everything was ordained to shape me as a citizen of the world. *World Neighbors* was conceived as a programme to instil in American students knowledge of world history and civilizations, talk about art, culture, economics, political systems and society as a whole, in different countries of the world. I helped to make programmes on Scandinavia, Italy, Greece, the United Kingdom, the USSR, China, Japan, Korea, Egypt, South Africa, Australia and India. Our budgets for the series were very limited but we had unlimited access to films and other materials of every consulate in New York, besides the permanent missions of the countries (to the UN) relevant to the TV serial. Lee Polk, producer of the series, developed confidence in me within the first few weeks. He produced four programmes of one-hour duration each, every week on widely varied subjects. Naturally, he delegated responsibilities to his associates, in whom he developed confidence. I thoroughly enjoyed working on that series and got to know the consular officials of several countries. Almost all of them warmly extended their hand of cooperation, giving me materials for study, and films from which I got clippings, besides access to prominent citizens of their countries to be interviewed, when they were passing through New York.

The most cooperative consulate was that of Japan. They went out of their way to import a portable bicycle and the world's first portable TV receiver all the way from Tokyo and handed them over to me for the show to demonstrate Japanese technology. Ironically, for our programme on India, when I wanted to showcase some ivory and sandalwood artefacts by borrowing them from India's tourist promotion wing, the consulate expected me to bear the cost of insurance and transport of materials from their office to the TV studio and back, which I could not afford, since there was no procedure to get such costs from the TV channel. The UN officials of Indian nationality compensated for this, by lending me footage from films and making guest appearances. They even organized for a veena player passing through New York to perform in my show.

Some of us Indian students organized a lecture by C. Subramaniam, Minister for Finance and Education in Tamil Nadu, who was on a visit. R. Venkatraman, my father's friend who later became the President of India, was a delegate to the UN and I had several opportunities to interact with him.

We had some film screenings open to all students of the university. One such was that of a documentary on India produced sometime in the 1940s as part of the *March of Time* series by *Time* Magazine. It was a disgusting, distasteful and distorted portrait of India; and it angered me. On the spur of the moment, I went up on the dais and declared my criticism. Erik Barnouw took the microphone from me and said, 'This film would serve its purpose if only your anger motivates you to make a proper, well-informed, balanced film on Indian history and culture.' I declared I would do so within a short time after my return to India. The challenge remained with me although the gestation period of the project from that day proved to be sixteen years, until I completed *Indus Valley to Indira Gandhi*, in 1976. I call it gestation period because although I was involved in several other activities, making many short films, this was in my mind and a script was taking shape.

By this time, I had become a regular visitor to my professor's house. Dorothy Barnouw had taken a liking to me and would make vegetarian dishes for me based on Asian and European recipes. During one such visit, Barnouw casually told me that he was getting a year of sabbatical leave from later that year and he had not made up his mind on how to use it productively. A researcher, academician and creative writer to the core, he had several books to his credit. Suddenly, he asked, 'What do you think of my planning a year in India? I don't find much research has been done on Indian cinema.' I instantly replied, 'Please pursue that idea. I will also return to India with you and help you write the book.'

Very magnanimously he said, 'Excellent! It is not a question of your helping. We will be co-authors.' I was thrilled. I was not aware how serious he was about this until some months later he told me that he had applied for and got a Fulbright Fellowship to spend a year in India to write the book. I couldn't believe my ears when he said that he had also spoken to Columbia University Press that it was to be jointly written by him and me, and that they had agreed to publish it. How can I forget the day when he took me to the publisher's office to sign the contract, where another major surprise awaited me? The university press was to give us an advance of $500 towards royalty, by two cheques for $250 each. But I found a single cheque in my favour. Barnouw turned to me and said, 'I know you need that money till you are in this country for a few more months. So I asked them to extend the whole advance to you.' Typical of him, he said it without any patronizing tone and with no melodrama. I made sure nobody there saw me wiping my tears.

Because of my work in educational TV, I came to know Paul, Dean of the Teachers' College of Columbia University. It was a period of several days of uncertainty and surprises— more often than not, very pleasant. When the second semester was over, Paul called me and said, 'I know you are a "Special Student" without registering for a degree. But I think you have done exceedingly well, and it would be unfair to send you back without a master's degree. Join the Teachers' College during the summer semester. Let me do what I think is right.'

In the summer semester, I attended courses in curriculum development, audio-visual education, and history of education. Paul represented to the president of the university that cumulatively between the mass media department and the Teachers' College, I had earned more points than required to collect a master's degree. He appealed to the president to waive the condition that I should have originally been enrolled for a master's degree. Four days before I was to catch my flight back to India, he called me to his room and proudly announced that the president had given the waiver and that some administrative formalities had to be completed to grant me the master's degree. Indeed, I was on cloud nine! I promptly called India and informed my father. Incidentally, I should mention that making a call to India in 1960–61 from America meant booking an international trunk call, and waiting for six to seven hours to get a connection. My parents were elated.

Clan with Elan

While there was a small group of family and friends when I left for America, there were many more people to receive me at the same airport. Going abroad for studying was not common in that generation. Among those in the small group that had given me a send-off at the airport was MGR, who later became the chief minister of the state. He treated my father as his father-figure. MGR had called me aside at the airport for a short chat and said, 'I know you will come out with flying colours. I only want to give you one piece of advice. Don't bring a foreign girl with you,' and continued after a pause, 'I am speaking on behalf of your mother.' I thanked him for his advice.

There was not much time for a long chat as the flight was

announced. Only after my return, I learnt from my mother that she had not asked MGR to convey any such advice. She said, 'Apparently, he was concerned about my feelings. But I didn't ask him to talk to you.'

Now, back in India, at the same airport, it was embarrassing to be received with garlands and shawls since I felt that I had achieved nothing yet. It was indeed a very happy family reunion with my parents, siblings and a lot of exchange of news. During my entire stay in America for my education, I had spoken to my parents on the phone only four–five times.

Professor Barnouw and Dorothy along with their young daughters, Susan and Karen, decided to take a holiday by sailing all the way from New York to India in a luxury liner. Their son, Jeffrey, joined them later. The US Education Foundation in India helped them get an apartment in Delhi as the family decided to spend a year in Delhi to enable the children to go to

MGR is hugging the author at the airport, as the author catches his flight to America. The author's parents, brothers (Balu and Chandru), sisters (Neela and Padma) and Janaki Ramachandran are also in the group.

the American School attached to the US Embassy. After settling down in Delhi, Barnouw got into active work, visiting me in Chennai. In the meantime, I had two months of exclusive family time. It is time to talk about my siblings with whom I reunited.

My eldest sister, Lalitha, had been trained in Bharatanatyam since my father was deeply involved in the resurrection of the art form, extending moral support to Rukmini Devi Arundale and E. Krishna Iyer, who were spearheading this art form by erasing its stigma as the dance of the devadasis. In 1945, Lalitha got married to M.S. Krishnamoorthy. My father was at the height of his prosperity and fame, and the scale of the wedding celebrations reflected it. As a boy of seven, I could not reconcile to the idea of my sister leaving us and moving to a new home. I cried so much that my brother-in-law decided to take me with him. I spent a few days with my sister before returning home, satisfying myself that my brother-in-law was a 'good man', who would take care of her. Having been a brilliant student, she was heartbroken when her parents-in-law refused permission for her to join a college and continue her education. Her husband had a master's degree in economics from Loyola College, Chennai. After the wedding, he pursued higher education at the London School of Economics. He worked in the corporate world before setting up practice as a financial consultant.[4]

Balakrishnan (Balu), one year younger to Lalitha, inherited along with the material wealth of his adoptive parents of an earlier generation, their orthodoxy too. He was affectionate to his siblings—often as their self-appointed guardian.

Third in the line of my siblings was Bama, married to Sundaram, whose family had been known to my father for a long time. Sundaram worked for a few years in my father's

---

[4]Lalitha Krishnamoorthy passed away after a brief illness at the age of eighty-nine, as I am writing this book in 2017.

company before joining the Overseas Communication Service as an engineer. Bama's memory was archival and she kept the whole lot of grandchildren from all branches of our family entertained with stories from our childhood, almost until a month before she passed away in 2015.

Next to her in line was Neelayadakshi (Neela), who was another great artistee of our family. Her mastery of Carnatic music surpassed those of the star singers of her generation. A rank holder at the College of Carnatic Music at Chennai, and gold medallist in pedagogy, life was not very kind to her, despite her retiring as the head of the department of music of a major institution in Madurai—a story to be dealt with later.

My immediate elder brother, Ramanan, was born in 1935. I was born in 1938, within a year of my father building his new palatial bungalow, when he was at the height of his success and fame. Everyone pampered me, including my elder siblings. My sister Padma was born in 1943 and at a very young age she became a star dancer. My mother's next child, Chandrasekhar (Chandru for the family and Shan in Canada), was born in 1945 and migrated to Canada when he was twenty-two. My stepbrother, Ramjhi—son of SDS—was just coming out of school and he joined us all once in a few weeks.

My return from America became an occasion for a family reunion for several weeks.

Exploring Film History

About three months after my return from America, I began active work on my collaboration with Professor Barnouw. But almost immediately on my arrival in Chennai I started correspondence with several individuals and institutions in the country, announcing our research project of writing a book for Columbia University Press and seeking their cooperation. I

First Edition, Columbia University Press (1963); Second Edition Oxford University Press (1980), London and New Delhi

started getting replies—first from people in West Bengal and then from leading film personalities of Mumbai and film industry organizations, including the Film Federation of India.

Barnouw and I decided to spend a week or so to plan our research and writing, in a place where we would not be disturbed by any other activity. We chose Bengaluru and decided to stay in a decent vegetarian hotel—the Madras Woodlands.

To start with, we got some hilarious insights about the film industry. For instance, when I had gone for a walk, Barnouw opened a letter from the SIFCC, which said, 'We acknowledge your letter that you are writing a book on Indian films. We regret we are unable to extend any cooperation to you since the office-bearers of our chamber are busy with Navratri celebrations' (signed by the secretary of the Film Chamber).
Barnouw immediately took up his Fodor's guide to India, to check for 'Navratri' celebrations. He was laughing heartily

when I returned to the room, and read out loud what the guide said—'Navarathri is a festival of dolls, celebrated by women and children for nine nights!'

He wondered how the entire film industry and office bearers would be occupied by this over several months. The story did not stop there. When we returned to Chennai, Vellore Venkatraman, a prominent film financier, paid a courtesy call on my father, and he was very happy to see me after a couple of years. When he realized that I was writing a book on his industry, he very enthusiastically said, 'Come over to the Film Chamber and let us talk about it.' He was a member of the executive committee of that chamber.

I told him, 'I know you are all busy with Navratri. How can you find time for us?' He was intrigued by this. When I showed him the letter, he was upset with the secretary and treated it as an insult to every member of the chamber.

He went straight to the Film Chamber and quarrelled with the secretary. The Committee passed a resolution that they will hold a reception to meet Erik Barnouw and S. Krishnaswamy, who are writing a book on Indian films. They fixed the date and time and got the invitation printed. They neither consulted Barnouw and me nor sent an invitation to us! We were both ignorant of the event. In the meantime, the Cine Technicians' Association (CTA) of South India, whose membership consisted of creative elements including directors, cameraman and so on, had fixed a meeting, wherein we would raise questions and seek clarifications as a productive, interactive session on exactly the same date and time in a different venue.

When they came to know of the confusion, two people from the Film Chamber rushed to meet Barnouw in his hotel after ascertaining that I was also there. They apologized profusely for not consulting us about the date and time of the reception. To ensure that the invitees of the two functions were not inconvenienced, I requested the CTA to advance their meeting by half an hour and the Film Chamber to delay their meeting by half an hour.

Indeed, spending a year with Erik Barnouw to write *Indian Film* gave me the pleasure of exploration. It gave me an insight into different dimensions of India's film history—the prime objective of our research. We were looking at not merely the history of cinema during the preceding half a century, but also at the roots of cinema in aesthetic, sociological and psychological terms in the Indian context.

The process of writing involved our interviewing over a hundred people from across the country, including film pioneers, contemporary stars of the period, several journalists, critics, sociologists, bureaucrats and a few ministers. At least with some of these people I continued to maintain contact for several years. There was no film archive in India and writing about cinema was looked at as the work of film publicists. No serious academic approach to the history of Indian cinema had been done before. One small incident that happened at the end of 1963 would reveal this attitude in a capsule. A few months after our book was published, I casually walked into the Madras University library. Although I was actually looking for some other title, I was curious to know whether our book had been acquired.

As I was searching the card index, a library assistant offered help and I said, 'I am looking for *Indian Film* by Erik Barnouw and S. Krishnaswamy.'

'Indian what?'

'*Indian Film.*'

'You know, this is the university library. You won't find fan magazines here,' he said with contempt. Of course, I did not reveal my identity. I explained to him that academic books had been written on cinema in several other countries and the two chaps had written on Indian cinema also. He said, 'But I am not aware of that and we don't keep such stuff anyway.'

Returning to the process of writing, I would rather dwell on the moments that lightened our spirits—sometimes profound and sometimes profane. We began our fieldwork in Koltaka, since Barnouw got involved in this project because of his admiration for Satyajit Ray. We got to know the great director very well and he invited us to spend one week with him in Darjeeling when he was shooting his film *Kanchenjunga*. I enjoyed observing him at work and had long conversations with him at night.[5]

In Kolkata, we enjoyed several meetings with Mrinal Sen and Ritwik Ghatak—who were called 'the new generation' at that time. I equally enjoyed long conversations with B.N. Sircar, probably the most efficient and educated film pioneer whose banner, New Theatres, was in commanding heights from the early 1930s for over two decades.

We came across the name Dhiren Ganguly as a pioneer film-maker in West Bengal who made silent films. While most of the film-makers at that time were making films based on mythology or folklore, Ganguly was making films on contemporary Indian society, which came to be known in India as social films. We were eager to know more about him. The Bengal Motion Picture Producers' Association (BMPA) had been extremely cooperative in giving us information about anybody we wanted to meet, and put us in touch with some of them. When I asked them about Dhiren Ganguly, the secretary of the association said, 'He died a few years ago, but I will give you the address of his daughter. You can perhaps talk to her and get more information.'

---

[5] I developed a wonderful relationship with Manekda (as we call Satyajit). He never missed meeting me in Chennai during his visits, which were frequent since he was dealing with film laboratories in Chennai. He invited me to join the Advisory Council of the Federation of Film Societies of India, of which he was the president; and later nominated me to be secretary of the federation—southern region.

We took a cab and went straight there. After reaching the locality in about an hour, it took another hour to actually locate the house—only to learn that she had vacated the house a few days earlier. Looking at our frustrated faces, a very helpful watchman volunteered to give her the information that we were looking for her. I wrote down our names and said that we were staying in the Ramakrishna Mission International Guest House. The next morning as we were having breakfast, a peon conveyed that there was a gentleman waiting for us. I walked to the reception to find a dignified, frail old man, extending his hand, saying, 'I am Dhiren Ganguly. I understand that you wanted to see me.'

The author with Satyajit Ray (1968)

We spent the next few hours with this amazingly active octogenarian. He showed us reviews of his films in the 1920s, spared some stills from those films and outlined what life was like for a film-maker in that era. The lively old man had no regrets. He had lost touch with the film industry. We not only wrote about Dhiren Ganguly but also informed the BMPA that the veteran was alive and suggested that they correct their records.

In 1976, the annual national awards for Indian films were announced by the jury appointed by the Ministry of Information and Broadcasting (MIB). But the Dadasaheb Phalke Award (in honour of the man who made India's first feature film) is usually decided by the minister and his officials in the information ministry. At that time V.C. Shukla was the information minister and S.M.H. Burney was the secretary of the ministry. He later became the Governor of Haryana. I happened to be visiting Delhi for something else. I got a call from the ministry stating that Burney wanted to see me urgently. When I called on him, he very graciously said, 'We are about to decide who will receive the Dadasaheb Phalke Award this year. I thought I should pick your brains for this. Can you give a few names for us to choose from?' I told him about Dhiren Ganguly and said, 'If only he had made films a couple of years earlier, this award may have been named after him. Being the oldest pioneer and producer of progressive films, it's time that we honour him.' I gave him some more details. Burney immediately met the minister and got his approval. A media release announced the conferring of the prestigious award to Ganguly. I was truly amazed that it could happen that fast and it was a very satisfying moment for me, since I could contribute to getting significant recognition for a highly deserving person.

Returning to 1962, when we were writing the book, there were several very sensitive as well as comical moments. From the Taj Mahal Hotel in Mumbai, I was ringing up several pioneers as well as contemporary stars to interview them. People like the veteran actor David, celebrated writer Khwaja Ahmed Abbas, Ezra Mir (chief producer of the Films Division) dropped in for tea in the hotel for long chats. One major star of the day gave us an appointment at his apartment. We turned up there in the evening as fixed. His assistant made us wait for forty-five minutes, saying that his boss was held up in traffic returning home from a shooting and would be with us any moment. His assistant went into a side room even as we were browsing through a magazine with the star on the cover. Much to the embarrassment of the assistant, the star arrived in his nightgown from inside, totally drunk and out of control. The assistant got the help of one more person and they both supported him and brought him to a sofa in front of us. Of course, he had totally forgotten that he had given us an appointment. We managed the moment, exchanged greetings and left the scene.

The office of another major star ruling the skies gave us an appointment. When I first contacted them, an assistant there took down the details, called me back promptly and confirmed the appointment. Just when we were ready to leave, we got another call and the conversation went something like this.

'Am I speaking to Mr Krishnaswamy of Columbia Pictures?'

'This is Krishnaswamy, but I am not from Columbia Pictures.'

'Oh, I see! But I was told that you and your colleague are from Columbia Pictures?'

'No! Professor Erik Barnouw and I are from Columbia University.'

'Yes! Yes! That's what I mean—Columbia Pictures.'

'No! I said, Columbia University—not Columbia Pictures.'

Now, I heard another voice taking over the phone and telling me, 'It will honour our star to appear in Hollywood movie. I tell time. You wait!'

'I am sorry there seems to be some misunderstanding. We

are actually from Columbia University and we are writing a book.'

'No misunderstanding, sir. You will discuss when you meet him,' and he disconnected the phone.

I briefed my co-author, asking, 'What do we do? Shall we go there and take the chance?'

'I don't think so! It will be embarrassing when they discover that we are poor academicians writing a book!' Barnouw laughed. I called the star's office and politely wriggled out of the meeting.

In 1969, I met Raj Kapoor, the unbeatable star, in a completely different context—he was the chairman and I was the secretary of the jury for the International Film Festival of India in New Delhi.[6] After establishing a rapport with him, I told him the story of how his office had dealt with me when I was engaged in research for our book—and he had one big laugh. Being a great thespian and one of the most sophisticated personalities of the cinema world, he shared the story with the renowned novelist R.K. Narayan, who was a member of the jury.

Another iconic Hindi film producer-director, V. Shantaram gave us an appointment not because of the Columbia University connection, but because I used my father's name. (I realized that I should have used the same mantra with other personalities also.) It was a fascinating Bollywood-style meeting with the film-maker. It could have been a scene from a movie. In the posh studio, we were with the secretary to the great man—a popular and one of the greatest creative film-makers of India. His office was on the first floor and we were sitting on the ground floor. After a few minutes of waiting and enjoying our cup of tea, the secretary led us to an elevator guarded by a ceremonially

---

[6]Refer to my article 'Mohenjodaro to Mickey Mouse' on that event. Published in *The Hindu*, 26 May 1996.

dressed attendant. There was another elevator for the rest of the building. This one went only up to the first floor straight in front of the boss's room. There was no visible door at all and we were facing a blank and large wooden wall. The secretary walked to the intercom and announced, 'I have brought Professor Barnouw and Krishnaswamy to meet you, sir.'

Within seconds, the wooden wall gave way, opening on both sides like in a suspense thriller. The motor which operated it made a terrible noise. We entered a large room in which the famous man was seated in front of his desk at the other end. The moment we entered the room, the wooden door behind us closed again making its irritating noise. We walked up to the big man and after shaking hands, I innocently asked him, 'Sir, in case of a power failure, is there another way of getting out of this room?' Both our host and Barnouw laughed. Stiff formality gave way a little, and our host settled down with some ease, asking, 'How is your father?' The conversation continued as he became friendly,

The author with V. Shantaram during a children's film festival (c.a. 1980)

moving away from what began like a straitjacket interview in the room of a 'don'. But for this theatrical 'intro', the interview was most smooth and enjoyable. Some years later, Shantaram asked me to be secretary of the jury for an international festival of children's films, when he was the chairman of the Children's Film Society) as a token of his confidence and affection.

Down South, we had interesting meetings with stars like Sivaji Ganesan, producers such as S.S.Vasan and A.V. Meiyappan, as well as directors, including B.N. Reddy. Compensating for the faux pas at the Film Chamber, the reception at AVM, Gemini and Vauhini was very warm, worthwhile and businesslike.

Between the two authors, we broadly divided the work by each of us writing the first draft of certain chapters and then exchanging them for comments from the other. For instance, the first draft for the Mumbai-based film industry was done by Barnouw and for the Chennai-based film industry was written by me. Although these drafts went through changes, they retained the thrust of the first draft in terms of details as well as exploring the relationship between cinema and society. The cinema of West Bengal needed more analysis and discussion between the two of us for several reasons. For one thing, it was the work of Satyajit Ray that had attracted Barnouw to write our book.

Among the celebrities who became close to us was Devika Rani Roerich. She was the ruling star of Indian cinema for two decades from the time she appeared in silent films in 1925. Her husband and film-maker Himanshu Rai passed away in 1941. A few years later, she married the world-renowned Russian painter Svetoslav Roerich. Svetoslav's father, Nicholas Roerich, was fascinated by the Himalayas and he settled down creating a home for himself in the Kullu valley. Svetoslav apart from receiving international encomiums for his own work, inherited his love for India, making India his home. The Roerich couple spent the summer in Kullu and the rest of the year in Bengaluru where they had a large plantation of aromatic trees. Barnouw and I visited them in Bengaluru in the middle of their captivating estate. It is difficult to come across a couple who carry their fame so very lightly as Devika Rani and Svetoslav Roerich.

When the postman delivered the first copy of *Indian Film*, Shyamala (the gifted singer who, shortly thereafter, married my brother, Balu) patted me on the back and urged me to take it straight to the pooja room. Instead, I took it to my father and sought his blessings.[7]

Several Streams of Seven Years

The period 1963–69 was crowded with events for me—my stint in journalism and its consequences, such as the blossoming of some lasting friendships, and, ironically, some powerful adversaries; and in the midst of it my modest company began to function.

Within months of *Indian Film* getting published, A.S. Raman, editor of *The Illustrated Weekly of India*,[8] was visiting my father. I met him casually and we built a kind of instant rapport, since he was an admirer of my book, even as I was an admirer of his column 'Chiaroscuro' in *The Illustrated Weekly*. He invited me to dinner at his hotel to continue our chat. A very pleasant surprise awaited me there. Without any fanfare, he asked me whether I would be interested in writing a column in his magazine. It was indeed very gracious of a senior, highly respected editor of India's most popular magazine of the day to offer this to someone who had hardly turned twenty-five. Need

---

[7]The book received rave reviews from which extracts are reproduced in the Annexure.
[8]*The Illustrated Weekly of India* was India's most popular English magazine published by *The Times of India*.

I say, I was elated! But I accepted it after very politely proposing a condition. 'I will maintain the number of words you prescribe. But I don't want it to be edited by your assistants. Of course, you may reject the piece if you don't like it, or return it to me with your comments asking me to rewrite. I hold you in high esteem and I hope you understand the spirit in which I am saying this!' Raman laughed and said, 'Well, it is an unexpected condition from a young writer, but I concede to your request.' I thanked him profusely. I wrote the column 'Madras Film Letter' for about six years, till my company had picked up so well that I had no time to handle this additional work.

Soon after I started my column, I was delighted to receive a phone call from Jayakanthan (JK) saying that he followed my column regularly. I told him that I was an ardent admirer of his writing. He was arguably the twentieth century's most gifted Tamil novelist, short story writer and radical thinker. This school dropout had brought in a new level of sensitivity in understanding human nature and created some fantastic characters of people ranging from the platform dweller to the palace resident. He explored the psychic geography of contemporary society and wrote with perspicacity and perspicuity, in particular, combining insight with sympathy for the woman characters of his novels and short stories. The immediate purpose of JK's call was to invite me to an exclusive preview of the first, feature film, *Unnai Pol Oruvan* (One Like You), that he had directed based on his novel with the same name. After the show, we had a long chat as though we had known each other for decades. A Marxist as he was at that time, we had differences of opinion in the nuances of our socio-political perceptions.

I wrote in my column, 'Sergei Eisenstein, a world-renowned pioneer of Russian cinema, wrote that a well-made Hollywood film is like a PhD thesis. He implied that they lacked literary and creative dimensions, but they were technically brilliant and can teach you how to make a film. JK's film is not a PhD thesis. It is a technically imperfect, rickety cradle from which a beautiful live baby smiles at me, while the average Tamil film is often an ornamental coffin carrying a dead body.' JK fell in love with this review and quoted it in the promotion of his film. I developed a strong bond of friendship with this giant among writers, and we remained intimate friends till he passed away in 2015.

While my dream was to produce films to promote culture, history and heritage besides science and technology, that would contribute to education in the widest sense of the term, my immediate plan was to produce the long film covering five millennia of Indian history—a promise which I had made to my professors in the presence of an audience in New York. I was waiting for a miracle by which somebody would finance my film. Many people advised me that I should join a film company, as they sincerely felt that my dream of making non-fiction films on history and heritage was unrealistic. Just then, an advertisement declared that the Films Division, Government of India, had vacancies for two directors. My father advised me to apply for the position, stating that it was the closest to what I wanted to do and that when I found the resources to make the films of my choice, I could resign from the government, gaining experience in the meantime.

I applied to the Union Public Service Commission, was interviewed in New Delhi by a high-profile committee, which included the iconic director Bimal Roy, and selected for the position of director, Films Division; indeed, I sent my acceptance stating that I would join in two months, although my heart was not in that job; but, I thought, I had no other option without resources to start my own enterprise and work on my ambitious documentary film project.

And then suddenly, there was a twist in the tale. MGR[9] volunteered to underwrite my dream project, stating that this was his new route to reach unconventional film markets and that he should have the pride of financing it, while I would be the writer-director. He admired my faith and confidence to do something 'different'. Everyone in my family was happy to hear this news. The star advanced ₹2,000 as a token of his commitment.

I wrote to the chief producer of the Films Division, regretting that I was unable to join their service, since I was otherwise occupied. As a proprietor, I valiantly started my enterprise—egoistically named Krishnaswamy Associates.

I took a room on rent at the Leadbeater Chambers of the Theosophical Society at Adyar for about two months to write my skeleton script for a feature-length documentary on Indian history and heritage. It is a very poetic location. I brought a few suitcases of books purchased with MGR's advance payment into the room which had open corridors on three sides and the Bay of Bengal visible from my balcony on the top floor. A few thousand birds flew out of the campus at sunrise—some of them westward to the land and most of them eastward to the sea. At sunset, they all returned to sing their heavenly chorus, creating an inspirational back plate for me to write the human drama of our nation. Occasionally, Ramanu or Padma dropped in there. I returned from that solitude with full confidence that I had the basic script with me to work. By the standards of the early 1960s, my budget of about ₹6-7 lakh for the 35 mm Eastman Colour[10] project involving filming in about a hundred locations across India, over one year, was considered reasonable. When I informed the star's manager R.M. Veerappan, who later became a

---
[9]Refer to my article 'When Stars become Tsars' in the collection *Frames of Mind* published by Indian Council of Cultural Relations.
[10]Eastman Colour was a process owned by Kodak Limited, US.

minister in MGR's cabinet, about the progress, he promptly sent one of his assistants to visit me the next day.

The conversation went something like this: 'Thambi![11] When do you plan to write a nice article about Puratchi Nadigar in your column? I suggest you plan a cover feature on him! We all know the editor is close to you.'

'I am sorry. It may not be possible, sir!' I politely replied.

'Why not?'

'You don't mean that is a condition for financing my film? Do you?'

'You should understand these things without such questions. Frankly, how are we interested in your making a documentary? It is not by itself a profitable proposal anyway. By now, any worldly-wise businessman in your place would have brought out a cover feature on Puratchi Nadigar. Come down to earth. Write a fabulous article that he is the greatest actor of all times.'

I controlled myself from responding. What if this fellow had been speaking on his own, not representing MGR's views? I found myself in a mess, having missed the bus for a government job, and having misjudged the offer of a film star.

In another stream of events, soon after the release of the book, *Indian Film,* with excellent reviews in the US, the UK, India and Australia, I got a call from the well-known monthly magazine *Imprint*, published in India by an American couple who tried with considerable success to bring some of the best writings of the world to Indian readers in abridged formats. Their regional manager, R. Desikan, wanted to discuss the possibility

---

[11]'Thambi' means younger brother. Puratchi Nadigar translates as 'revolutionary actor'—as MGR was called by his fans; it is a sobriquet which in the 1970s changed to 'Puratchi Thalaivar', meaning 'Revolutionary Leader', when he started his own political party after breaking away from the Dravida Munnetra Kazhagam (DMK).

of publishing an abridged version of our book in *Imprint*. We met at Garden Woodlands, a popular middle-class cafe. We were destined to become very close friends for the next half a century. *Imprint* soon published an abridged version of our book. Desikan was a popular figure among advertising circles in Chennai, and we began to meet often. Soon he realized my career predicament, and sincerely suggested to me to begin making advertisement films, a proposal for which I had strong reservations.

As a student in New York I had gradually realized that the so-called 'freedom of expression' was somewhat of a myth even in America. I wrote in a term paper, 'If the TV medium carries the propaganda of a totalitarian state in the Soviet Union, in America it carries the subliminal sales messages of the corporate world. I learn that a TV programme depicting poverty in America does not get a sponsor. Sponsors advertise their products in programmes that showcase glamour and luxurious living styles; because the greedy corporate world would like to sell products which people don't need at prices they can't afford. Any down-to-earth image of reality is inappropriate to sustain the "Maya" of this capitalist bubble.' It was as much a political statement as an analysis of the media. I salute my university for not only tolerating my scathing attacks on the consumerist lifestyle of America and pretentious freedom but also paying accolades for my revolutionary words and giving me high grades in every semester, culminating in awarding me a master's degree. I told myself, 'Hats off to you, America, for being the pinnacle of academic freedom! But I will only be a visitor to your shores, since I can never be part of a society which values possession and consumption as the highest ever goals of life.'

The more I studied the psychology of communications, the more I hated advertising as a profession. Confessed to be the 'Art of Permissible Lies' by a leading American advertising professional, I believed that it mostly aimed at promoting half-truths, exaggerating the values of products and services to unsuspecting consumers. I told Desikan that my commitment was to make a major film on Indian history, probably something that would be three to four hours long, highlighting culture, philosophy and the journey of India over five millennia, and that I was unwilling to fritter away my time on selling soaps and shampoos.

Perceiving my ideological and academic approach to the media, Desikan organized a meeting for me to address the Advertising Club of Madras on 'Evolving Challenges of Mass Media'. Umesh Rao, the legendary art director who had created the Maharaja mascot for Air India, was the president of the club. Friends in that meeting began to nurture the idea that I should make corporate films for companies. Umesh Rao was a very sensitive man, unlike advertising folks who were mostly shallow.

The author and his brother, Balu, filming

He told me that consistent with my ideals, he would suggest I make films to educate farmers, promote modern agriculture and help sell products like fertilizers and pesticides. Desikan and Umesh Rao convinced me that my company should be devoted to development communications, educating rural folk and helping to improve their standards of living. A major brand of fertilizer manufactured in our region was Parry's fertilizers. I signed a contract to produce a two-minute advertising film for them titled *A Pathway to Plenty*—the first film produced under the banner of Krishnaswamy Associates. I had realized in New York that when my potential benefactor at the UN had to suddenly leave for Congo, it affected me personally. If the conflict in another continent could affect the individual life of an Indian student in distant America, the social reality of India was such that you had no option but to accept that 'No man is an island'.

Professionally, although I founded Krishnaswamy Associates as a proprietorship firm, there were three other pillars of strength—my two elder brothers and Desikan. Balu was a gifted cameraman with an excellent visual sense, trained by the pioneer cinematographer Venkat. He had a degree in law, but never practised as an advocate because of his interest in photography. Ramanu was interested in a wide range of fine arts. Although a commerce graduate, his heart was in film-making. A brilliant music composer with no formal training in music, he had assisted my father in directing his last feature film, *Pandithevan*. Balu and Ramanu had founded a company, Morak (P) Ltd, which specialized in producing documentary films for the information ministries of the central and state governments. To avoid conflict of interest with Morak, Krishnaswamy Associates concentrated on doing business with corporate houses. Balu was the cameraman for all my films and Ramanu was the music director. We made a twenty-minute film on the Neyveli Lignite Corporation, written and directed by me, photographed by Balu,

The author receiving his first national award for his documentary *The Brown Diamond* from Zakir Husain, President of India; K.K. Shah, Minister for Information and Broadcasting, looks on

with music by Ramanu. This film, *The Brown Diamond,* got me my first national award, in 1968.

I acknowledge Desikan as the fourth pillar of the company, since he was my unpaid ambassador talking about me to corporate houses. Asked by someone in an advertising agency what he gained by talking about me to the rest of the industry, he replied, 'It's two birds at a stroke. I get Babu's goodwill, for getting him more business; and I get the goodwill of these companies for introducing them to the most gifted film-maker to promote their products. I don't have to make money from every minute of my activity.' He was talking the truth. Soon thereafter, Desikan left *Imprint* and joined *The Reader's Digest* in Mumbai, as the advertisement manager.

A Bridegroom-in-Waiting!

In the early 1960s, my mother was deeply concerned about getting her two younger daughters, Neela and Padma, married. In the order of priority, the boys were given a much lower place in that regard. Neela had emerged as an eminent Carnatic vocalist of extraordinary talent. Padma was on her way to stardom as a classical dancer. Generally, all of us in the family were proud of these two artistees and their calibre. As a musician, composer and lyricist, my mother was keen to see the two girls shine as accomplished artistees. She was only upset with my father that he was not taking equal interest in looking for suitable bridegrooms for them.

At the time of my return from New York, I began to perceive Balu's new-found interest in Padma's performances. It didn't take very long for me to realize that this was due to his interest in Shyamala, who was associated with Padma's dance performances. She had got introduced to the family when I was away in New York and Padma made it a point to introduce her to me, giving a hint that Balu was getting interested in this girl. Padma was very fond of her but was constrained by being too young to initiate talking about such things with our parents, thereby discussing it only with me. Shyamala had impeccable credentials with a degree in music, besides command over her voice, and as a researcher in the folk music of Tamil Nadu—for which she got an MLitt degree. She had spent much time with her aunt Soundaram Ramachandran, founder of Gandhigram, near Madurai, as an institution for social activism. Soundaram was the daughter of T.V. Sundaram Iyengar, founder of the nationally reputed TVS group of companies. A staunch Gandhian, she had married Ramachandran, who was a Dalit. Shyamala had been groomed by her in the most liberal traditions of an emerging society. She had also become a favourite visitor of both my parents, who showered affection on her.

I became proactive about doing what best I could in the interests of my brother—for despite our differences in personality and attitudes I genuinely loved and respected him. I spent long hours with him to ascertain his level of interest in Shyamala. I had long independent conversations with Shyamala too. Fortunately, I was able to win her trust, prompting her to say, 'Think of me as your sister; and your brother as a prospective bridegroom. Yes, he is a good man and I like him. But do you think I should marry him? Don't look at it only from his perspective.'

Balu was not the kind of person who would open up and say what was in his mind. I more or less read his mind and came to the conclusion that he would not marry any other girl. In conversation he would shower praise on Shyamala, but at the end repeat in a defeatist tone, 'But my marrying her will not happen.' However, the truth was that Balu was in love with Shyamala. In that era, over half a century ago, it was not merely fear of our mother's reservations about her son marrying an Iyengar girl, but also of the mental block of other older relatives that Shyamala's famous aunt had married a Dalit leader.

After several long conversations, I got the concurrence from the bride and bridegroom. We knew that our father was delighted with this development. Padma and I were confident of getting our mother's approval also because she was very fond of Shyamala. We did not expect that certain negative personalities would poison my mother's mind so strongly that she would turn vehemently against the proposal.

The wedding was organized in the temple town of Tirupathi.

Even though my mother accompanied us to Tirupathi, some relatives brainwashed her and tried to prevent her from attending the wedding by asking her to stay in her room and not go to the wedding hall. Without mincing words, I directly crossed swords with the most cunning among them, alongside persuading my mother to come with me to the wedding hall and bless the couple. It was the only occasion in my life when my mother slapped me in a fit of anger. Ironically, the slap helped because she felt sorry for it and accompanied me to the marriage hall.

When the wedding was over, the bridal couple and a few hundred guests had darshan at the temple and started leaving for different destinations. When all the cars and vans had left, I stayed back for an hour to settle the accounts of the marriage hall, caterers and so on. I got dropped at Renigunta railway station. I boarded a first class compartment which had six berths with an attached toilet in the old design of Indian Railways, as an independent unit, with no connecting corridor to walk to other compartments. I felt it somewhat strange that the only occupant in the compartment was sleeping on an upper berth.

As the train moved, I heard the man in the upper berth calling, 'Babu!' I looked up and found the celebrated poet Harindranath Chattopadhyaya, my father's friend, known for his leftist leanings, his guest appearances in some Hindi movies, and also as brother of Sarojini Naidu, an associate of Mahatma Gandhi.

The poet climbed down from the upper berth and sat opposite me, cordially enquiring about everyone in the family. Our wonderful conversation lasted all the way till we arrived in Chennai. However, I would rightly describe it as a monologue of that genius, with my occasional short interruptions. Suddenly he asked me, 'Are you capable of intense love?'

I said, 'Yes.'

He thought for a second and asked, 'Are you capable of

intense hatred?' I instantly said, 'Unfortunately, yes.'

'Oh! That's good; you are honest! You would be either a saint or a hypocrite if you had said "No" to the second question.' He continued, 'Okay! Tell me something that you hate the most.'

'Loneliness!' I replied.

'Now tell me something that you love most.'

I smiled and said, 'Solitude!'

He got up and hugged me, saying, 'That's wonderful. You should dedicate your life to the sublimation of all loneliness in the world to solitude.'

Time is truly a healer. We were all part of one joint family and my mother began to accept her eldest daughter-in-law, gradually, because after all she had been very close to her before the marriage proposal was mooted.

Within a year thereafter, Ramanu fell in love with my father's secretary, Bama, who was also a dance student of Padma. Unlike Balu, Ramanu did not depend on any assistance from his brother or sister to take a decision. He just absconded from home one day and a few days later announced that he was married. Bama belonged to the Nayar caste of Kerala and it became very difficult for us at home to tackle the near-hysterical condition of my mother. Despite his being one of the most liberal among all men, my father remained non-committal in the spirit of giving solace to my mother—realizing that the youngsters were capable of taking care of themselves. To me, Balu's reaction was the most unacceptable. He became antagonistic to his brother. For a few years, I was the only periodic visitor from our family to Ramanu and Bama's. However, Ramanu was visiting us regularly commencing from a few months after his wedding, but Bama began visiting Balu's house again only some years after her marriage.

In 1966, my brother Chandru got an opportunity to visit Canada as part of a youth delegation from India. While the sponsors in Toronto took care of the hospitality, his airfare had to be paid by him. The ticket cost was enormous by the standards of our joint family's income at that time. Apart from his being my pet little brother, I also thought about the fact that my family had spent on my studies in America, and I felt it was my duty to sponsor Chandru's trip. I borrowed from a bank to buy his air ticket, and repaid the loan in monthly instalments over the next two years. Chandru had studied at the Madras School of Social Work and was looking for opportunities in Canada to further his education. Even though his trip was originally supposed to be only for a few weeks, he managed to pursue his studies at Toronto until a spectacular career unfolded before him. He worked as a professional social worker visiting orphanages for a few years, took interest in music groups and made an impression as a producer of ethnic Indian TV shows in Canada, became a Canadian citizen, married his fiancée of many years (Jayalakshmi, a South African citizen of Indian origin, who had been a dance student of Padma in Chennai) and, eventually, founded a TV channel called Asian Television Network in Toronto, becoming a prominent Canadian of Indian origin. That's about as briefly as I can speak of his very colourful success.

In my childhood, my father used to take me along to my stepmother SDS's house only to be fondled and spoiled by her with sweets. Within two years of my founding a company of my own, I was looking for a more spacious office than the one where I had started. SDS helped me locate a large place for rent, next door to her own house in Mylapore, and we shifted our office there. I met her more frequently during the next six years, before we shifted our office to my own house at Shastri Nagar. We had many intimate chats on the balcony of my office building in the evenings and she remained a loving figure all the time. Thus, when Ramjhi, my stepbrother younger to me by ten years, became a neighbour, there were more occasions for interactions with him. Ramjhi started a 'Light Music Group' famously named 'Abaswaram' (Out-of-tune). With his formal qualification in hotel management, he dabbled in running a restaurant for a while. But music had become his primary preoccupation. In later years, he disbanded his Light Music Group and concentrated on his very successful classical Carnatic music group 'Isai Mazhalai' featuring teenage and child talents.

When my company was in the news, taking off in its own way, information circulated that Director Subrahmanyam's third son was an eligible bachelor. It created several occasions for me to laugh in terms of friends of the family bringing proposals.

One amusing incident is worth recalling. Ranganathan had worked with my father for several years as his trusted lieutenant. Later he had shifted to Mumbai, and was in the inner working group of the media mogul Ramnath Goenka of the *Indian Express*. He knew me from my boyhood and he was very close to my mother. I had gone on a short business visit to Mumbai and was staying in the Taj Mahal Hotel. Ranganathan called me and said that there was something important and that I should go with him somewhere. I obeyed him as I held him in high esteem. He picked me up at the appointed time and dodged disclosing his mission, keeping me in suspense. Eventually, only when we were inside the lift in a modern apartment building somewhere on Marine Drive did he tell me that we were there to chat with a family and meet a potential bride for me. By the time he rang the doorbell of the house, I had no time to rebel or retract. He told me that my mother had been talking to him about finding a good alliance for me. We settled down in the posh apartment of a senior government officer, who introduced his wife and daughter to me. Ranganathan knew him well. Ranganathan taking me there was the by-product of one of their chats. I had made up my mind much earlier that I would never subject myself to this awkward interview of brides and I was looking for a formula to get out of this situation.

Within minutes of the girl joining us, the girl's father asked, 'What can I offer you gentlemen? Scotch with soda or some coffee?'

Ranganathan instantly opted for coffee. But on the spur of the moment, I said, 'If you are having scotch, I will join you.' There was a sense of shock. But the host was so generous. He brought a bottle and poured a drink for himself and for me. Ranganathan's coffee arrived. We had a pleasant evening chat and left the house.

Ranganathan chided, 'You rascal! You ask for scotch where we have come to see a bride?'

'I am very sorry, Ranganathan! I didn't mean to embarrass you.'

'That's not the point,' Ranganathan retorted. 'If I knew you would ask for a drink, I too would have opted for it and not settled for coffee! Anyway, the meeting was bound to fail the moment you dared to ask for scotch.' We both laughed till we reached my hotel. This was my state of mind hardly a year before I got married.

While I was all admiration for my father, my sympathies were entirely with my mother. She meant everything to me—nothing less than a goddess and she had gone through a lot of emotional trauma over the decades. I had heard elders, including my great-grandmother, narrate how Rao Bahadur received a bag of gold coins from one of his clients for whom he had won a major court case. It was a popular story that he opened the bag and poured the coins on the floor to create a small heap. He made his five-year-old granddaughter Meenakshi sit on top of that and prayed, 'Let Goddess Mahalakshmi always bless you.' At that time, there was no electricity in Nagapattinam. He celebrated her marriage when she was nine. He persuaded an Englishman in Chennai to spare his generator for ten days, loaded it in a lorry and brought it all the way to Nagapattinam to illuminate his house where the wedding was held. My mother had a deep attachment to that house where she was born and where she got married. Rao Bahadur gifted the house to her as part of streedhan property. When I was a teenager, she lost all the wealth she had, except the house. She had given them to her husband for investment in business as and when he wanted. My father was a great man in every respect but not in the management of finances. It was easy to cheat him and he lost heavily. In the process, he had to sell the house he had built also. This affected my mother psychologically. She may not have minded all this if my father had not developed an extramarital interest. All this made her emotionally weak and she clung to her children for love.

Her children belonged to the first Indian generation, who were legally obliged to marry only as adults. In the 1930s and 1940s, adult unmarried daughters were the new social phenomenon. My mother was happy that her elder daughters were married at the earliest legally permissible age of marriage—sixteen—but was distressed that her two younger daughters were yet unmarried although they were both above twenty-five. Amidst all this, the biggest distress to her was that her two elder sons had got married in a manner unacceptable to her. Her older relatives derived sadistic pleasure in teasing her for all this and suggesting sarcastically that 'Your next son—the foreign returned—will surely bring a foreigner into the family.' My heart craved to see her smile again. But I seemed almost helpless.

My sister, Padma (who became immensely popular as Padma Subrahmanyam), was the rising star of classical dance. I designed her dance brochures, and sometimes compèred for her shows in English, while Ramanu did the same, most of the time, in Tamil. This brought me in touch with many people from the dance and arts circles. In this process, I met a pretty young foreigner who was in Chennai along with her mother with the object of studying Indian art and culture. Over a period of months, I realized that I was meeting her often and taking more than casual interest in her, sometimes explaining Indian mythology and philosophy, and observing her perception as a foreigner. Her mother took a special interest in me—inviting me home and cooking a special meal. Some six months after our first meeting, her mother called us both for a chat. She was a person with deep religious convictions. She started by saying that she was going to share a secret with us and that I should understand it in its true spirit. She continued in an enigmatic style, that her daughter 'may have guessed a little—but then it is time to explain the whole story. When this girl was about five years of age, she was laid up with high fever diagnosed as pneumonia. The doctors were trying several medications, while I spent my time in prayer. My husband, who was then alive, was heartbroken. I went to our church and prayed at the altar. I explained the matter to our priest who was closely known to us and told him that I want my daughter alive and healthy. He also prayed for me to the Mother and after a few seconds, turned to me and said, "Yes; your prayer will be answered, but you have to make a difficult decision; rather, a difficult promise." I said, I will do anything!' He said, "Don't be perturbed. I will suggest something holy. Take a vow to dedicate your daughter to the church in the order of the nuns to serve the Lord when she grows up." It was a big shock for me. But then that was the order of the Lord! I had no choice, but to obey it. A minute later, I gave my commitment.'

After total silence for a few minutes, she got up and brought coffee and snacks and changed the topic casually. Was it a scheme by this lady to keep me away from her daughter? I answered the question in my mind in the negative. Having known her for several months, I saw her as a simple, pious woman, incapable of theatricals.

I had developed no romantic dreams about this pretty girl.

And yet this story created an emotional discomfort. It occurred to me for just a moment that perhaps God wants me to see a smile on my mother's face. How ridiculous—the idea of getting married to an unknown girl in an arranged marriage—I laughed it off.

Yes! I was looking for inspirational guidance. As usual with me, in such situations, I began my conversation with the greatest thinkers either of my times or of centuries ago. Well, they are conversations like the dialogues of the Upanishads. Most of the Upanishads are in the form of a dialogue between two people—often between a student and a teacher. There are no holds barred in the arguments. A student can ask virtually anything; nothing is treated as impertinent including questioning the existence of God. In my walk through a bookstore in a random manner, I stumbled upon the title *The Art of Loving*. 'Is love an art?' I questioned in my mind. I picked up the book for just a glance, expecting to reject it as some rib-tickling pornography. But when I found that it was written by one of the greatest psychiatrists of twentieth-century Europe, Eric Fromm, I brought it home and spent the next couple of days with it. That was my long conversation with Eric Fromm. He answered all my questions with a great deal of clarity. I will keep quoting him all through my life, but here is an excerpt.

> People think that to love is simple, but that to find the right object to love—or to be loved by—is difficult. This attitude has several reasons rooted in the development of modern society. One reason is the great change which occurred in the twentieth century with respect to the choice of a 'love object'. In the Victorian Age, as in many traditional cultures, love was mostly not a spontaneous personal experience which then might lead to marriage. Marriage was contracted by convention by the respective families and love was supposed to develop once the marriage had

been concluded. In the last few generations, the concept of romantic love has become almost universal in the Western world. This new concept of freedom in love must have greatly enhanced the importance of the object as against the importance of the function. This is because one does not see that love is an activity, a power of the soul, one believes that all that is necessary to find is the right object—and that everything goes by itself afterward. This attitude can be compared to that of a man who wants to paint but who, instead of learning the art, claims that he has just to wait for the right object and that he will paint beautifully when he finds it. If I truly love one person, I love all persons. I love the world; I love life. If I can say to somebody else, 'I love you', I must also be able to say, 'I love, in you, everybody; I love, through you, the world; I love, in you, also myself.'

The next day, I walked up to my mother and told her that I was ready to marry any girl of her choice. I put a caveat—I wanted her to be selected also by my manni (sister-in-law)—Shyamala. By that time, my mother was on better terms with her, although the wounds had not healed entirely. I announced this to manni as a simple statement. She laughed. 'You got me a bridegroom and so you want a return favour?'

A Beautiful Child

It's time that I pick up the threads and talk about Mohana. I have taken more space for my own story because I have to cover thirty years of my life, as against only twenty of hers, before the stories converge. In 1969, if an angel had seen us both from the sky, she would have probably observed:

Chemistry is her passion and poetry,
To him, it's a mind-boggling mystery;

> He adores the human drama of history,
> To her, all that story is dull and sultry;
> Her scientific mind is sharp and realistic,
> His ethereal thoughts are exotic, erratic;
> She is scholarly and fluent in Hindi,
> His writing in Tamil is quite trendy;
> In grasping which, she is a little slow,
> While her Hindi, he doesn't follow!
> How good would be their chemistry?
> Let me track their lives' unfolding tapestry.

Subramania Ganapadigal[12] was a Vedic scholar in Siddamalli village near Kumbakonam, and was highly respected for his erudition throughout Thanjavur district in the late nineteenth century. His wife, Nagalakshmi, gave birth to their only son, Balachandran, on 30 December 1898, in their ancestral home. The village had about seventy brick houses with tiled roofs (and an equal number of thatched-roof huts for the farm labourers). Ganapadigal was the eldest of three brothers, who all lived under one roof with their wives and children, as a joint family. He had taken the mantle as head of the family, when his father Seshadri Sharma, an Ayurvedic physician, passed away at a ripe old age. Sharma's second son, Atmanatha Iyer, pursued English education and became a clerk in the education department of the provincial government. His English must have been so good that some Englishmen in Kumbakonam, posted as government officers, engaged him as 'tuition master' for their children. The youngest of the three brothers, Narayanaswami, stayed at home and managed the family's small farm.

Ganapadigal died when he was hardly thirty, leaving behind his wife and only son Balachandran. A daughter, his only other

---

[12]'Ganapadigal' is an honorific given to the one who has reached the highest level of proficiency in Vedic chanting.

child, had passed away earlier. The social security of children like Balachandran was taken care of by an age-old tradition by which other earning members of the family considered it their Dharma to protect them. Atmanatha Iyer, too, wanted to treat Balachandran as his own son. But he had to bow down to his wife's dictum that his salary was not enough for such 'charity'. That is when Atmanatha Iyer used his proficiency in English to great advantage. He began to work for more hours as a tuition teacher and earmarked all that extra income to send Balachandran to school, telling his wife that this income was out of her purview.

Balachandran married Mangalam, when he was studying for his bachelor's degree at St Joseph's College, Tiruchirappalli. After graduation, he got a job in the office of the accountant general of the Madras Presidency, at Madras city, and set up home with his wife. In that era, old and large traditional houses with terracotta tiled roofs were apportioned as rental spaces to accommodate different small families, and Balachandran occupied one such. His neighbour in the same house was a tall leader of the freedom movement, Satyamurthy. The two young couples became good friends. Balachandran's eldest son, Subramanian (Mani), was born in 1924 and his daughter, Janaki, in 1929.

Balachandran was sent on deputation by his office to Bengaluru, where he worked for four years, gained experience and then he got promoted. His son and third child, Rajagopal (Raju), was born in Bengaluru in 1930. When he returned to Chennai and rented another 'portion of a house' as it used to be called, Mangalam was pregnant with her fourth child. The house owner refused to permit the delivery of a child in his house due to a superstition. Hence, Balachandran borrowed money and bought a piece of land in Venkatesan Street, T. Nagar, and earned the cooperation of a relative to build a small house there, within three months, so as to shift there for his wife's delivery. Getting admitted in a nursing home in that era for childbirth was a rarity. Kothandaraman (Kondu) and the next son, Viswanathan (Vichhu), were born there. It was suggested that to improve his career prospects, Balachandran should shift to a state which had a shortage of trained accounting manpower. Orissa (now, Odisha) needed such experienced professionals, and Balachandran got into a higher position. But the accountant general's office of Orissa was functioning in Ranchi (then, it was part of Bihar and now, it is capital of Jharkhand), and so Balachandran and family began to live there. While they lived in Ranchi they had five children including their sons, Venkatoramani (Ramani) and Radhakrishnan, and three daughters, Lakshmi, Radha and Mohana—who was the youngest.

In that era, Ranchi had many practitioners of tantric cults. If, for instance, there were heavy floods, it was common for a tantric magician—known as a Moori Katava—to declare in a séance that sacrificing a child to a village deity would result in the receding of floods or bringing any such other calamity under control. He would sometimes specify a male child, sometimes a female child—between one and five years of age. Later, a severed body and its head would be discovered at a riverbank. Hence, families with young children had to take extra precautions. In such a milieu, Mohana as a child was specially guarded by her parents, and not allowed to play outdoors in their days in Ranchi.

Mohana as a teenager

Ranchi was also a notorious area for

dacoits. There were celebrity dacoits who would send an advance letter to a household stating that they would raid that place on a given date, asking that all the valuables be kept ready and handed over to them. Disobedience may cost a life or two. Hence, Mangalam made it a habit to hide the family jewels in tamarind sacks (tamarind is an important spice in South Indian cooking) or hidden in other spices in the kitchen. An occasional dacoit would make a casual visit and go away without causing much disturbance to this family, because he was in any case more interested in looting a prosperous local landlord than a middle-class government officer from South India.

Close to his retirement from Odisha government service, Balachandra Iyer opted to join the state government in Hyderabad, which gave a longer number of years to work, and higher position and pay. He moved there with his wife and their two youngest children—Radhakrishnan and Mohana—while the elder sons and daughters continued their studies in Ranchi.

Balachandran's eldest daughter Janaki's marriage had been celebrated in 1943, when she was just fourteen years old, to Balakrishnan, a son of Mangalam's maternal uncle, in Chidambaram. Although India had passed a law in 1928 fixing the minimum age of girls for marriage at sixteen, it took several years for this to be implemented, and many girls got married when they were fourteen—as a compromise between the earlier custom of getting them married when they were seven or eight and the legal age of sixteen. And so, Janaki had delivered a baby boy shortly after Mohana was born. Although Janaki was happy having become part of a prosperous, locally well-known family (besides her husband's status in an administrative position in Annamalai University), she had a grudge against her parents that she alone was not educated beyond school while one of her younger sisters proceeded to get a master's and the other two doctoral degrees.

One of the earliest things that Mohana recalls from her

childhood is the daily visit of a street vendor who used to sell bananas and visited their home, in Hyderabad, early in the morning. He believed that gifting a few bananas to this child would bring him luck the whole day in his sales. Embarrassed to receive the bananas free, her mother bought another dozen or two from him on payment and distributed them to all the children and their friends. Balachandran interpreted this as a vendor's sales strategy to sell that number of bananas early in the morning by giving a few to the child free. He even cautioned Mangalam to stop this habit since this fellow may use it as a ploy to kidnap children. But with due precautions, this routine continued. Although the Hyderabad princely state had already merged with India by the historic effort of Sardar Vallabhbhai Patel, the Nizam and his family were major forces to reckon with as the ex-rulers. Hence for a few years two currencies were legal tender. The currency of the Nizam was called hali (meaning local) while the Indian rupee was described as kaldar (meaning national currency). The Indian currency had not been converted into the decimal system. Since both the currencies were in circulation in Hyderabad, there was much confusion among the public. Proving her prowess in arithmetic and accounts at the age of five, Mohana became a 'consultant' to her mother on converting the two currencies and make proper payment to vendors. Her mother always took her along for shopping. A rupee consisted of sixteen annas and an anna consisted of twelve paise. Similarly, hali was also not in multiples of ten and the conversion was in complicated fractions.

Mohana was only five years old when her parents moved to Hyderabad. Although her parents spoke Tamil at home and the children picked it up, they were all more proficient in Hindi than in their mother tongue. Hindi has several local dialects across the country, which differ from the peculiar dialects of Hyderabad, owing to the influence of Urdu besides Telugu—the regional language. Her parents were not proficient in Hindi, since they began to learn this language out of necessity while living in Bihar. They often depended on little Mohana to speak to vegetable vendors, since the elder children were in Ranchi. Mangalam made use of Radhakrishnan and Mohana as interpreters to talk to common people in Hyderabad—more often, Mohana because Radhakrishnan was sent to school.

Initially, due to the insecure conditions in Ranchi, and later, since Mangalam wanted her pet youngest baby's company, Mohana was not sent to school till she was about ten. Her siblings were also her tutors, and among them Kondu was her maths teacher and was a strict taskmaster. She directly joined Class V in Raja Bahadur Sir Bansilal Balika Vidyalaya (RBSBBV), a girls' school under Marwari management. Her elder sister, Lakshmi, had studied in the same school paying full fees. The next one, Radha, was entitled to 50 per cent discount on school fees and if a third child joined the same school, tuition fee was totally

From left: Radha, Mohana and Lakshmi

waived for that child. Thus, the family did not spend on her education from day one. From their house in Chikkadpally, the sisters went by bus for about 8 km and walked another couple of kilometres from the bus stop to their school.

Mohana was treated as a darling child in her school also since she became the teachers' pet. Radha had finished her graduation and was a teacher in the same school. The fellow teachers put gentle pressure on Radha to carry her pretty little sister's lunch box to the school and gave the child the privilege of eating in the teachers' room. On the extra-curricular front, Mohana joined a dance class at the Government Music College where the classes were held before or after school hours.

The Music College was near King Koti, the city palace of the Nizams. One of the common sights which the dance students witnessed was that of servants carrying large tiffin carriers bundled in colourful cloth to several women of the Nizam's harem. It was a routine to deliver food from the central kitchen in the palace to about a hundred women in their dwellings in the lane. The dance students were frightened to walk alone in that area and always formed groups to walk through that street.

RBSBBV had an unusual way of encouraging extra-curricular activities. The dance students never cut their academic classes nor was there any compensatory leave of absence for such students. If, for instance, the dancer had a performance representing the school on an examination day, she would be permitted to answer merely four questions instead of six in the question paper, finishing the exam in two hours instead of three. The marks given for the four questions would be proportionately extended for fair comparison with the other students answering all the six. Under Marwari management, the school followed strict Hindu traditions. Cows were worshipped on important dates and cows' urine sprinkled on all the students for blessing. Near the school was the core Islamic Charminar area. While normally things were peaceful, there were also several occasions of communal conflicts. At such times the students were asked to stay in the school itself, as a measure of protection, until their parents or guardians came to fetch them. The luxurious Falaknuma palace, where the Nizams resided, was visible from the school.

An annual event the students watched with interest from the school terrace was the visit of the Nizam to his wife's tomb in an ornamental chariot with much paraphernalia. Everything was black including the chariot and the horses to denote the death anniversary of the queen.

There was a weekly Sadachar (Moral Science) class for students, wherein the Bhagavad Gita and other scriptures were taught. Mohana's parents were religious in a broad sense, but without much faith in ritualistic practices. There was more of that in the school than at home. But the child Mohana from the age of ten began to spend several hours every day in the Balaji temple at Chikkadpally, not far from her home. Every time her mother asked her to buy vegetables or coconut from the nearby market, she made a detour to the temple in the same area and walked around the ambulatory passage as part of her worship. The age difference between her parents and herself made her look more like their grandchild. The parental role was often played by her elder brother, Raju, and sister, Lakshmi Bai. It was Lakshmi who came to the school for any parent–teacher meeting, or at school functions in which the little girl danced. Raju pampered her with sweets and new clothes all the time. She was indeed a favoured princess at home as well as in school. It was taken for granted that she would get first rank in every subject, except English, in which she was weak.

Her Hindi was so good that she could speak every dialect of the language, be it Bihari or Bhojpuri, Hyderabadi or Marwari. Because of her local friends, she was proficient in Telugu although she did not learn the Telugu script. As she came up to higher classes, her interest was increasingly centred on science and not humanities. Since her school was a multipurpose higher secondary school, as it was classified, she finished up to Class XII there with her name appearing on the roll of honour listing the best student of every batch. Incidentally, her two elder sisters had also found their names in the roll of honour in the years before she did.

By the time she finished her school, she was also an accomplished dancer. She got a government diploma in dance from music college and often performed at school and college functions.

Mohana's main dream was that of becoming a physician by joining a medical college after finishing Class XII. She would have got admission on the basis of mere merit in the Warangal Medical College if an additional fee of ₹6,000 had been paid to that college. But her father was not keen to spend that much more, since he always calculated that he should allot his resources equally to all his children. Moreover, her parents were not keen to send her to a hostel. There was a scheme by which she could join the Nizam College in Hyderabad itself for a bachelor's degree in science which would enable her (if she got high grades) to join medical college in the second year of the five-year-long MBBS course in Hyderabad. They decided to take this route.

The Nizam College in Hyderabad is a prestigious institution with a long history—a co-educational institution with a very colourful atmosphere. It attracted students from very prosperous families. The annual elections for the students' union used to be on a grand scale as though they were contesting for the legislative assembly. Mohana recalls how one group mounted on horses to canvass for votes in the university campus, while the rival candidate came mounted on an elephant to promote his candidature.

Having studied in a Hindi-medium school, Mohana found it

difficult to compete with the students coming from an English-medium background. And the English lecturer was upset that a student who was very bright in all other subjects was unable to shine in his class. But he did not know how to go about encouraging a student weak in English. He took the route of asking her to stand in the open classroom and answer questions from the English lessons including Shakespeare, as though it was necessary to embarrass her and thus make her put in more effort. Eventually, by hard work, she got some decent marks in English, although she was not among the top rankers.

Candidates who got very high marks in chemistry in the first year exam of BSc were automatically transferred to the university as BSc [Special] students, to get training of a higher level. Mohana was included in that scheme, automatically, since she scored 99 per cent in chemistry. This course included several branches of chemistry, which were not in the syllabus of the normal BSc class. It also guaranteed Mohana a seat in the master's degree after completing BSc [Special]. Her chemistry answer papers were obviously so good that the professors read them out in MSc classrooms as model answers. During her three years of undergraduate studies, she earned the popular sobriquet 'Miss Chemistry' among the students and staff.

There was an excellent rapport between students and professors of Osmania University. An incident which Mohana would never forget relates to her gold medal for the university first rank in chemistry. The gold medal had been instituted for a girl student getting the highest marks in chemistry and it was Mohana who got that. But a printing error in the mark sheet spelt her name as Mohan Iyer, instead of Mohana Iyer. 'Mohan' being a masculine name, the girl who got the next-best marks—Geeth—was listed to receive the gold medal and her parents were invited for the convocation. With exemplary innocence and integrity, Geetha brought this error to the notice of her friend, Mohana, prompting her to protest. Mohana walked into the room of the principal, explained the error and demanded the correction. The principal apologized and said, 'I will take corrective action.' The student said, 'I will receive the medal only at the convocation. If you take time to engrave my name and give it personally later, I don't want it!' The principal smiled and said, 'You will get the medal with your name etched on it tomorrow, at the convocation.' In the academic atmosphere of Osmania University, it was possible for a young student to protest and get justice. When she received her gold medal, her parents could not attend the convocation as there was no time to issue invitations to them. The reason for narrating this event in detail is that it stands in contrast to what happened after Mohana shifted to Chennai later and pursued her education.

It was assumed that she would continue her MSc studies in the same university. Subba Rao, head of organic chemistry, came

Mohana with her parents

to know that she had a plan of switching over to medical college after completing her BSc. He tried to influence her. 'You have a great future in organic chemistry. Don't rush to medical college like a normal student.' But her heart was in medicine. She made use of a scheme in the medical college by which applicants with high grades in BSc could join second year of MBBS, shortening the medical course by one year, and she very merrily joined the medical college.

When she was sixteen or so—Mohana narrates with a touch of humour—a boy started stalking her from home to college, and then back home. Wherever she went, whether it was to her college, temple or dance class, the boy followed her about fifteen feet behind her. Increasingly conscious of being stalked, she reported it to her mother. Mangalam said, 'Treat him like your bodyguard in busy streets. He will ensure nobody else bothers you. You avoid lonely streets for some time.'

Introvert by nature and having a select group of friends with whom she interacted, she was nevertheless popular in the college because of both her academic brilliance and her Bharatanatyam performances on many occasions in the college. Hindi film songs with remarkably poetic lyrics and melodious tunes along with soul-stirring songs of Tulsidas, Meera and Kabir, besides those of the Sufis, inspired her. She developed a special interest in ghazals and became a fan of Begum Akhtar. Without any formal training, she built a reputation as a singer among her peers. And then, circumstances brought about a change of mood. Balachandra Iyer retired from service and he, with Mangalam, moved to Chennai to expand the house they had built several years earlier in T. Nagar, which was considered a quiet area for people to settle down after retirement with basic facilities, but without congestion and with hardly any traffic. Past seventy and a decade after his retirement, Iyer thought it was time to live in a home of his own in the city where he had most of his close relatives. The elder siblings of Mohana were to look after her in Hyderabad.

Even before this, her eldest brother had got employed in Sambalpur, at the construction site of the Hirakud dam. And now, Raju was posted at the Indian Audit Office in the Indian High Commission at London, which was responsible for auditing the Indian embassies all over Europe. Vichhu also got employed in London. While Raju and his wife returned to India a few years later, Vichhu made London his home and became a British citizen. Kondu got employed in a cement factory in Mancherial, while Ramani, a geologist, who sometimes cooked for Mohana and himself when she had to study for her exams, when their parents were away, moved to Ahmedabad as an officer of the Geological Survey of India. Radhakrishnan, next in the line, got employment in the National Productivity Council at Pune. Her sister, who was like a mother to her, Lakshmi, a brilliant academician with a master's degree in linguistics, got a fellowship and went to America to pursue her doctoral studies. Hence, Radha and Mohana were the only two who continued to live in their house in Hyderabad.

Being eight years elder, Radha showered much affection on her little sister, getting her gifts and new clothes every month on her salary day. With a master's degree in statistics, she was employed in a senior position in a government research institution and her office was on the outskirts of Hyderabad. She had to leave early in the day and return late in the evening because of the commuting time. Although Mohana had an elderly lady as a neighbour, who had a motherly affection for her, loneliness crept into her mind. Having grown up with several siblings—all elder to her—she missed them all.

One evening, Radha and Mohana went to a movie hall, and were in the women's queue to buy their tickets, when a suspicious-looking middle-aged woman deliberately dragged them into a quarrel. They soon realized that she had a few henchmen with her. Radha identified her as a notorious sex-racket agent. The two sisters managed to leave the cinema hall unobtrusively before the show was over and hurried home, in what they perceived as a narrow escape from a potential trap. The youngster did not attend college for the next three or four days, while the elder sister after giving her company for two days, requested their kind neighbour to take care of her when she herself had to go to work.

On another day, a classmate introduced her father to Mohana casually at a bus stand. Soon enough, the old man volunteered to accompany his daughter and her friends to a temple. To Mohana's utter shock, the lewd old lecher made advances to her in the crowded bus, unmindful of his daughter travelling with them. She hurriedly changed her seat. The youngster began to feel a deep sense of insecurity, although nothing had happened. Her parents, who were in an age group where they could have been her grandparents, were now away in Chennai building a home, while her elder siblings except one had gone away in pursuit of their careers.

Young men from across the college campus greeted Mohana after every dance performance, gave her flowers and shook hands. Mohana was not the kind to date any young man, although every boy who liked her performances or admired her for her academic brilliance would have cherished taking her out for a quite dinner or to a Hindi movie. But she had no time to think of romance, since her goal was to become a physician or a scientist and she did not want ephemeral romantic relationships to become obstacles to her larger goals in life. And she wished to remain committed, pure and innocent to the core of the family's traditional values, inherent in her upbringing. A combination of these factors provoked a fit of anger against her parents for leaving her alone.

She had a close Muslim friend, who used to wear her purdah (veil) up to the time of reaching college, remove it during the class hours, and wear it again to go home. This girl planned to secretly get married to her maternal uncle in a relationship not permitted by Islam. When asked how she would face the rest of the family, she said her uncle and she would migrate to some far-off country. Mohana couldn't imagine a girl deserting her parents and the brothers and sisters she had grown up with to marry someone not acceptable to any of them.

Lakshmi and Radha who were ten and eight years older than Mohana, respectively, were not yet married. The family astrologer rejected any alliance for them. On one such visit to an astrologer, Mangalam took a few horoscopes for comparison, and Mohana was by her side. The astrologer said, 'Get this girl married first. I can easily find matching horoscopes for her.' Subconsciously, it must have worked in the young girl's mind.

Soon after her twentieth birthday, in a momentary outburst, she told her mother, 'Either you come back to Hyderabad and take care of me, or get me married so that I will find my own security!' Mangalam jumped with joy. Traditional Indian parents consider it their most important duty to get their daughters married at an early age. Both Iyer and Mangalam had been very concerned that three of their four daughters were not yet married. It is no surprise that even though the twenty-year-old said something in anger in the heat of the moment, Mangalam grabbed the idea and said, 'Look, I am not coming back to Hyderabad. I will certainly find a suitable match for you soon.' Iyer started examining the matrimonial columns.

Mother's Choice

I recall a story I heard long ago. A man remained unmarried all his life and when he was in his deathbed at ninety-six, his close friends asked him, 'We have always hesitated asking you, this, in order not to interfere in your privacy, but now you won't lose anything by answering us. Why did you never get married?' The old man smiled and said, 'I waited all my life to marry the perfect woman.' One friend asked, 'You mean you never found one all these decades?' The old man said,'Well, I actually did find one,

From left: The groom's father, the bride, the groom with his brother, Balu, and Deputy Prime Minister Morarji Desai

but she was waiting for the perfect man!'

Shyamala (Manni) was delighted to take on the responsibility and deemed it a loving privilege to find a bride for me. Together with Balu, she was actively hunting for a few months, reporting periodically to my mother. My mother was keen to match the horoscopes of the bride and bridegroom, before finalizing the wedding. So Balu and Manni shortlisted to meet only girls whose horoscopes matched with mine. In this context, my mother pulled out my horoscope from the bundle of personal papers from her cupboard. Balu noticed the difference in my date of birth as per all my official records from that in the horoscope. The story goes back to the time when I was admitted in Class VI in the National High School, Nagapattinam. When my teacher, Ramamoorthy Iyer, was told that I was July-born, he filled up my date of birth as 15 July 1937, as an approximate date for the school records. Nobody at that time imagined the importance of recording the accurate date in such records and hence, took no initiative to correct it as 29 July 1938. From my school records, it went on to my college records and eventually to my passport and my insurance policies, etc. I consulted a lawyer, who told me very casually, 'This discrepancy matters only if you were a government servant thereby affecting your retirement age. Since you are a self-employed person, it is of no consequence, except that you will be paying a slightly higher insurance premium.' Hence, I left the matter at that and never got the records corrected.

Between Balu and Manni, they shortlisted two profiles, and wanted my mother and me to accompany them to see the girls. I took just a few minutes to think and said that the three of them could visit the two families and my mother would have the veto.

Eventually, for reasons I don't remember, they went on the first visit to somebody and while going to the next place, decided that they should take me along. Their argument that the girl and her parents would like to meet me convinced me that I should go along.

We went to Balachandra Iyer's house in T. Nagar. The Iyer couple on the one side and Balu, Manni and my mother on the other did the talking. It seemed as though neither Mohana nor I had anything to say. Of course, I saw a very beautiful girl and knew from the letters of her father to my brother that she was a university rank holder and that she was a dancer. My mother had a brief conversation with Mohana. Her body language and the manner in which she started talking to Mohana left no doubt in anyone's mind that she was very impressed. As we left the compound of Iyer's bungalow, she declared to me aside, 'This girl is my choice.' That was 3 January 1969.

When Mangalam and Balachandra Iyer asked their daughter, for whom it was the one and only experience of meeting a prospective bridegroom, she replied, 'Wait for them to call you; let's decide after that.' Balu and Iyer spoke to each other within hours and organized the bride and her family to visit our house to meet my father. For reasons which I never understood, they

The mother with her son and daughter-in-law the day after the wedding

did not inform me of this meeting and it happened when I was away in my office.

Although by that time it had become conventional even among very conservative families to organize for the boy and girl to meet in one of their houses just aside in the garden or in an adjacent room to talk to each other for a while, no such thing was arranged for us. The only opportunity we had to exchange pleasantries was on 3 January 1969, before we met as bride and bridegroom, exactly thirty-four days later, on 7 February. Mohana's eldest sister, Janaki, and her husband, Balakrishnan, had taken the responsibility to fix the wedding hall and make all the arrangements in Chidambaram.

Padma had not seen the bride and was very keen to do so. After a dance programme in Delhi, she boarded a flight to Chennai, which had a stopover in Hyderabad for forty-five minutes. Iyer informed his daughter to meet Padma at the airport. Padma was delighted to meet her would-be sister-in-law and the two got along famously in those thirty minutes they spent at the airport lounge. By coincidence, Shyam Rao, a very good friend of mine from the Presidency College days, who was in a senior position in a company in Hyderabad, was also at the airport. Padma introduced him to Mohana. The very next day, Shyam visited Mohana to congratulate his friend's bride, in advance, since he would not attend the wedding. The bride used the opportunity to talk to her groom's friend to know more about the person to whom she was getting married to and his family. Shyam talked about my father as a generous man with very modern views, reinforcing Mohana's confidence that a family which was progressive enough to encourage a daughter to take up dance as a career would certainly be the right environment for her to pursue her medical education by changing to a college in Chennai.

There were discussions between Balu and Shyamala with

Mohana's parents about the wedding arrangements. On the bride's side, some relatives gossiped how Balachandra Iyer got such a famous man as sammandhi, parent of the son-in-law. One of them reported to Iyer, 'The groom has no landed property and the family is not living in luxury as most cinema people are.' Iyer cryptically replied, 'I rely on his master's degree from the US, with no assumption of any property.'

One day my father surprised Mohana's parents by an informal visit and chat in which he told them, 'It is generally known to everybody that I have a relationship with S.D. Subbalakshmi outside my marriage. I hope you will understand that she will also attend the wedding.' Iyer turned to his wife, who nodded a gesture of 'yes' and he turned to the visitor saying 'yes' without hesitation. When they were alone Mangalam shared her thoughts with her husband while Mohana was present. 'Many men in a weak moment develop an extramarital relationship, which often is short-lived, since men disown such women in no time. Having developed a relationship like that, only a great man can acknowledge it publicly and say that she will participate in his son's wedding.' Iyer nodded in approval. They were not endorsing his extramarital relationship. They were appreciating his transparent attitude without any hypocrisy. Mangalam—even more than her husband—was capable of judging people in a jiffy and assessing their character. She respected and followed perennial values. But she was against obscurantism and caste prejudices. She respected the dignity of individuals and their liberty. Above all, she was immensely humane and non-judgemental in reacting to people. Wrapped in a nine-yard sari, she belonged to an earlier century. In her attitude, she belonged to a future generation.

A luxury bus had been chartered for the groom's party to travel from Chennai to Chidambaram, although several others were going by cars. My father insisted that he and I should be in the bus. Apart from close relatives, persons who travelled with us included JK as well as Manian of Ananda Vikatan and his wife, Lalitha.

Mohana and her sister, Radha, caught a train from Hyderabad to arrive in Chennai on 3 February to join their parents, four days before the wedding. That day, C.N. Annadurai (a popular mass leader and chief minister of Tamil Nadu) passed away in a hospital in Chennai. The state came to a standstill. There was a shutdown. There was neither any public transport nor taxis. The sisters reached their home in T. Nagar a few hours later, in an adventurous way, carrying with them heavy, expensive silver articles made for the wedding.

In the wedding ceremonies, when the auspicious time (muhurtam) was approaching, the bride suddenly fainted in the quarters for the bride's party adjacent to the wedding mandap. Her relatives were worried that it should not be misconstrued as her being unhealthy in some manner. They protected her from the sight of others until she slowly gained consciousness. It was just a combination of her fatigue and anxiety, with the many questions in her mind without answers. 'Have I done the right thing? What kind of a man will my groom be? How will my in-laws treat me?' And so many such questions. At the muhurtam, the bride was indeed photogenic, but posed a problem for the official wedding photographer—because of shyness combined with anxiety, she kept her head bent down most of the time. A year later, Manian, my friend, remarked, 'She bowed down for one day and then is holding her head high, forever.' Padma also was photographing with her 'box camera' as an amateur. Since she could persuade the bride to look up and face the camera, the only good stills of our wedding in the album are those clicked by her.

My father organized a reception for us on 10 February at Chennai. Morarji Desai, deputy prime minister of India, was among the many senior leaders and freedom fighters who were in my father's list of invitees. He graciously visited Chennai and attended the reception. There were, of course, several film stars, directors and technicians—besides a vast circle of friends.

All this was going on for two people getting married who had never had the opportunity to talk to each other till that moment!

I felt sad that when I got married, although Ramanu attended and took active interest in the celebrations, he did not bring his wife. A few days after my wedding, I made it a point to visit his house taking Mohana along to join them for dinner.

There was a male chauvinistic streak in me. I thought, 'After all, I am marrying a girl ten years younger to me, who was traditional enough to ask her parents to choose a groom and, therefore, it should be possible for me to mould her and influence her to my way of thinking, however academically brilliant she is.' It did not take very long for me to realize that influencing was going to be totally mutual.

A few months later, I told an elderly friend, 'Arranged marriage is like buying a lottery. I think I am destined to get a prize-winning ticket.' He said, 'Any marriage is a gamble. Not only an arranged marriage.'

However, over a period of time, I realized that marriage is not a gamble. It is a mixture of true love with hard effort to succeed in a new relationship; and unless both partners put their heart and soul into it, the partnership will not work. This is true whether the boy and girl choose each other, or allow their elders to choose for them.

Gold Medallist Waits for a Seat

What I realized within days of our wedding was that studying medicine or science was almost Mohana's 'spiritual commitment'. I talked to my father, who said he would do his best to get her a seat in one of the only two medical colleges in Tamil Nadu. Both were government colleges and both were in Chennai.

When her brother, Rajagopal, who had played an important role in bringing her up from her childhood was hospitalized in London, Mohana—as a teenager—had taken a vow that she would either become a medical practitioner or a researcher in medicine to render service to humanity at large.

Since Mohana had finished her first year study in a medical college in Hyderabad, technically it was feasible for her to get a transfer to another medical college in India because of her exemplary academic record. However, she received her first taste of politics in an attempt to get a transfer to the Madras Medical College. There were several kinds of reservations. For those unfamiliar with reservations in India, it is important to give this background. In 1969, there were two kinds of reservations in the admission to professional colleges and most other institutions. One was a small quota for people from outside the state and the other was 16 per cent of the seats for Scheduled Castes (SCs) and Scheduled Tribes (STs). These SC and ST reservations were, in spirit, comparable to affirmative action in the US, which gives certain privileges to African–Americans in the sphere of education to encourage their assimilation in society with equal opportunity. The Constitution of India provides for such reservations for SCs and STs, who were socially in a disadvantageous position, being treated as untouchables for generations. These reservations were provided in the Constitution to give opportunities in education and employment as well as representations in the legislature and Parliament. These were originally supposed to be for two decades, during which time the assimilation process was expected to be completed. However, Parliament extended these reservations, periodically, in such a manner that they are still a reality, even seven decades after independence. Not only that; new groups demanding reservations have been created in several states for people belonging to backward castes and most-backward castes, in addition to the reservations for STs and SCs originally envisaged in the Constitution. Tamil Nadu has been in the forefront of creating these reservations, thereby implementing a drastic 'reverse discrimination' against Brahmins. If society had discriminated against lower castes over the centuries, independent India, particularly Tamil Nadu, began to discriminate against the so-called higher castes to ensure that their opportunities were drastically curtailed. Merit was unceremoniously sacrificed in

Mohana and her brother, Rajagopal, c.a. 1990

this process in selecting candidates for higher education as well as employment. India has lived with this aberration over the decades.

'Affirmative action' of the American model meant creating educational and skill development opportunities for the deprived sections of the population. The Indian model, by and large, means thrusting positions of authority on them without preparation or skill development. During the period of Nehurvian socialism, there was some justification for this policy as it was limited in scope as well as time frame. We have to go to the depth of this problem which continues to exist even in the twenty-first century. Suffice it to say for the purpose of this biographical narrative that in 1969 Mohana was unable to get into the medical college in Chennai because she belonged to Andhra Pradesh and had to find a seat within that quota and because Brahmins were the new undeclared untouchables of state policy. The impact of this political policy continued to affect her individual life and career for several years.

Having found it difficult to enter the medical college in Chennai, there were two possibilities. She could choose to return to Hyderabad and continue her second year medical college or pursue higher studies in pure science. By the time the new academic year started, Mohana was pregnant, carrying our first child. It was considered absurd to send her to Hyderabad with no elders to guide her in that condition. I felt depressed that she could not continue her chosen first preference. And now, facing the very real possibility of both of us getting into a depression, I asked her whether she would choose to join a college for a master's degree in science at Chennai. We thought about it a great deal and came to a consensus that she would continue her master's degree in Madras University, in biochemistry to eventually pursue a career in research.

Even admission for postgraduate study in biochemistry was

not an easy task. My father met A. Lakshmanaswamy Mudaliar, vice chancellor of Madras University, taking me and Mohana along, and explained the background that Mohana was a rank holder, and could not be refused an opportunity of studying in the university just because she came from another state or because she belonged to the Brahmin community. Mudaliar was an admirer of my father's films and had respect for him as a freedom fighter. Although he belonged to the Justice Party (it was the forerunner of the Dravidian parties and had its roots in the anti-Brahmin sentiments of the 1910s), he was first an

Mohana with her father-in-law

academician and physician and last of all a politician.

Mudaliar[13] spontaneously said that it would be a shame if Mohana was not given a seat for pursuing a master's degree with such a brilliant academic background. He wrote in the file that she should be given a seat. It was a period of transition when Mudaliar laid down office as vice chancellor, after serving in that position with great distinction for over twenty-five years.

His successor, Sundaravadivelu, a reputed educationist and one of the leaders of the anti-Brahmin movement, could have stopped her admission in spite of his predecessor's promise. However, he endorsed the opinion of Mudaliar and gave admission to Mohana to join MSc in biochemistry). In the process, he telephoned my father and told him in his own way, 'Your daughter-in-law is the only Brahmin candidate for whose admission to MSc I have taken the initiative. This is because I know that you are far above caste politics and I respect you for that.'

Mohana eagerly looked forward to her studies, which would lead to her career as a research scientist. However, there were major differences between her studying in Hyderabad from elementary class to the bachelor's degree and her new experience at Madras University.

Professor E.R.B. Shanmugasundaram (a Brahmin with a non-Brahmin wife) made an informal introduction of all the candidates who had joined MSc class to one another. The introduction was something like this.

'This is X, a candidate recommended by the education minister, Y has come as a candidate recommended by Z, the film

---

[13]Malcolm Adiseshaiah had narrated the following incident to me in a personal conversation. A.L. Mudaliar was also leader of the opposition in the Madras Legislative Council. He was also a leader of the Indian delegation to UNESCO. When Adiseshaiah mentioned this in a UNESCO conference, a French colleague remarked, 'This is democracy running riot—a leader of the opposition representing the country in a UN body!'

star,' and he continued with some more names, adding, 'Mohana Krishnaswamy is a candidate admitted by the vice chancellor.' He did not stop there. He went on to say, 'Incidentally, she is the only Brahmin candidate recommended by the vice chancellor.'

The caste prejudice vitiated the entire atmosphere of Tamil Nadu to such an extent that nobody was shy of even talking about it blatantly in an academic or official atmosphere. The 'reverse discrimination' and prejudice against the higher caste was going to affect the nation as well as many individual lives in the years to come. In this book, I intend to touch upon this wherever it is relevant because 'the universal emerges from the specific'. It changes perceptions, private lives and deeply affects the consciousness of the people, while affecting society adversely.

Mohana had always enjoyed a merit scholarship throughout for her education, including a scholarship from the Atomic Energy Commission for studying for her bachelor's degree and now she got a Council of Scientific and Industrial Research (CSIR) fellowship for pursuing her master's degree.

Although she felt a deep sense of gratitude to her father-in-law for helping her to pursue her education, there was a sense of remorse that it had not happened based merely on her merit! Nevertheless, she was happy in the college in terms of conducive atmosphere and friendly colleagues. She gradually discovered that there was a mercenary angle. A professor called and advised her in an apparently friendly manner that it would be a great advantage if she could take private tuition. Her colleagues knew that her level of understanding was adequate to be a teacher rather than a student. But there was an excuse to offer tuition classes because she was pregnant, and so the offer of tuition was couched in terms of being helpful to a student who may miss some classes. It took several months to understand that the real intention was to privately collect tuition fees. The student, however, had a level of self-confidence that she did not need any tuition at all.

At the personal level on the first day in the university, Manni accompanied her to the college performing a motherly role and introducing her to the faculty. My father and I took turns to drop her and pick her up from the college which was merely a five-minute drive from our house, in the traffic conditions of 1969. My mother and my sister-in-law were both sources of emotional support to her in a manner that Mohana proudly declared to her colleagues.

It is time to mention that we had an elderly cook at home, who had joined our family household a year before I was born. Her husband died when she was a teenager. And so she joined our household as domestic help. But it would be grossly erroneous to describe her as a servant. Vedambal (that was her name) identified herself so much with the family and welfare of the children that no one would consider her as one. She developed an extraordinarily special affection for the three youngest children—I, Padma and Chandru—born after Vedambal joined the household. She treated us like her own children (like in the British tradition of a nanny) and we responded with our love and affection. She welcomed Mohana as the new member of the family and became an important source of support for her to continue her education.

Vedambal

Vedambal could never have expressed her subliminal feminist attitude better than by supporting a girl's higher education after her marriage.

Triumph and Trauma

The atmosphere was conducive for Mohana to study, even though there was no one with a science background in the family to which she now belonged. Our first child arrived within a year of our marriage. Balu's son, Kannan, was about five years old and reflecting the loving spirit of a well-knit joint family, we all let him choose the name for the little girl and he chose the name 'Lata'.

But I had decided to move out of the joint family and I started looking for a rented house. The moment I discussed the idea with Mohana, she vehemently opposed it saying that she was born in a family with nine siblings and now she was very happy with her in-laws, and she found no reason for us to move away. After several discussions, she agreed that she would move with me to an independent place if I 'acquired' a house and not if we moved to a rented place. Her logic was that our moving out should give happiness to the family. After my father's house was sold in 1953, we had been living in a rented house for seventeen long years. The idea appealed to me that it will be a cause for celebration among all members of the family. But buying a house immediately seemed very difficult, since I just did not have the money.

Well, when everything was going so smooth and easy, why had I thought of moving out? I was far too independent by temperament and my family also appreciated this. By early training under my great-grandmother, and by the influence of Swami Chinmayananda in later years, I had a spiritual bent of mind, strengthened by my studying Vivekananda. But I considered some of the orthodox practices to be socially abhorrent, especially demeaning the status of women. One such practice in our family was that the women in the household had to remain aside for three days in a month. Apart from the discomfort, it was cause for much embarrassment to declare that they were going through their menstrual cycle, during which they were not allowed in most areas of the house. A separate room had been allotted to them for this purpose so that they didn't interact with others in the household during those three days. I did not want my wife to be put through this. At the same time, I did not wish to revolt and change the practice of the whole family. It was not my right to do so. The first year after my marriage passed without this problem because my first child arrived. I started laughing within myself thinking of an Italian film featuring Sophia Loren. It was a light-hearted comedy in which the police visit her with arrest warrants for many thefts she had committed. But they are never able to arrest her because Italian law prohibits pregnant women from being arrested. The heroine remains pregnant for six or seven years, delivering a baby every year.

I started house hunting in right earnest, hoping to raise loans to buy one. However, I had to abandon the project for some time because my concentration shifted to my father's health. Our family physician suspected that my father had a tumour in his colon and suggested that we treat him at the Christian Medical College Hospital in Vellore (about 120 km from Chennai). There was no comparable medical facility in Chennai. We took him to Vellore, where an eminent surgeon, Fenn, who operated on him detected malignancy, disheartening the entire family. In spite of his failing health, my father remained cheerful in the special ward of the hospital. He organized a party for the doctors and nurses who attended on him in his ward itself. Several political leaders and film personalities visited him in the hospital.

The post-operative care in the hospital took a couple of

months. We all took turns spending two days with him every week in such a way that either of my brothers or I was present with him to attend on him. My mother was allowed to stay in an adjacent room, since the doctor treated her also as an inpatient, while my sister, Neela, spent all her time there. Mohana and I made two trips to Vellore every week with our little daughter, Lata, who was less than a year old.

Mohana had not yet learnt driving. The road was not as good as it is now. While I was proud that the child insisted on sitting on my lap, it was not the most comfortable way of driving a car with a mischievous child on your lap. I managed because she would sleep in the first fifteen minutes of the drive, enabling me to leave her with her mother.

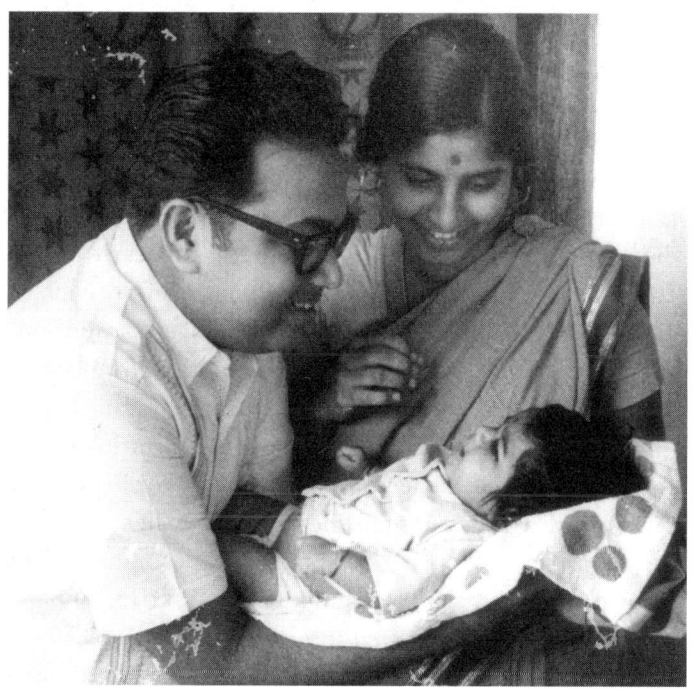

Little Lata smiling at her parents

Every member of the family was keen to visit my father, often overcrowding the ward. There was an unwritten exemption to his ward from restriction of visiting hours and number of people visiting at a time, because the doctors realized that the patient enjoyed their company. Later, when we brought him home, his health improved and we started taking him for a drive up to Marina beach. He became strong enough to hold Lata and play with her for a few minutes at the beach.

I started my property hunt again, but found nothing within my means. The issue was clinched based on a suggestion from my nephew, Ramachandran, alias Kumar, son of Lalitha. We identified a property which had the unique status of being under the Tiruvanmiyur village panchayat 'but with entrance from a city road!' C.S. Parameswaran, secretary of the Railway Board, owned this 12,000 square feet of land with a 1,400 square feet house built in one corner. We were impressed with the place because the comparable space within the Chennai municipal limit would have cost several times more. A tenant was living in the house, who staunchly dissuaded us from buying the house, showing every defect possible in the property. However, we learnt from the house owner that he had not paid rent for nearly a year. A worldly-wise friend negotiated with the tenant on my behalf and finalized that we would not merely pay the overdue rent on his behalf to the landlord but also pay three months' advance for the new house he would take on rent. But Parameswaran thought it was unfair to collect from me the rent dues from his outgoing tenant. We only paid the tenant's rent advance for his new place and he shifted within a month. Besides the small savings that I had, I got a loan from the Life Insurance Corporation of India and borrowed the balance required from a private financier. We got the property registered in January 1971. We took a few weeks to renovate the house and had a religious housewarming function on 5 March. Both my parents were visibly delighted.

Little did we realize that the joyful mood would change in just five weeks. My father's health deteriorated suddenly, and we lost him on 7 April. He was a colossus of a man in many respects—deeply and genuinely human, immensely talented, unpretentious, generous to the core, loving, caring, cheerful, radiating warmth and happiness among everyone who came in touch with him; creative and witty, commanding the respect of even his adversaries. All of us siblings had, perhaps, inherited different facets of his outlook.

Within months of my father's passing away, a celebration that brought the whole family together was my sister Neela's marriage. The family had chosen A. Krishnamurthy, a landlord with agricultural lands and other real estates in Madurai, as her groom (he was also a moneylender). Unfortunately, later he

Standing: Balu, Chandru, Krishnaswamy (holding his second child, Gita), Ramjhi and Ramanu; Sitting: Shyamala, Neela, Meenakshi Subrahmanyam, Mohana, Shobha Ramji and Bama Ramanan; Squatting: Lata, Kannan, Padma; Lakshmi and Saraswati (both Ramanu's daughters)

proved a male chauvinist to the core, with nineteenth-century values in many respects. Neela did not even enjoy the freedom to use her discretion about spending her salary as professor of music in a college in Madurai. He was rich in terms of material wealth, but the poor man was hesitant to spend any money to make life comfortable for his wife. As I was filming at the Temple of Literature in Hanoi, Vietnam, in 2006, I received the sad news that Neela had passed away after a few months of dementia. She was among those to whom God was not kind through most years of her life.

Storms in a Teacup

Several concurrent developments changed our lives after we lost our father. We had remained under his shadow, despite his encouraging individuality in each one of us. And now, each one of us began to tread a different path and I will try my best not to be judgemental in this narration from a distance of forty-six years.

On my own family front, our daughter Gita was born in November 1971, restoring the mood of joy in the family. Mohana got her master's degree, a couple of months before Gita was born.

Since, in any case, both my brothers—Balu and Ramanu—were fully creatively involved in the productions of Krishnaswamy Associates from day one, I thought it was proper to convert my proprietary firm into a joint-stock company. Mohana, Ramanu, Balu and I were the four founding directors when the private limited company was formally registered in 1971, within months of my father passing away. Since we were involved in making several corporate films for leading public and private sector organizations, our hands were full and we had to sometimes engage talent from outside to carry out our work.

However, I was restless, since I found myself nowhere near making the kind of films on heritage and culture that I had planned, in particular, my ambitious documentary on Indian history. Hence, I launched a small project of my own—a sixteen-minute film titled *I* which needed filming in different states of India—north, south, west and east. The concept was to make an experimental narrative from the perspective of a soul born several times over the centuries in different parts of the subcontinent at different times, and the soul narrating his/her story through the ages. Fortunately, at this time, Indian Airlines entrusted to me the production of a tourism promotion film for them, covering their operations in remote corners of India. It came in handy and I could simultaneously shoot for my film *I*,[14] in several areas from Kashmir to Kanyakumari. We were about fifteen people and we had a wonderful time, since this was a combination of family time with work. With me as writer-director, all of them were involved in the work including my two brothers and Mohana. Ramanu's daughters, my daughters, and Balu's son, Kannan, besides my sister, Padma, featured in small roles in the two films.

My son, Subrahmanyam alias Bharat, was born several months after our return from this tour. Eventually, *I* won the special national award on the silver jubilee of Indian independence for the best short film. The award was presented in 1975.

A few months before we left on this filming tour, Desikan had resigned from *Reader's Digest*. I invited him to join the board of Krishnaswamy Associates, which he happily accepted. Thus, we were now four full-time directors—Balu, Ramanu, Desikan and I, while Mohana was a part-time director, since, by then, she had registered for working on her PhD in biochemistry at Madras University.

---

[14]*The film* I *can be viewed on www.indianimprints.com.*

When Mohana registered as a PhD candidate, despite her getting the second rank in the university in MSc (biochemistry) and her impeccable track record, there were non-academic hurdles. However, she hoped that by the quality of her work and the doctoral thesis she would submit a few years later, merit would outshine other considerations in building up her research career.

The author receiving the Rajat Kamal (Silver Lotus) Award for the best short film on the occasion of the twenty-fifth anniversary of Indian independence for his film I from Fakhruddin Ali Ahmed, President of India. At the twenty-second National Film Festival, 1975

Krishnaswamy Associates completed a decade in 1973. I was reflecting back with mixed feelings—on the one hand, we had achieved reasonable commercial success, recognition with national awards and a reputation as an upcoming enterprise, but I was not at peace with myself, since I was not able to launch my dream film on Indian history. I talked to a few friends, including Desikan, who were willing to take the commercial responsibility of continuing the production of sponsored documentary and advertising films if Balu and Ramanu would continue such production in my absence. I say 'absence' because my plan was to devote at least two years, if not more, totally to making this long documentary on history—which meant my getting away from my commercial contracts of ad films and corporate films. I managed to get a few people to promise financial support for the project, sharing the risk with me, each supporting it to a small extent in a spirit of a cooperative endeavour.

My brothers thought it was a financially risky proposal to produce something like that at the company's cost. I was unwilling to compromise on this issue. Desikan lauded my idea but was not in a position to offer any financial support. I was at a crossroads. I would be depressed if I did not do what I wanted to. But almost everyone was warning me about the potential financial catastrophe, urging me to see the reality and abandon the idea. Mohana saw my dilemma and said casually, 'After all, I will get a PhD in a couple of years and can manage to earn on my own. Don't bother about our financial security. You have to think and make up your mind whether you really want to take this risk or not. You have two choices: be bold and swim against the current; or drop the whole project without regret. Don't grow up to be an old man stating that you had a great dream which you could never realize.'

I thought about it deeply overnight and decided that I would take the plunge even if nobody else was willing to share the risk.

Balu was willing to work on the production as a cinematographer but was unwilling to participate in the risk. Ramanu was not involved since he thought that there was not even a remote chance of the project's financial success. His aim was to make feature films in the standard Tamil film formula for success, and, of course, I had no right to interfere in that. It looked as though the company would not survive. I made a difficult decision to say that I would proceed with the project and those who were not interested, not involved or had no faith in my project, could leave the company. Balu and Ramanu resigned from the company selling their shares to me and Mohana and we settled them all as amicably as possible. Situations of this kind are certainly uncomfortable for everybody and none of us were exceptions. Some of them thought that I had undisclosed supporters, without whom I would not be so foolish! Although Desikan liked my idea, he felt he had no role to play in my new project. He resigned with goodwill, and I bought his shares in the company.

I worked out the project cost to be about ₹9 lakh, which was a lot of money in 1973. A few people were willing to give about ₹50,000 each, sharing the risk with me. But that would total only 30 per cent of my need. The convention in the film industry was that if you had 20 per cent of the capital and if you progressed with the work, some distributors would come forward and finance the rest. But this was not a commercial feature film to expect that kind of finance. I thought that it would happen. I started devoting my time on rewriting my script of 1963 vintage. It took me a few months to complete it.

After managing some part of the finance, I invited I.K. Gujral, Union Minister for Information and Broadcasting, to the first day of shooting. I had met him earlier as I was a member of some government committees including the Film Institute of India, Pune, and the Film Finance Corporation, and I had also interacted with him when I was secretary of the jury for the International Film Festival of India in 1969–70.

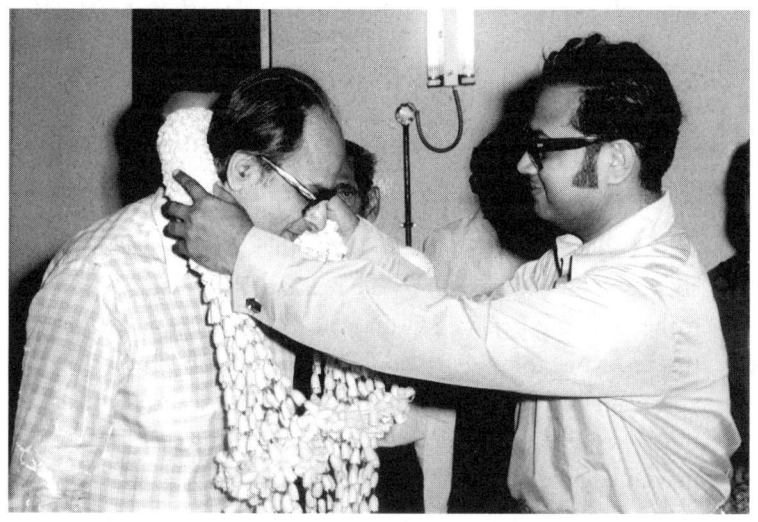

The author with Union Minister I.K. Gujral at the inaugural shooting of Indus Valley to Indira Gandhi

The Myth of My Film on Indira Gandhi

To quote from my talk on mass media on All India Radio in 1968, 'When you and I talk to each other, there are actually six people in conversation—the real me, the person I want to be, and the person I want you to think I am; besides the real you, the person you want to be and the person you want me to think you are. If that is the problem of interpersonal communication, imagine the problem of the mass media!'

I had to urgently coin a catchy title for the film denoting that the documentary narrates 5,000 years of history. I thought of a few alternatives, including *Where Centuries Coexist*, the name given to the abridged version of this film. But I needed something that would denote a dialogue between contemporary India and its historic past—on culture, heritage, politics, world view and societal values. During that time, the *Time* magazine declared Indira Gandhi as the 'Leader of the Year'. The title suddenly flashed in my mind—*Indus Valley to Indira Gandhi*—from a lamp post to a lamp post.

The title was also inspired by the excellent book on German cinema, *Caligary to Hitler*. To me, it meant the story from the Indus civilization to the present with India's powerful first woman prime minister.

I requested I.K. Gujral to symbolically switch on the camera for the first shooting day at Chennai in July 1974, close to my thirty-sixth birthday. The film's muhurat was organized where we screened my short film *I* to represent the spirit of the film being launched. *I* had just been completed but not yet released. Gujral literally fell in love with *I*.

He said, 'After seeing this film, I feel more proud to be an Indian. Krishnaswamy plans to expand this concept into a four-hour film, tracing our nation's 5,000 years' history. Hats off to his spirit of patriotism in an independent film initiative.'

The event was attended by several film personalities besides a large contingent of the press. Sundarlal Nahata, a very successful producer of feature films and president of the Film Federation of India, presided over the event. The film fraternity had never heard such a tribute being paid to a film-maker by someone in power. Till that moment, I had had no support from financiers, but suddenly there was a renewed enthusiasm about this film and me. Within minutes after the meeting was over, Nahata called me aside and said, 'This is a great project in which I would like to invest.' He was going out of town for a few days and he wanted me to meet him on his return to finalize an agreement.

The next morning, I was catching a flight to Bengaluru to address a seminar. Who do I find in the aircraft as a fellow passenger? Nahata! He said, 'It is God's plan that we should be in the same flight this morning. Let us finalize the agreement for financing your film while we are both in Bengaluru.'

I met him after my seminar at his hotel. He had a lawyer in attendance as well as secretarial staff from his Bengaluru office, who were waiting for my arrival. An agreement was drafted and typed on stamp paper by midnight. Nahata considered early morning the following day as auspicious to sign it. The terms of the agreement—a film-maker cannot dream of anything better—it was so one-sided in my favour. Nahata's company would finance the entire production and my role would be that of writing, producing and directing the documentary and I would get a mutually agreed professional fee. Beyond this, I would get a percentage of the profits from the film. In the unfortunate event of loss, the entire loss would be absorbed by Nahata and I would have no liability whatsoever. I could not believe this. But here was a leading film industry man, and so I had no reason for disbelief. We signed the agreement at the appointed time the next morning.

Naturally, I announced the news to Mohana and to close friends. I called the few people who had made advance payments as their commitment to finance the production, gave them the good news and forthwith returned all their money. They were very happy because they were not involved with any commercial intentions, but to support a laudable project of a dreamy friend.

As per the agreement, Nahata had to give an advance of ₹1 lakh for production within a fortnight of signing and ₹1 lakh every month—thereafter—for one year, for completion of the production. It all seemed too good to be true. Indeed, it proved false. Every time I asked for the first instalment of advance, Nahata had one excuse or another for the delay. He also urged me to visit America and get advance reactions from the market for this film.

Some five months later I went to Delhi in some other context and paid a courtesy call on Gujral. The minister seemed unusually perturbed. He came to the point. 'You said you wanted to launch your film on "History" as a private project, when you invited me to inaugurate your shooting. Why have you started canvassing for government finance? And if at all you wanted to do that, why couldn't you do that directly? Why did you use that film industry man, Nahata, to talk to us?'

It was a moment of revelation that there was a massive attempt to take me for a ride. When I told Gujral what my arrangement was, he showed Nahata's letter to him. The shrewd financier had claimed that he was willing to sell this film to the Government of India for ₹30 lakh, although it would hardly meet the cost (for he was doing it in the national interest!). To cut a long story short, Nahata was persuading the minister and his officers for a pre-sale of *Indus Valley to Indira Gandhi* by his company, asking for an advance of ₹15 lakh. I apologized profusely to Gujaral and clarified that I had no intention of asking for government money, since I didn't want to be told by bureaucrats how to make the film that I had dreamt of making for fifteen years.

The trap became transparent. Gujral lauded my independent spirit and advised me to smoothly get out of the agreement with the film man. I sought one help from him. I requested him to send a regret letter to Nahata, urgently. A week later, at Chennai, I got a personal letter from Nahata, which was hand-delivered by a messenger.

The operative paragraph of the letter said, 'I am very sure that you will get huge financial gains and international acclaim for your film. I think it will be unfair on my part to take any share of your credit or profit from such a laudable venture. I request you to treat our agreement as cancelled.'

There were friends whose blood boiled and Desikan said, 'Take the fellow to court. After all, you have a signed document with him; claim damages.' I told him, 'I thought about it all calmly even before the letter arrived. The choice before me is either to spend all my energy and time in fighting with a business tycoon for the next year or two, or constructively put in my creative energy in producing my film. I have chosen the latter.'

I was, once again, back to square one.

Where Angels Fear to Tread

I began my search for finance all over again. The friends who had promised some financial support earlier had invested their savings elsewhere and even that fragment of the cost was not available now. After a fortnight of considering a few options, I thought of approaching a bank. Banks in India generally do not finance film production, since it is considered a high-risk investment. My proposal was by all standards even more risky, since it was not for a commercial entertainment film. I had made a few advertising films for Canara Bank and come to know Vaideeswaran (GM—Advertising) at their head office in Bengaluru. My bank accounts were with a different bank in Chennai. When I was making films for Canara Bank, Vaideeswaran had persuaded me to shift my accounts to Canara Bank and I said light-heartedly, 'When I decide to make a long film of my dream, I will open an account with you and ask for an overdraft.' He had laughed, but was not dismissive. That was in 1970, and now, even as I was thinking of bank finance, I got a call from Vaideeswaran stating that he had been promoted and transferred to a new branch in Chennai, which would be one of their largest branches, and he reminded me that I was supposed to shift my accounts to his bank and that the time had come to do so. It was like a floating straw before a drowning man, and I grabbed it, discussing my proposal with him. Since he had been handling PR for the bank for many years, I presented a new angle which appealed to him. I said I would give credit lines for Canara Bank in the beginning and end of the film. We would also plug in Canara Bank in the main film when we depicted the 'nationalization' of major banks. The idea caught his imagination. He forwarded my proposal to their chairman with his own strong recommendation. It was approved subject to my giving reasonable security. The house that I had purchased in 1971 for ₹90,000 was worth about seven times more in 1975. The bank was liberal to the extent of advancing almost 80 per cent of its market value. It was a huge risk to take, since it amounted to burning my boats and risking the only savings I had made in my career. Anyway, as I was bitten by the bug, I instantly decided to take the risk. Some finance was required beyond the bank loan for which my friendly finance broker Nandalal Madhavdas agreed to lend liberally without security. I can never forget him saying, 'Something tells me that you will succeed. I go more by the integrity and ability of the borrower than by his proposal and net worth.' And so, when the bank loan was exhausted, I had this additional resource.

Although the project had been formally launched several months earlier, I could practically start shooting only by early 1975. My brother Balu had confidence in my project to some extent. He was also deeply interested in history. I was very happy that as a brilliant cinematographer he agreed to photograph my film and take his fees for it on completion of the project. We began shooting in many parts of North India, flying from place to place and engaging taxis locally. Because Indian Airlines were one of my clients, I struck a bargain with them that they would allow me to carry all my excess baggage of cameras, trolleys, tracks, etc., without any extra baggage charges. In return, we showed a few minutes of Indian Airlines in my film, as the proud 'national carrier'. I had obtained such concessions from five-star hotels and a few other clients, all of which contributed to managing the cost of production. Coming to think of it, it was very tough combining the role of the producer, writer and director, as well as an anchor, speaking in various locations; and managing finances, schedule and everything else to the last detail. We were a crew of six people including K.J. Mohan, a former employee of the

American Consulate, as my liaison officer to arrive a day ahead of the shooting day in each location to fine-tune arrangements; and K. Balan, who had been my production executive (Jeeves) since the inception of the company.

The Archaeological Survey of India gave permission to film over seventy-five monuments after thorough verification. By all standards, it was a project where angels fear to tread, and I had rushed into it.

We were filming in Bodh Gaya when news appeared that Indira Gandhi's election to Parliament had been set aside by the Allahabad High Court, creating rumours of instability across the country. There was an undeclared undercurrent in the thinking among my friends and co-workers, including Balu, that in some manner I would be supported by Indira Gandhi in the project. Actually, except for a few meetings with her when she was the minister for information and broadcasting, and for a courtesy call in 1974 to tell her that I was launching a documentary, *Indus Valley to India Gandhi*, I had never talked about the project nor approached her even indirectly for financial support. The title truly meant 'from a lamp post to a lamp post'. But it acquired so much significance that the film, apart from the genuine acclaim it received, was both praised and condemned at times for the wrong reasons. People around me considered that the project had failed when Indira Gandhi's election was set aside. There were several more tours and hardly 20 per cent of the shooting had been done.

By the time I landed in Delhi, Indira Gandhi had declared a national emergency. Leave alone those who were against this in the opposition parties, there was resistance even among ruling party leaders. Since Gujral was one of them, he was unceremoniously transferred from the MIB to the glamourless Ministry of Planning.

During his tenure as information minister, his office was

The author with I.K. Gujral

always crowded with visitors competing to get a few minutes of his time. But when I walked into his office on his first day as planning minister, there were hardly any visitors. He was hurt by the prime minister's action; but was very calm and as gentlemanly as ever. Soon thereafter, he was shuffled out of the cabinet and sent to Moscow as India's ambassador. I met him again on the day when he was leaving for Moscow. He told me, 'What you are doing with dedication to history and culture is likely to be dragged into politics. I am sorry; I failed to advise you against the title you have chosen. Your film would have been non-controversial if you had stopped the story on 15 August 1947 and not covered the post–independence period at all.'

I said, 'Won't you agree that history is a continuous river. I thought that I should take a holistic approach by bringing it to today.'

In short, most unintentionally, I had dragged myself into a tricky situation just by coining what was intended as a catchy film title.[15]

Micro- to the Macro-Level Challenges

After a short gap, I returned to my production work in full swing. Most unfortunately, the next major hurdle was Balu. He developed a lack of confidence in the success of my project and wriggled out of it. I felt upset, indeed saddened, by the fact that he was doing this to me although he knew the quantum of risk I had taken.

Apart from his losing confidence in my film, there were other angles for Balu cutting himself out. He had inherited landed property by being the adopted son of K.S.V. Iyer (KSV). While he gave the rest of his property to Balu, KSV had given his house in Nagapattinam to my mother as streedhan property. My mother was deeply attached to this house, since that is where she was born and brought up and that is where her wedding was celebrated in 1920. When my father had several liabilities to clear, my mother had also become legally liable by her being the co-signatory in some of the documents. Her total identification and faith in my father had led her to sign on the dotted line without knowing its implications. And now our family lawyers, Venkatramani in Chennai and N.R.S. Mani

---

[15]Eventually, when the film was released, three facts saved its reputation—first, that the press, like the *Statesman* and the *Indian Express*, who were staunchly anti-Emergency, gave excellent reviews for the film; second, a politically uninvolved Hollywood company distributed the film; and third, international scholars expressed admiration for it. Extracts from the reviews are reproduced on a later page. *Indus Valley to Indira Gandhi* is available in four parts of one hour each on *www.indianimprints.com*.

in Nagapattinam, who was also my mother's cousin, wanted to save her house from any court proceedings. They said that if the property was transferred in the name of a confidant and after a few years if that confidant could return it to her, her property could be saved. When I was in school at Nagapattinam, another family friend and lawyer drafted a deed by which the house was 'sold' to Balu. I was present in the registrar's office when this document was registered. Sundaram Iyer took Balu aside and demanded a promise from him that since he was not paying any money to our mother to buy her house, he would reconvey this property to her at the appropriate time. Balu spontaneously promised him that he would do so and the lawyer asked me to be the moral eyewitness. About sixteen years later, when my father was recovering from surgery, Venkatramani and N.R.S. Mani declared that it was time to reconvey the house to my mother. Amma was very deeply moved, not because she was getting her property back but because of her memories of her childhood associated with that house.

Mani had a word with my father, in my presence, when my father emotionally said, 'I would be very grateful to you, Mani, if the house is transferred back. There is a sense of guilt in me, that due to my recklessness, I got Patta involved in my liabilities.'

Advocate Mani wanted me to be present to finalize this with Balu, who perceived it as a prestige issue for him that he would lose respect as a landlord of his large farm, if he lost hold of that house. After much persuasion, Balu agreed to pay her compensation of ₹50,000 and retain ownership of the house. Amma agreed to it as a compromise.

My father passed away a few months later. From 1971 to 1975, I was persuading him to keep his promise, but Balu was evasive. He had a degree in law but had chosen not to practise as a lawyer. He quoted from Manu (Hindu law giver) that 'a woman has to be protected by her father in childhood;

thereafter, by her husband; and in case of widowhood by her son; she has no individual rights of her own'. He felt that as a son he was duty-bound to take care of his mother and there was no need for her to have any property of her own, nor was it mandatory for him to pay her for her house.

This conflict precipitated in Balu wriggling out of work from *Indus Valley to Indira Gandhi* and from all my projects thereafter.

Except for a few weeks each year, when she was with Ramanu or with me, our mother lived in Balu's house most of the time and died there, sixteen years after my father passed away. Since he was giving protection to his mother, he justified his action of not monetarily compensating her for her property. What he failed to realize was the trauma created in his mother's mind.

About the same time as he distanced himself from working on my projects, he realized that Padma was the rising star of the family and began to administer her dance programmes and contracts. Indeed, she richly deserves the stardom that she has consistently enjoyed over five decades now. Balu became her unofficial guardian. I perceived that he was subconsciously irked by my righteous stand with regard to our mother's house, and attempted to create a distance between me and the rest of the close family and friends. However, he surely deserves credit for efficiently administering Padma's interests with dignity as a star dancer.

Meanwhile, I engaged a very able cinematographer, E.N. Balakrishnan (ENB), to shoot the rest of the film. In the titles, Balu gets credit for filming northern India, while ENB gets credit for filming southern, eastern and western India.

The new cameraman became very friendly with the rest of the team but the technical and aesthetic challenges continued to be formidable. Since my conception of this film was in the nature of a dialogue between the present and the past, the narrative was not in one chronological order. For instance, a long sequence on the 'status of women in India over the centuries' was conceived as a branching off in the middle of my dealing with the Taj Mahal. This whole narrative of the high status of women during the Vedic period; and the dichotomy of the woman being a goddess as well as a slave at once in the Middle Ages; the problem of widowhood, sati and the period of renaissance was dealt with in that sequence of twenty-five minutes. It was a highly acclaimed segment. Similarly, I dealt with the performing arts and explained the dance of Shiva in a sequence branching off from the Thanjavur temple. I was keen that Padma perform this dance sequence. Balu had by then dissociated himself from the project. Generally, Padma did not do anything without Balu's consent. However, she kept her commitment and performed in the film.

There were any number of comic incidents during the filming. In the Ajanta caves, for instance, an official of the Archaeological Survey was unwilling to honour the written permission that I had with me from their director general. After arguments for almost an hour, I suddenly found some foreigners filming in the caves even as we were waiting. So I asked the official, 'What kind of permission do those tourists have?' and he said, 'They don't need permission. They have paid ₹50 at the gate to carry a camera.' I said, 'Indeed, we are ready to pay ₹50.' And the official argued, 'But your camera has a tripod stand whereas their camera is hand-held.' I told him that permission was obtained from Delhi for shooting a 35 mm movie. He retorted, 'But it does not say camera with tripod.' I quickly turned to ENB and winked. ENB spontaneously said, 'We will also shoot without tripod.' The official said, 'You didn't tell me that. In that case, you don't have to pay ₹50. You can shoot with your hand-held camera because of the permission letter.'

Not every cameraman is capable of handling a bulky

35 mm hand-held camera. But I knew ENB could do that. He did a magnificent job of the shots inside the caves carrying the camera on his shoulder. We got wonderful shots of Ellora too.

Soon enough, we were in Lothal—an Indus Valley site in Gujarat. It was one of the oldest ports of the world. The ruins show how 5,000 years ago they received boats from Rome at the one end and China on the other, for trade. We had taken a taxi to Lothal and the weather was completely dry. However, when we finished filming and returned, suddenly there were flash floods and we could not cross a causeway. We camped overnight on the roadside till the water receded.

We were processing our film at the Gemini Color Laboratory. Like everybody else in the film industry, lab technicians, including the chief, gave stepmotherly treatment to documentaries, and we had to argue with them on more than one occasion. The worst was when they sent the negative of Ellora through the processing machine, using it as a 'test bit' before loading some feature film. Our negatives got damaged. The chief said that he would buy one role of raw film and give it to us for reshooting. ENB got wild and shouted, 'But who will pay for all the cost of travelling again to Ellora?' The lab man said, 'There are no stars, and it can't be expensive.' That was a reflection of the attitude of not only the film industry, but society at large, towards non-fiction films—not that societal attitudes have changed now, but it is certainly better today than it was four decades ago. Fortunately, only a segment of our shots of Ellora got damaged and we could retrieve 60 per cent of them. Yet the damage had been done.

Our locations included the deserts of Rajasthan and the Himalayan peaks shot from Darjeeling. In all, we covered 120 locations travelling about 60,000 km, criss-crossing the country. By January 1976, we completed filming and I started editing and post-production. K. Selvaraj, film editor, was a nationalist with general knowledge, besides being a brilliant technician, despite his limited formal education.

Before I started shooting this film, I had vacated my rented office space and shifted my office to a couple of rooms in my house. I was operating a Moviola editing machine which produced quite a bit of noise in addition to playing my commentary and music. Selvaraj and I were working together in my editing room. Mohana and the children had to put up with the noise as our bedroom was the adjacent room. I would be working from about 7 a.m. to about 2 a.m., taking brief breaks.

When the film was ready with the commentary synchronized, I requested Salil Chowdhury, the nationally celebrated music composer to compose the background score. When Salil-da saw the four-hour film at one stretch, he hugged me and said, 'It will be a privilege for me to compose music for this masterpiece.' We had a fairly large orchestra. Samuel Joseph (Shyam), his music conductor, became a famous music director for Malayalam films. Later, he composed music for most of my documentaries and TV serials.

When I asked for M.S. Subbalakshmi's voice for a background song, the icon and her husband told me to choose anything from her recordings, granting blanket permission to use her voice. I paid a nominal royalty to HMV—the gramophone company. When the music recording was in progress at the Gemini Recording Centre, the leading playback singer Jesudoss walked in one day and said that he wanted to have the pleasure of lending his voice somewhere in this film. Salil-da said, 'If you don't mind, I will use you as the lead voice in the title music.' He not only readily agreed, but also graciously refused to receive any money for it.

'Light' at the End of a Long Tunnel

Several things were happening simultaneously. On the one side there was a high degree of cooperation and understanding with regard to the spirit of the project; and on the other, tremendous prejudices—both in favour and against the documentary. I completed the film by about July 1976. A censor committee met and asked for a few brief cuts. For instance, I had managed to shoot the original Kashi Vishwanath temple on the banks of the Ganges, which was pulled down by the Mughals. My shots clearly showed how pillars and several parts of the temple had been retained from the original construction reflecting Hindu architecture with sculptures of deities, while the tower had been demolished and a typical dome of a mosque built in its place. My commentary described in essence that the original temple was demolished some four hundred years ago, and the Hindus built a smaller temple elsewhere, which is currently under worship as the sacred Vishwanath temple. The censors objected to this stating that although it was historically true, it would contribute to communal tension. We had to remove a few such scenes—truthful, but unacceptable.

In search of an audience, I was talking to leading commercial film distributors of India for theatrical release on the one hand, and to the government-owned Doordarshan to sell TV rights on the other. I chose to screen the film for Tarachand Barjatya, one of the leading film magnates of India with a distribution chain.

Barjatya was virtually moved to tears at the preview. His reaction epitomized the reactions of the more sensitive film industry people. He said, 'What a great service you have rendered! You even deserve the Bharat Ratna for this. But unfortunately, I cannot distribute it because Indian audiences are neither educated enough nor mature enough to see something as exceptional as this in the film medium.' He went on to say, 'Find someone who will distribute this abroad; Indians get curious only if a white man appreciates you. I am sorry. I am not able to help you commercially.' This was the single civilized reply I received from the commercial film industry.

From the time the film was completed, I had spent almost sixty days at the Ashoka Hotel in Delhi negotiating with private parties as well as with the government for selling the film. Kasturirangan, a respected journalist and correspondent of *The New York Times* in India, had seen the film in a private screening and liked it very much. He took the initiative with Parliament secretariat to organize a screening for the members of Parliament (MPs). The show was attended by about two hundred MPs—cutting across party lines. Soon after the show, I developed acute chest pain and was advised to get admitted in a hospital. I telephoned Mohana and urged her to join me. She left our children with Desikan and his wife, Nirmala, and took the next flight available. My childhood friend Nirmala (Nimmu) and her husband, Vaidyanathan, admitted me into the Willingdon Hospital. Mohana joined me within hours. I spent about three weeks in the hospital undergoing various investigations with no conclusive results. Nimmu and Vaithi were a great source of strength to both of us. When I was discharged and allowed to return to Chennai, the doctors insisted on my taking a wheelchair at both the airports. Mohana was very worried but was courageous throughout. She took me straight home and not to a hospital. We sought the advice of an eminent cardiologist and a family friend, C.R.R. Pillai, who examined me and said, 'You have suffered from VIP attention by an unsure hospital. Fortunately, I don't find anything wrong with you. The ECG is normal and this is just a muscular pain or pain due to gas. Get up and run! You are an active person and we can't see you confined to bed.' He gave me some medicines; but more than that, his words were reassuring. In all fairness to the doctors in Delhi, there was no commercial exploitation, except that they had frightened me.

Resuming my marketing efforts for the film, I consulted my

friend T.T. Vasu, industrialist and president of the prestigious music academy in later years, who liked my film immensely. Since he was the president of the Indo-American Chamber of Commerce, he said he would try to get an American distributor to preview the film. There was no precedent at all for American distributors buying an Indian film. Vasu talked to the Kinematograph Renters Society, that represented Hollywood companies in India. Nadkarni, head of Warner Brothers in India and chairman of that association, took interest and organized a screening for all the eight Hollywood companies at Mumbai to see if anyone would be interested. I was requested not to be present at the show for the members to feel free to discuss it.

Keeping my fingers crossed, I joined them at the appointed time after the show. It was an unbelievable turning point. Nadkarni announced to me that each one of the eight Hollywood companies present was interested in acquiring *Indus Valley to Indira Gandhi* and I had to choose any one of them. However, he said a film print would have to be sent to whichever company I chose to deal with in Hollywood. I was dazed and I said that it was a very difficult choice and requested them to discuss among themselves and to shortlist two or three, with whom I could talk.

The task of sending twenty-six reels of a 35 mm film print weighing 90 kg was a formidable task for my small company. As luck would have it, within a week or so after the show for the Hollywood distributors, Nadkarni got a letter that a vice president of Warner Brothers was visiting Cairo and Singapore and that Nadkarni was welcome to meet him in either one of the two cities, if he had anything to discuss. Nadkarni requested him on the phone to spend a day in Mumbai en route from Cairo to Singapore to preview my film. Lee spent nine hours in Mumbai—just enough time to drive from the airport to the preview theatre and back to the airport. But he had the authority and the inclination to take a spot decision—and he approved the

proposal of distributing the film under the banner of Warner Brothers.

I promptly announced this arrangement to the information ministry in Delhi. Tarachand Barjatya was right in predicting that if I got support from abroad, Indians would follow! And now, the ministry decided in principle to buy the TV rights and details were to be worked out. Warner Brothers fixed the release of the film in India as 10 December 1976. V.C. Shukla, minister for information and broadcasting, was the chief guest at the premiere.

When I paid a courtesy call on the minister to thank him the next day, he said he had taken the liberty of requesting the prime minister to appear on screen and introduce the film in two minutes in view of the title. I recalled Gujral's advice that it should not only be independent but also remain so in public perception, although I couldn't share this angle with Shukla.

We had asked for an appointment with the prime minister to make a courtesy call. Now that Shukla had sent her a request,

From right: Mohana, the author, Union Minister V.C. Shukla, and other guests at the premiere of Indus Valley to Indira Gandhi

I was in a dilemma whether it would be appropriate to raise the issue with her or not. The issue got resolved without any effort on my side in the best manner possible, reflecting Indira Gandhi's magnanimity and vision.

Mohana gave the great lady an unusually large bouquet of flowers. The prime minister smiled and said, 'This is really heavy like the burden of history your husband has thrust on me by the title of his film.'

Then, hesitantly, I expressed our request that she speak for a couple of minutes as a foreword to the film. She replied forthwith, 'Shukla spoke to me about this. Frankly, I have your interest in mind in expressing regret. Even the anti-Emergency press has given very good reviews for your film. I learn that you have gone through a lot of hardship in making this independent film. My address would dilute all that and make it look like a propaganda film. I hope you understand.'

'Of course, Madam, I do and I will go by your advice,' I told the tall leader. Yes! Emergency was a humongous mistake, but who doesn't make mistakes?

Regarding the TV rights I had offered to Doordarshan, the ministry appointed an eleven-member committee headed by an additional secretary. There was no precedent of acquiring TV rights of any film. There were only schemes by which a film could be telecast by paying a small royalty for each screening as TV was not a wide-spread medium and the budgets were limited. When I sat in front of the committee, I told them light-heartedly, 'It's like one man against a whole cricket team.' Eventually, the committee decided to acquire TV rights for fifty years for the territory of Asia and sent their recommendations to obtain the sanction of the finance ministry.

Since I knew the finance minister (CS), I requested him to see the film. It was not uncommon in that era for political opponents to be friends. P. Ramamurthy (PR), a renowned communist leader, was a friend of CS. It was a pleasant surprise for me to receive PR along with CS for the show. PR liked the film and clapped for a few scenes. CS was a man of few words. In a different context, almost a year later, I learnt about his note on the file. An officer of the finance ministry had commented, 'There is no precedent in buying the TV rights of a film, hence this may not be approved.' However, the file was put up for the minister's order and he wrote: 'Let us set up new precedents since this is an unprecedented film.'

In early 1977, I signed an agreement with Doordarshan. It had just been made an independent department, since it was only a wing of All India Radio till then. P.V. Krishnamurthy, the first director general of Doordarshan, signed the contract on the government's side. What the government paid me for the telecast rights for the four-hour 35 mm Eastman Colour film for a period of fifty years for the whole of Asia was just about adequate to pay back the bank and other creditors. Warner Brothers brought in prestige and what came through them constituted profits.

In the meantime, as our 1,500 square foot house on Mahatma Gandhi Road was getting cramped to accommodate my office and technical facilities along with our residence, we started looking for office space in a commercial locality. But nothing seemed to suit my requirement at a price that I could afford. On a Sunday morning, a stranger—Venkatanarasimhan, retired chief engineer of the state—and his wife visited us to pay their compliments for *Indus Valley to Indira Gandhi*. They had shifted to Mysore after his retirement and they were visiting Chennai to find a buyer for their house in Chennai, which was near my own, in the same locality. Mohana and I visited his house in First Avenue, Shastri Nagar, and it occurred to me that we could shift our home there and convert our existing office-cum-residence entirely into an office and expand by building a studio there. Mohana approved of the idea. Like in the case of my first property, in this 1977 transaction too, there was no payment without receipt. Once again, we took a loan from the Life Insurance Corporation of India. In April 1977, we shifted to the new house, converting our earlier house into an office. Studios and other technical facilities were created in the same place over the next three decades.

After-effects and Side-effects

The audience's reception of the film in the cinemas was beyond anybody's expectation. In India, in the 1970s, if a film had a screening of hundred days, it was considered a huge record. *Indus Valley to Indira Gandhi* exceeded hundred days in several cities. In Chennai, it was screened in one cinema hall for over twenty-five weeks. The only place which attracted only a rather small audience was New Delhi. Analysts later said that it was a reflection of New Delhi being most affected by the Emergency, and unfortunately there was a common impression that it was a propaganda film for Indira Gandhi's regime. We had special screenings on the first day of release in Bengaluru with Karnataka Chief Minister Devaraj Urs as the chief guest. In his presence, I made it a point to announce that my film had no contemporary political party patronage. Several congressmen in the audience felt uncomfortable about this statement.

Even as *Indus Valley to Indira Gandhi* was getting released, Mohana had submitted her PhD thesis. Hence, it was possible for her to be present at the film's premiere at New Delhi and, again, in Bengaluru. We advertised in *The Hindu* and *Hindustan Times* (reproduced on a later page herein), explaining how our film had no relationship to political parties.

Warner Brothers invited Mohana and me to a special screening of the film organized at the Motion Picture Association of America, Washington, DC. It was Mohana's first trip abroad and we took a short holiday in Rome and London before reaching America. By then, Erik Barnouw had retired from Columbia University and was the head of the newly created Motion Picture Division at the Library of Congress in the US capital. He invited us to stay with him in his apartment and we had a wonderful time combining business with holiday.

There were several senators and congressmen at the show besides media personalities. Warner Brothers had organized cocktails and snacks in the intermission between the two sessions as the entire four-hour film was screened in one go. The *Saturday Review* said, 'Not everyone, it seems, was charmed by Sir Kenneth Clark's TV series *Civilization*. What put them off was Sir Kenneth's implication that the Mediterranean Basin has been the main cradle of human culture and progress. Krishnaswamy's film may prove a corrective to the cultural myopia.'

During the cocktail intermission, I was introduced to former President Roosevelt's granddaughter who said that she was thoroughly enjoying the film. After a few minutes of conversation, Mohana joined us from another group and I introduced her to the VIP. The lady was astonished and asked me spontaneously, 'Oh! I didn't know that some 'swamis' in India are allowed to marry!' She had obviously taken that part of my name to mean that I was a monk.

We went by car from Washington, DC to New York City. As you approach New York, you see virtually hundreds of huge industries on both sides of the road and the enormous quantum of smoke emanating from their chimneys. In that era, although experts were talking about environment and pollution, it was one of the fringe subjects and nobody really cared. The first reaction of most people on seeing New York City and its industrialized neighbourhood was one of amazement. To my surprise, my wife shed tears. I asked her why. She said that she recognized the dangers of pollution and if this kind of pollution continued it would endanger human society and even life on the planet. While she enjoyed the atmosphere of Washington, DC and considered it civilizational progress, she was upset with New York City as a mechanical place where humans behaved like robots.

Within a couple of weeks after our Washington preview, reports trickled in that my film was being discussed in the Indian Parliament and was accused of being an instrument of the Emergency. Yes! A few weeks before we left for America, Indira Gandhi had lifted the Emergency and announced general elections. Not only did her party lose, but she herself lost the election to Parliament. Morarji Desai, who had parted company with her earlier when he was her deputy prime minister, was the consensus leader of the newly formed Janata Party, and was now the prime minister.

Among the audience in Washington, DC, who expressed appreciation for the film was Dikshit—first secretary at the Indian Embassy—who I met again, years later, as the Indian

High Commissioner in Colombo. After we reached New York, I got a call from him that there was a discussion in Parliament in which members of the ruling Janata Party alleged that my film was 'an instrument of the Emergency.

Since Morarji Desai had attended my wedding reception about a decade earlier, for a moment I thought of writing to him explaining my position. But it occurred to me that it may be lost in the volume of correspondence in the PMO. So I wrote to L.K. Advani, minister for information and broadcasting. I said in my short letter that it was absurd to think that my film was directly or indirectly financed by Indira Gandhi or her government. I went on to say that 'Parliamentarians would have benefited by watching any forty-five minutes of my four-hour film, instead of discussing it without seeing it.' The Indian Embassy obliged me by sending it in the embassy bag to ensure that it reached him promptly.

We cut short our tour and returned. In the meantime, Railway Minister Madhu Dandavate's wife, who was also an MP, had seen the film and she told Advani that the party was not being fair with regard to this film. In that background, my letter appealed to Advani and he organized a show for himself and Dandavate. When I returned to India and met him in his office, he said, 'I have seen your film. It is a great film with a very bad title.' He continued, 'If you want us to continue screening it on TV for which the government has the rights, you should change the title.'

Our discussion eventually resulted in my agreeing to the title *Where Centuries Coexist!*, which I had given for an abridged version. I tried to impress on the great leader that his party had been unfair by mentioning my film in the government's white paper on 'Misuse of Mass Media'. Advani said, 'If we telecast it on national TV with the new title, it will amount to our approving the film.' It was too much indeed to expect more than that from someone who had been imprisoned till a few months earlier under Indira Gandhi's regime, against all principles of democracy.

There were unfortunate consequences. Sovexportfilm (the Soviet entity for film import–export) had agreed to acquire *Indus Valley to Indira Gandhi* and dub it in Russian. It would have given us the satisfaction of reaching a wider audience. But when the white paper on 'Misuse of Mass Media' mentioned my film, they cancelled the deal.

However, as a goodwill gesture, they extended an invitation to me to attend their international film festival at Tashkent in 1978 and to address their international documentary symposium at Alma Ata, capital of Kazakhstan. In all, I spent about six weeks as a soviet guest. Here are extracts from my article in *The Hindu*.

> The V International Film Festival at Tashkent was a non-competitive festival attracting a choice of excellent films from the third world. If Tashkent introduced the lavish Soviet hospitality and the opportunity for observation of the international film scene, it is Alma Ata, Kazakhstan, which gave me tremendous gratification as a documentary-film-maker. We were only two Indians who participated at the five-day international documentary symposium organized there, by the USSR Association of Film Makers. Participants from about forty countries and almost every republic of the Soviet Union had opportunity to view several hours of film. With much less gala distractions than Tashkent, we talked cinema over tea, breakfast, lunch and dinner. My film *Where Centuries Coexist*—an abridged version of *Indus Valley to Indira Gandhi*—was the lone Indian film. I was overwhelmed by the tremendous reception given to it, which led to the

sponsoring of its premiere show in Moscow by the USSR Association of Film Makers.

As a consequence of the show in Moscow, during his visit to India, Dimichov, Vice President of the USSR, attended our private reception in his honour at Krishnaswamy Associates, in Chennai.

The author receiving Dimichov, vice president of the USSR, at Krishnaswamy Associates at a dinner reception in his honour; Mohana and the USSR Consul General Cherapov are standing behind

Objective Press Reviews

Everybody knows the attitude of different newspapers to Indira Gandhi during the Emergency. On the day of release of the film in Mumbai, *The Indian Express** captioned a photograph from the film with these words: 'A marathon, scholarly film on Indian history—a beautifully photographed, inspiring document on celluloid, the first-of-its-kind in movie history nobody should miss.'

A week earlier, *The Statesman**,[16] New Delhi, had said: 'The director unearths layer after layer, and often through deft flashbacks and flash forwards, the soul of India, the spirit that lies beneath the sediment a moving, powerful and thorough piece of work—an objective and painstaking odyssey.'

The Patriot*, New Delhi, commented without any ambiguity, 'The second part (of the film) also dispels rumours that it may have been in the nature of a government propaganda. It is not. The closing shots of the prime minister take barely a few minutes. Krishnaswamy does not try to sell any political philosophy or personage.'

Here is an advertisement published 10 August 1977 in *The Hindu*, and *Hindustan Times*

INDUS TO INDIRA WAS NO POLITICAL STUNT, NOR PART OF ANY BANDWAGON
An Objective Film Essay on Indian History

The white paper on 'Misuse of Mass Media' during Emergency presented by the MIB based on the K.K. Das Committee report referred to *Indus Valley to Indira Gandhi* and said, 'The main object of the film appears to be to project that while India had been great in the past, it reached its culmination under the leadership of Srimati Indira Gandhi'.

That this is not a justified criticism will be realized by anyone who has seen both the Parts of my film on History. Before talking about the genesis of the film, I would merely like to give extracts from comments on the film at the time it was released in late 1976.

---

[16]The three newspapers quoted here, had all taken an anti-Emergency stand.

No Propaganda, No Sycophancy

In fact, the only newspaper in the whole country whose review was an outright condemnation of the film, dissuading its readers from viewing it, was *The National Herald*, widely known to be associated with Indira Gandhi.

There was a press preview of my film in Bengaluru in the first week of January, and Devaraj Urs, chief minister of Karnataka, was the chief guest. In order to set the right tone of expectations for the film, while introducing the film to the press and other invitees, I said, 'Please do not consider this film to be part of the Emergency bandwagon. This is a film on history, and I gave it its title long before the Emergency was declared.'

Commenting on this, in its column *The Deccan Herald* said, 'Mortally afraid of being mistaken for a sycophant, Krishnaswamy goes out of his way to explain that he chose the title of his film one full year before the "bandwagon began to roll", with the declaration of the Emergency in 1975. I tend to believe him absolutely. The film does not even have a touch of sycophancy about it. On the other hand, it is brutally frank where brutal frankness is called for.'

The Timing—A Proof of Bona Fides

The important thing about this statement was also its timing. Although I had negotiated for several months with the MIB for the sale of TV rights of this film, the contract for this was signed only on 14 January 1977. I had spoken clearly dissociating the film from Emergency propaganda in unmistakable terms, nearly ten days before signing that contract—that too in the presence of no less a person than Devaraj Urs, at Bengaluru.

The idea to produce a film on the Indian civilization occurred to me in 1964 and I devoted all my spare time to collecting materials for it. I waited for long because I could not raise the required financial resources. In late 1973, I made up my mind that I must make the film of my dreams even at the risk of all my savings and the future of my career. It was simply a passionate involvement with an idea to project my interpretation of India.

I launched the film entirely on my own in June 1974, inviting the minister for information and broadcasting, I.K. Gujral, to inaugurate the shooting at Chennai. I had thought of the title *Indus Valley to Indira Gandhi* in 1973 and I had announced it in June 1974. It merely indicated the wide canvas of time the film would cover.

Sale of TV Rights—No 'Hush-Hush' Deal

A four-hour documentary if it was mere political propaganda is unlikely to have been well received by the audience in several parts of the country. Although none of the eight American film companies operating in India for over half a century have ever taken up an Indian film for distribution, one of them took up my film for distribution. Anyone who knows the commercial values of the distributors would also know that they shun political material. While I could discuss theatrical rights with several parties, as for TV, I obviously had to offer it to the only monopoly TV organization available in India. As for the financial transaction of the government acquiring TV rights of this film, L.K. Advani himself explained in Parliament that it was done by constituting a special committee and that the approval of the finance ministry was also obtained.

> **A Request to Set the Record Straight**
>
> It will be a blemish on the democratic traditions of the present government to question the bona fides of an independent film-maker of small financial means, who dared to make such a film on Indian history at his own risk, and succeeded in completing it and reaching the people with it. The fact that the previous administration purchased certain rights of the film should not colour and prejudice anybody's views on the film or on the integrity of the film-maker. I earnestly request that the government should delete all references to my film from the white paper.

Here are a few extracts from other reviews.

Not everyone, it seems, was charmed by Sir Kenneth Clark's TV series Civilization. What put them off was Sir Kenneth's implication that the Mediterranean Basin has been the main cradle of human culture and progress. Krishnaswamy's film may prove a corrective to the cultural myopia.

—*Saturday Review*, New York

Your film awakened me to India. I was acquainted with many of the cold facts you touch on. But your film gave them the heat of life.

—Elia Kazan

Bold in conception and execution [...] Attempts what no film-maker, Indian or foreign, has so far attempted [...] Credible and of absorbing interest [...] There is not a dull moment...'

—*The Hindu*

Nobly conceived and most ably executed!
—Professor James Beveridge, UNESCO

Commendable effort to pick up the undercurrents of our culture, and trace them to their sources! There is an inherent photogenic quality in the subjects Krishnaswamy seeks to expose.
—*Times of India*

A Non-Political Woman's Political Biography

B.R. Ambedkar[17] became serious as he recollected an incident.

> Yes... the relative of an untouchable student found out that I was the examiner appointed by the University of Bombay. He came to me and insisted that I should give the boy passing marks. He thought, since the boy was an untouchable, I would help him. It was not possible. I made it clear saying that If I wanted I could easily do it, but I do not find it right. I hate anybody asking such a favour. I feel that an untouchable student should not be less intelligent or less industrious than his counterparts. I think, compared to others, he should be an ideal student. The person left quietly when he heard me.[18]

In 1977, soon after our return from America, Mohana got her PhD from Madras University for her thesis related to pyridoxine biosynthesis in *Aspergillus nidulans*. She wanted to continue her postdoctoral research. That was the beginning of a new chapter of frustration. There was a position for a research scientist at the Central Leather Research Institute (CLRI) in Chennai which was

---

[17]B.R. Ambedkar was the torchbearer of the rights of the untouchables and an architect of the Constitution of India.
18Refer to Vasant Moon's article in the anthology *Ambedkar—The Attendant Details*.

a reputed laboratory. Although she did very well in the interview, one of the panel members told her straight to her face, 'It is unlikely that a Brahmin can get involved in leather technology since it means dealing with leather derived from dead animals, and a Brahmin woman is likely to feel uncomfortable.' Mohana replied that she had been a medical student for a couple of years and that she had even dissected cadavers. The panel must have invented some other reason to disqualify her.

A fellowship was available, suitable for her qualification, at the highly reputed Indian Institute of Technology, Chennai. After the interview, the director of the institute told her, 'You richly deserve to continue your research with a placement in this Institute. But you know I have to be considerate to people from poorer sections of society. Your husband has become a famous man with his film released by a Hollywood company. The fellowship money which the IIT can give you will be peanuts for you. So you will understand if I give this position to someone who is in need of this money to support his family.'

As she was leaving, an IIT professor told her, albeit with sympathy, 'They think a man needs a job because he has to support his wife and children; but that women work only for luxury as a pastime.'

Down but Not Out

With these two rejections coming one after the other in a very short span of time, Mohana became cynical about our society. I needed wisdom to deal with this and help restore her balance and self-esteem, and tackled the situation as best I could.

Soon, the University of Madras had a vacancy for the post of a lecturer in biochemistry. She appeared for the interview and did very well. What we were not aware of was that while it was not reserved for SCs it was, however, a position 'reserved for sale'—for an underhand payment equal to one year's salary to an influential member of the selection committee. We came to know of it only after the appointment was announced. I may have, perhaps, made the compromise and paid the money to get her the position to restore her equilibrium, although I had a strict policy of never giving kickbacks to get business for my company. I may have done it just to get a position for Mohana that may have given her the opportunity and freedom for research. Even when I expressed this thought, she got wild stating that she would never buy a position for herself nor allow me to do so.

And then, she got a confirmed offer of the position of a lecturer in biochemistry in Andhra University at Visakapattinam (Vizag). We thought about it and decided that she should accept the position even as our children would remain with me and go to school in Chennai. We thought we would visit each other every alternate weekend; and I would take the children along during my turn to visit her. It was not the most comfortable arrangement, but we almost settled in favour of it. When she went to her parents to announce this decision, I nearly convinced her father that she was likely to be happier doing this.

But Mohana's mother was staunch in her resistance. She refused to even shake hands with her or congratulate her for getting a job—that too, not any job, but what she wanted to do. Mother and daughter sat alone and had a chat—at the end of which the daughter respectfully obeyed the mother and reversed her decision. Her mother did not approve of Mohana's idea of

Dilemmas of difficult times

leaving me and our children most of the time to take up a job in a different city, even if we planned to meet every week.

These were very difficult times for us, since Mohana almost came to the conclusion that the very idea of marriage was wrong and had begun to subconsciously identify her husband as the villain of her career and her very quest in life. It took a long time for her to come out of this disturbed attitude, which I was bearing with fortitude, since I understood her angst and the socio-political causes which impacted our personal lives.

Even as she lost her temper often, thinking of marriage as the villain of her life, I was not always at the receiving end. While I put up with a lot of it, I lost my patience at times and erupted like a volcano. The word 'divorce' came into our argument once in a while, but I suppose neither of us meant it seriously, and we patched up soon.

Sometimes, the children suffered as dumb spectators to our quarrels. But after a while they learnt to tackle the situation as one of them would tell us, 'Wait till we get some popcorn and watch the scene.'

I was feeling utterly guilty for the unhappiness of my life companion. 'Have I spoilt the spectacularly successful life of a scientist? Have I been an obstacle in her pursuing her path, her faith and destiny? Am I being selfish in not letting her go her way? On the other hand, is she likely to be happy if I leave her alone at this stage?'

I had no easy answers. For there was an unshakeable bond of love for each other between us and we knew that neither of us was likely to be happy without the other. Mohana was not aware that this state of affairs affected my concentration in my own work. I never revealed this to her, because she had sacrificed a lot for the sake of our children and she was not to be held guilty for my disturbed state of mind. Even as her problems were caused by a corrupt socio-political ethos of twisted mindsets, extraneous to our personal lives, my problems resulting from her frustrations were by-products of the same skewed public values.

Laughing at ourselves today, two incidents of matrimonial squabbles come to my mind from that period.

In a deeply depressed mood one morning, Mohana chose not to take her car, engaged an autorickshaw, cryptically took leave of me and left home saying, 'Goodbye. Don't expect me back here!' I was worried but confident that she would only go to her parents' house and not anywhere else. I thought she may have probably gone with the idea of convincing them that she should pursue her career and look for a position abroad. After contemplating for half an hour, I telephoned JK and the conversation was something like this.

'JK! I will tell you the opening sequence of a short story. A girl and her husband who love each other, quarrel over a societal issue that bothers and interferes in their personal lives. The girl abruptly goes away to her father's house to think of her next step. Tell me, what alternatives occur to you to proceed with the story, and how you would conclude it.'

'It could be a simple and straight story if written with sensitivity. The best next sequence that occurs to me is that the man gives her an hour or two to cool down, and then visits his in-laws' house to see what's happening. After his small courtesy chat with all of them, the girl returns with him as though it was the understanding that she wanted to spend some time with her mom and dad and that he was expected to pick her up after a few hours.'

'Thank you, JK! I think that's brilliant!'

After an hour, I drove straight to S.B. Iyer's house in T. Nagar and had a pleasant chat with him and with my mother-in-law. Mohana joined us from the kitchen with cups of coffee for all of us. It was too obvious that she was happy to see me. I asked if she wanted me to come back after some time to pick her up. 'No. You don't have to drive all the way again. I will come with you, whenever you are ready,' she said.

Another day in that period, I found it essential to call someone for help. I telephoned Mohana's mother and briefed her very politely that Mohana and I had just had an unusually nasty quarrel. She said she would visit us without delay. And she promptly arrived within twenty minutes. She saw raw rice and some provisions strewn about the living room and containers thrown at random. I was sitting in a corner and Mohana was upstairs. The old lady guessed the scene, cleaned up the place in a jiffy, walked into the kitchen, cooked some breakfast, laid the table, returned to the hall and quietly but dramatically called out to Mohana and me to join her in the dining room for breakfast. She didn't bother to ask who lost their temper and created a scene, nor showed interest in what the issue was. We both responded like resentful kids to her affectionate, motherly call. After another hour or so, I took the car and dropped the wise lady home.

Mohana is unlikely to have agreed to our meeting a marriage counsellor. That route did not look appropriate to me either. A more traditional route would have been to talk to the elders in the family. But I preferred talking to someone in my generation who could better understand the nature of the problem.

I wanted to talk to someone of our generation in whom my wife had total confidence and who could at the same time understand my mind. I zeroed in on Mohana's sister, Lakshmi. Younger to me by only a few months, Lakshmi had a PhD in linguistics from Cornell University, and was teaching at Osmania University, Hyderabad. She had fallen in love with and married Suryanarayana (Suri), a Telugu and English bilingual journalist, reputed for his integriy. I had a consistent friendly equation with them both. A brilliant intellectual with a warm heart, Lakshmi had been close to me to the point that I often wondered whether she was really Mohana's sister or my own sister.

Strangers become soulmates

My best bet was to take her into confidence about my problems on the home front. I had a heart-to-heart chat with her. I held her hands and said, 'I love your sister. You alone can ensure that we are not separated.' With affection and warmth, she understood what our problems were. She chose not to have a common discussion with both of us, since she didn't want tempers to be lost, taking us nowhere. She talked to Mohana and sorted out apparent differences, never disclosing that I had sought her help. I will be eternally grateful to Lakshmi for this step of wisdom—which helped us to evolve as true soulmates over the years, and not remain mere husband and wife.

It was an irreparable loss to both of us when Lakshmi passed away in a hospital in London in 2013, when she was visiting her daughter and grandchildren. Indeed, she lives in our hearts.

Pride and Prejudice

Even as she had applied for the post of a lecturer in Vizag, Mohana had also applied for a position in Denmark for postdoctoral research. It took almost one year for that application to be processed and then the interview for this was conducted in New Delhi. We were most delighted that she was chosen for the post of a researcher in protein chemistry against a lot of competition. The position had been created as per an Indo-Danish agreement to offer it to an Indian citizen and it meant spending three years in Denmark. I told Mohana that I would take the children along and spend those three years in Denmark as a house-husband, taking a break from my work. Our preparations for our three years' trip to Europe started in right earnest. We planned that our company in Chennai would remain dormant. The house would be under lock and key with a caretaker and not rented out, and we would coordinate with the Danish authorities for school admission for the children. My in-laws did not refuse this time, since we were not planning to set up our family in two different places.

When she received this Danish offer, Mohana was a pool officer[19] of the Council of Scientific and Industrial Research (CSIR) attached to Captain Srinivasamurthy Drug Research Institute at Chennai (CSMDRI—a unit of the Central Council for Research in Ayurveda and Siddha [CCRAS] at New Delhi).

About a year earlier, she had also applied to the CCRAS for the position of a research scientist in the CSMDRI, since she was deeply interested in Ayurvedic research. Just as we were ready to

---

[19]Since there were a large number of highly qualified Indian scientists who had no suitable jobs, the government had created positions for 'pool officers' in research establishments, giving them a modest fee as a stop-gap arrangement till they got suitable jobs. Although this was normally given to scientists with international qualifications, it was given to exceptionally meritorious candidates with Indian degrees also.

leave for Denmark, she got selected for this position. It meant research in traditional Indian medicine. This attracted her because although there was glamour and prestige attached to working in Denmark, it was not her first choice, since it was unrelated to medical research, in which she was passionately interested.

Once she was appointed as a senior research officer in the CSMDRI, she politely expressed her regret to Denmark. She thought she had secured the position dearest to her heart— to pursue research in the ancient science of Ayurveda from the perspective of modern science. She strongly believed that Ayurveda should not be treated as a faith but as a science. It was now celebration time for us. She took up this position in 1979. A list of her papers published in different scientific journals follow on a later page.

She primarily pursued research in finding a potential drug for cancer based on herbal materials described in Ayurveda, while she was also involved in attempts to develop a birth control drug. The common problem of all researchers in Ayurveda with a background in modern science was that if they did a study on the basis of Ayurvedic medicine from the ancient texts and found success, the traditional Ayurveda practitioner would say, 'What is this research for? We know this for over 2,000 years.' On the other hand, if a researcher with a background of modern science conducted research on the basis of discovering new applications for old medications, the conventional Ayurvedic practitioner did not cooperate. Mohana's mindset as a researcher with the true intention of finding therapeutic relief was one of finding a cure for human disease without bothering too much about the origin of the drug, either in terms of history or in terms of geography, that is, irrespective of how long the medicine has been known or from which origin it is known (Indian, Chinese or Western).

Unrelated to her position at the CSMDRI, Mohana was invited to attend the International Nutrition Congress at San Diego in

1981 to read a paper related to her doctoral thesis. It so happened that I had an invitation to address a conference of the International Institute of Communications at Strasbourg. We decided that we should travel together to attend both the conferences. We took the route via Singapore and Tokyo to San Diego. There was a gap of about four weeks between her seminar in San Diego and mine in France. We decided to spend that month in tourism and return to India from France. Mohana was amazed at the Nutrition Conference to find that modern scientists were presenting many facts of research regarding nutrition which were part of India's traditional knowledge and ancient wisdom. But she never took the route of claiming everything old to be true.

Within a few years of her work in anti-cancer drugs based on Ayurveda, she made substantial progress, which was recognized by awarding her the coveted Hari Om Ashram Gold Medal—an award of national stature—at the Ayurveda University in Jam Nagar, Gujarat. It was a proud day for me to witness her receiving the award.

In 1983, Mohana received an invitation from the Institute of Medicinal Plant Development (IMPLAD) at Beijing to visit China for three weeks as their guest. While her travel cost was met by IMPLAD, they invited the spouses of such invitees if they paid for their own travel.

I thought it was an excellent opportunity to visit China, especially when it was still behind the bamboo curtain and the India–China relationship was at very low ebb. She sent her 'Impressions of a China Visit' to the secretaries of the Ministry of Health and Ministry of External Affairs, Government of India. She also submitted to the ministries her 'Report and Recommendations' document on developing integrated medical education in India, based on the Chinese model.

M. Palaniyandi, a member of the Lok Sabha, who had also been the president of the Tamil Nadu Congress Committee, was

Mohana with scientists of IMPLAD

known to me from my childhood, since in the 1940s and 1950s he was in my father's close circle of admirers. Through him, I came to know G.K. Moopanar, one of the general secretaries of the Congress party and a leader of national stature. They were both staunch admirers of *Indus Valley to Indira Gandhi*. Palaniyandi's wife, Punitha, a feminist and the first woman mayor of Tiruchirapalli, looked upon Mohana with pride saying, 'Here is a woman scientist going places.'

One day, Palaniyandi disclosed, 'Yesterday, Punitha and I had a brain wave. Mohana should be in the Rajya Sabha. How many birds at one stroke! We get a good woman MP; we get a respected scientist; we get an MP from Tamil Nadu who can speak fluent Hindi in Parliament—all rolled into one. It is the most politically correct thing we could think of. I gave the idea to Moopanarji.

He received it well. Babu, it is now for both of you to think and take the plunge.'

'I will be delighted,' I said. 'But it is for Mohana to take the call. Although, she is not much interested in politics, I think she will say "Yes"—since she has great regard for you.'

Mohana did not take it seriously when I conveyed it to her, since she thought that Palaniyandi may have said it casually. The next day, when I got a call from Moopanarji that he would like to see both of us, she realized that they were serious. The big man came to the point. 'I hope you both thought about it and have come with a good answer!'

Palaniyandi and Moopanar expected me to answer. I looked at Mohana and said, 'You better tell them directly what is in your mind.' Mohana said, 'I am very embarrassed. I feel deeply honoured to be given such a high-profile proposal, but I have to deny myself the pleasure of accepting it.' She explained how her total involvement from her teenage years was with science with a single-pointed devotion to research. She was doing something worthwhile in that direction and she did not wish to dilute her attention to science. She expressed her gratitude for their offer, profusely and honestly.

At another level altogether, news came through the grapevine that some officers of the CCRAS were unhappy and envious of the Chinese invitation to Mohana and our consequential visit. It is an unfortunate but well-known tradition of Indian bureaucracy that people are deputed for any seminar or convention on the basis of hierarchy. If an Indian administrative services (IAS) officer from the health ministry was invited, they would have been happy; but they were offended by the fact that a scientist working for a lab in a not-too-senior position had been invited.[20]

---

[20] An example of the bureaucratic attitude is narrated in my book *Indian Film*. When the renowned film-maker Satyajit Ray was given the national

The consequences of this 'I-am-taller-than-you complex', combined with the prejudice against Brahmins in Tamil Nadu, began to show up in the day-to-day functioning at the CSMDRI. The director of the institute was afraid of a certain research officer since it was easy for the latter to complain that he, as a Muslim, was discriminated against. These factors often resulted in reverse discrimination against the Brahmins. Santappa, vice chancellor of Madras University, and an eminent scientist, gave an authorization letter to Mohana for guiding PhD scholars. She was very happy and began to guide a couple of junior scientists at the CSMDRI, who wanted to pursue their doctoral studies. However, internally in the institute the atmosphere was becoming more and more vitiated. The reservation policy resulted in a lady of mediocre calibre being posted as a scientist enjoying a higher rank than Mohana. Although Mohana was not obliged to report to this person, it created an atmosphere undesirable in any institution devoted to scientific research.

It would indeed be unfair to argue totally against reservations for the descendants of those who had been socially oppressed for several centuries. It is fair to allot a quota for them to reach higher levels of achievement and prosperity by giving them suitable jobs in the government. But this can neither be done at the risk of intellectual and scientific progress, nor at the risk of the security of the nation. Reservations are understandably acceptable in administrative positions, but not in artisteic, intellectual, sports or scientific pursuits. Yes, brilliant researchers or sportspersons may emerge from the communities classified SCs and STs, but they have to succeed in open competition and not by reservation. Even as there are no reservations in the armed forces and in

---

award for his first film, *Pather Panchali*, the person who received the award for the film was the director of information, government of West Bengal, since the state had financed part of that production.

the judiciary, concerned rules must be modified to ensure that scientific research is not pulled down by considerations other than 100 per cent merit.[21]

Mohana had succeeded in her experiments in finding an Ayurveda medicine which could be a promising anti-cancer drug. In research of this kind there are long procedures to be followed to make a drug available in the market because the drug has to go through several stages not only for its positive action against a specific disease, but also to show that its toxicity levels are tolerable for human consumption. It is only after testing several chemicals of plant origin that she had zeroed in on plumbagin (extracted from the plant plumbago zeylanica) as a very promising anti-cancer agent. She had also worked on birth control drugs, but had not made as much progress in that work as in the case of the cancer drugs. The next logical step would have been to do clinical trials with plumbagin. It was not easy to find hospitals coming forward for this trial. Since it was a question of a patient's life, often doctors were not willing to take the risk with unknown drugs and preferred to take the safe route of proven methods. More often than not, only patients who were considered to be terminally ill with cancer would be available to experiment with a new drug. Against all these odds, a team from the CSMDRI—led by its director, Purushothaman, and Mohana—convinced a hospital in Kerala to take the next step of research by clinical trials. But its implementation had not started.

The modest media exposure for her work and for the

---

[21] In early 2017, a group of top administrators in Indian scientific institutions submitted a detailed report to Prime Minister Narendra Modi, which states, 'The stature of Indian science is a shadow of what it used to be because of decades of misguided interventions. We have lost the ability to recognise excellence among our own. In a false sense of egalitarianism, we often choose the mediocre at every level.' (Published in *The Hindu*, 20 April 2017, page 11)

recognition of the Hari Om Ashram Award and invitations to San Diego and to China created false impressions in the minds of some lay people that Mohana was a physician. Patients began to visit us at home asking for cancer treatment. She had to explain that she was not a practising physician and that her work was only in the stage of research. In one case, we got a VIP recommendation and she had to explain at length why it would be unethical to prescribe the medicine.

Nevertheless, Mohana had tremendous confidence that her medicine was likely to turn out to be a big success in the clinical trials and was looking forward to the day when it could be prescribed to patients. However, a combination of factors contributed to her frustration. First, she was still holding a 'temporary' position, getting extension every year, in spite of national and international recognition. This meant that she had to depend on other 'permanent' officers for indenting even a small quantity of a chemical for her work. Secondly, there was an increasingly vitiated atmosphere in the CSMDRI because of caste and reservations politics. Thirdly, with a few honourable exceptions, her colleagues were more interested in salaries and promotions than in research, and so there was a cynical atmosphere of non-cooperation within the institute for continuing her work.

The CSMDRI was situated in Anna Nagar, while we lived in Adyar. It was a forty-five-minute drive each way. The financial compensation she got for the part-time consultancy did not even cover the fuel cost for her car. She continued this for a few years only out of her passion for research in Ayurveda. But the atmosphere at the lab was becoming increasingly hostile due to caste and communal prejudices.

By most people's standards of ambition for material success as the predominant aim of life, we were both mad in our own way. If I understood the limitations of human intellect because of my involvement with Swami Chinmayananda and others, she perceived the limitations of the mind because she saw poetry in all of God's creations—whether it was the nuances of genetics, the evolution of the species, or the inflorescence of a flower. She perceived a divine hand in everything and in that sense, she differed from the common image of the scientist as often an agnostic or an atheist. There were moments when she perceived marriage as having been an obstacle in her road to success as a scientist; she could have pursued her research and migrated to any part of the world for her scientific work. Sometimes she felt that she lost the freedom because of her innate love and devotion to her children. In her position, if she had pursued her career, ignoring her family, she would have risen to great heights as a scientist. But she was as much a committed mother, performing that role with perfection. Between the two of us, our uncompromising commitment to integrity, devoid of any desire for material aggrandizement, was the strongest link, although our fields of interest differed.

On 17 December 2004, Ram Nath Kovind[22] had said (in the Rajya Sabha), 'Reservations over fifty-odd years had led to bitterness between reserved castes (SCs/STs/OBCs) and general castes, and both are justified.' He said, 'SCs/STs were concerned that their share of 22.5 per cent in jobs was not filled in decades as the administration of quotas was in the hands of non-reserved castes.' On the other hand, he said, 'the non-reserved castes were also justified in saying how will reservation, which was to last only ten or twenty years, continue if they (SCs/STs) have suffered injustice for centuries, will reservation also continue for centuries? I think both sections of society are justified in their argument. After all, you cannot carry on with reservation for years.'[23]

---

[22]Ram Nath Kovind was elected as the president in July 2017.
[23]Refer to *Times of India* newspaper of Saturday, 24 June 2017.

An Ambivalent Transition

In 1982, S. Viswanathan (SV), a leading industrialist of Tamil Nadu, pleasantly surprised me by walking into my office. Without much fanfare, he said he was an admirer of *Indus Valley to Indira Gandhi* and that he wanted me to make two short films—one on Seshasayee Paper Boards Limited (SPBL) and the other on Tamilnadu Newsprint and Paper Limited (TNPL). He was the chairman of both. Considering his reputation as a high-profile industrialist, he was as unassuming as one can be. I gratefully agreed to the proposal.

The author and Mohana at an IQ conference in London

At SPBL, a private sector company, SV learnt that a new process of manufacturing newsprint from bagasse—residual fibre after extraction of sugar from sugarcane, which is a waste material—had been adopted by a company in Mexico. Some scientists felt that it could be an environment-friendly source of pulp from which paper can be made. SV convinced Chief Minister MGR of this laudable idea and the latter agreed to set up TNPL as a state enterprise. Critics pointed out that the Mexican company with similar technology had failed.

SV visited Mexico to see why that factory had failed and came to an understanding with Beloit Corporation, Massachusetts, to modify the technology and make it work. The World Bank extended a loan of $100 million to TNPL—the single largest loan, granted by it to any enterprise in India, till then. This was the stage at which I started making the two films.

Newsprint to News Coverage

We re-enacted the scene of the World Bank board interacting with SV to grant the loan in Washington. I filmed other scenes in New York and in the Beloit lab in Massachusetts. Indeed, the technology proved successful and TNPL began manufacturing newsprint from bagasse.

Barbara Blair, of the International Quorum (IQ) of Film and Video Producers, had invited me to join IQ, representing South Asia. IQ is an intentionally small organization, but it has presence across the world, which functions as a chamber of commerce and fosters fellowship among its members. Membership of the IQ is by invitation. The members cooperate with one another for location filming anywhere in the world. IQ membership gave me cameramen to shoot the scenes in the US, without my having to take my crew from India.

In the following years, Mohana and I attended the IQ

conferences in Paris and London. We extended our crew and technical support in India for some IQ members to shoot some scenes in India.

In the meantime, I had registered as a candidate for a doctoral programme at Columbia Pacific University, California, which allowed you to submit your published book as a part of your doctoral thesis. I submitted *Indus Valley to Indira Gandhi* as a component of my work. About a year later, they screened and accepted a 16 mm film print as part of my thesis and conferred a PhD on me, in 1983.

In early 1984, Lee Davies, a prominent IQ member, flew to Chennai to meet me at short notice and entrust the film coverage of a meeting of the Non-Aligned Movement (NAM Summit as it was called) scheduled in New Delhi, hardly a week later. He represented a US TV syndicate. I gladly accepted the work, but with the apprehension whether it was possible to get the necessary security clearances to film the event at such short notice.

I reached Delhi by the next available flight and found that the permission to film the summit and the security clearance had to be obtained one month in advance. But it was less than a week for the event to commence. It was a high-profile event, in which over a hundred heads of state were meeting in New Delhi. The chair of the summit was handed over by Fidel Castro to Indira Gandhi. There were several kinds of permissions required for filming. I discovered that if a crucial permission was obtained from the MEA, the rest would follow without much difficulty. I had no contacts in that ministry. I virtually dashed into the office of a joint secretary at the MEA, who was in charge of NAM. As luck would have it, he vaguely knew me because of *Indus Valley to Indira Gandhi*. In two minutes I explained to him the assignment and asked for permission. In a surprisingly friendly tone, the officer said, 'You are doing my work. How can I refuse it? We want the summit to be publicized with good media coverage.' This was Mani Shankar Aiyar, a diplomat who later turned politician after resigning from his job. Eventually, he became a popular minister in the central government.

Since security clearance had to be obtained individually for members of the crew, there was no time to get my crew from Chennai. I engaged a Delhi-based crew. The highlights of my covering NAM included brief interviews with Fidel Castro, Yasser Arafat (renowned Palestinian political leader) and J.R. Jayewardene, President of Sri Lanka, besides covering the main speeches of several African, Asian and Latin American leaders in the conference. We sent the 16 mm film footage every day to New York to Lee Davies, who edited them with my notes and gave them for telecast to the channels.

Also, in 1984, the government nominated me as the chairman of the jury for the national film awards for non-fiction films. I camped in Delhi for a fortnight to watch the nearly 180 documentaries. The awards were to be presented at a colourful function on 5 June. On the night before the awards ceremony, the Indian army entered the Golden Temple in Amritsar, the most holy shrine of the Sikhs, as a measure to counter terrorism. Terrorists headed by Sant Bhindranwale were converting the holy place into an unholy shrine of bloodshed. They attacked several civilians across Punjab. The Government of India decided to send the army into the temple.

Giani Zail Singh, the then President of India, was to distribute the national awards at our function and he expressed regret at the last minute, since he was pained by the entry of the army, of which, he was the supreme commander, into the most scared temple of his faith, a few hours earlier. Usha Bhagat, social secretary to Indira Gandhi, appeared briefly on the dais and explained to the audience that the president was unable to attend the function due to unavoidable reasons and had requested H.K.L. Bhagat, Minister for Information and

Broadcasting, to give away the awards.

Within hours of my flying back to Chennai, I got a call from Bhagat asking me to rush back to Delhi on an urgent professional assignment, the details of which would be given on my arrival. On reaching, Bhagat and a few others gave me a short briefing on the situation in Punjab and urged my reaching Amritsar urgently to make a film on the crisis.

It was agreed that it would be a fair independent journalistic film on what was happening in Amritsar. I was asked if I could reach Amritsar immediately. I confessed that I could speak no Hindi and I needed an interpreter. Someone suggested, 'Your wife speaks excellent Hindi.' Realizing that I was hesitant to take her along to an area of militancy, the officials assured me of high security for us. Mohana joined me in Delhi within hours for consultations. The briefing continued late night, presided over by Rajiv Gandhi (then heir apparent, who later became the prime minister) with ministers Buta Singh and Bhagat participating.

I needed a little more time to gather information on what was happening in Punjab by talking to experts, such as journalist Inder Malhotra, who toed the government line on this issue, and I.K. Gujral, who differed in his approach with that of the government, but decided that reaching Amritsar was the first priority. I told Bhagat that if they wanted a propaganda film with a one-sided story, then it would have no credibility abroad and would defeat the very purpose of the government entrusting this work to an outside documentary maker. The minister said, 'Let us cross the bridge when we come to it. You complete the film and show us your point of view.'

All modes of public transport to reach Amritsar, including airlines, had been suspended. The government gave us both seats in a charter flight. They deputed Patnaik, a cameramen of the Films Division, to work with us, who proved very cooperative. As we walked into the Golden Temple complex, although the jawans had worked relentlessly to clean up the place, there were still many signs of a battlefield.

Our thoughts went in flashback. A decade earlier, both of us had worshipped in the Golden Temple, when we were filming *I*. We had been thrilled by what was the cleanest and most well-maintained place of worship in the country; and had all admiration for public participation of the devotees in the maintenance of the temple—in every activity from sweeping and mopping of floors to management. The temple kitchen of the gurdwara had served us langar (complimentary hygienic food) with model levels of courtesy.

Now, we virtually shed tears since the place was full of bloodstains. While the most holy Harmandir Sahib in the middle of a water pond remained unaffected, the next important site within the temple campus—Akal Takht—was in ruins. We could fully empathize with the sentiments of the Sikhs on witnessing this devastation, but we also knew the full story as given to us during the dozens of interviews with the common citizens and the relatives of victims of terrorism, murdered in cold blood during the previous three years. Meeting the widow and children of Giani Pratap Singh, the chief priest of the Akal Takht, was most revealing. That revered man of peace devoted to harmony and welfare of the Sikh community had been shot dead at point-blank range in his house by terrorists, who had pretended to be his devotees to enter his house.

We filmed dozens of interviews including one with Ashwin Kumar, the young editor of the *Punjab Kesari* newspaper, whose father and grandfather had been assassinated in two separate incidents. Since the terrorists had sent a notice to this youngster that he was their next target of attack, we met him for the film interview at about two o'clock at night. Words are inadequate to praise this valiant young man, unmindful of the threat, vowing to uphold the spirit of Punjabiyat or the 'Punjabi way of life'.

All this and more made a deep impact on the young woman of my life for she had never dreamt that she would be witness to such real stories of violence as well as heroic valour. Initially, starting as an interpreter, translating my questions and the answers of the subjects, she evolved within a few days as one who could handle a Hindi interview on her own, adding questions and getting valuable inputs for me on screen.

This was a psychologically momentous evolution in her personality, expanding her interest beyond science to what was happening in the world—India in particular. I perceived this change in her, perhaps, even more than she realized. The human stories of tragedy and bravery moved us both deeply.

We also interviewed Major General Brar,[24] who commanded Operation Blue Star—the army operation at the Golden Temple. He was an example of how a soldier can behave valiantly even when placed in the most trying circumstances. His jawans were more or less fighting with their hands tied, since they were expected to safeguard the temple while attacking the several hundred terrorists who had made it their hideout and were attacking the army from inside. It was a transformational experience for us. The army suffered more casualties only because they had to go soft on the holy place.

We spent about twenty-five days in Amritsar to cover the whole story. We visited Delhi once in between for consultations with experts.

Another officer, Major Brar, was assigned by the army to keep us company throughout the filming. He performed two roles—one of coordinating with us to help our work and the other of ensuring

---

[24] I was pained that three decades after Operation Blue Star, terrorists attacked Major General Brar on the streets of London. But I was equally happy that living up to his reputation, Major General Brar defended himself and defeated the attempts of the armed opponents.

The author and Mohana with Major Brar and the helicopter crew

that we didn't become channels of confidential information to which we were privy. When we brought the entire footage of exposed film to Chennai for processing, he sat at the Prasad Colour Laboratory to ensure that no bit of film was duplicated at any point. It was a new experience for the laboratory officials to find an army officer looking over their shoulders as the film went into the processing machine and came out from the other end. As we were editing this in my office, Major Brar picked up every foot and frame of the discarded film which was not included in the edited footage, and carried them away with the whole lot. I admired this army man's meticulous eye for detail, without unduly interfering in my interpreting the whole event. I added interviews with two journalists—Inder Malhotra at Delhi and N. Ram at Chennai. Ram was known for his views opposed in principle to Operation Blue Star. Inder Malhotra believed that there was hardly any alternative to army action. Thus, we presented both sides of the coin to create a balance, tracing the origins of the conflict and the face of terrorism. I titled the nearly fifty-minute documentary *After a Thousand Days of Terror*.

The international media was projecting Operation Blue Star with several views for and against the army action. The MEA found our film to be a good vehicle to explain the position without bias and so they made about 1,000 VHS video copies and sent them through the embassies to the press, worldwide. But it was an irony that the film was not allowed to be screened within India. Intriguingly, the Censor Board under the MIB refused to give a certificate to the film for public release. They objected to thirty-two visuals and/or audios in the film including a shot of the dead body of Bhindranwale, and to some statements of N. Ram.

I legally appealed against the decision of the Censor Board. S.S. Gill, Secretary, MIB taunted me by saying, 'We own the rights of the film which you have written and directed. What difference does it make for you if the censors allowed its release or not?' I said, 'Mr Gill, although I have taken a small honorarium for this, I have worked on this film out of sheer interest in exploring a very important story of modern India—and I am interested in people watching my film.'

'Good luck for your effort,' he said sarcastically.

Tragedy struck on 30 October, when Indira Gandhi was assassinated by one of her security guards. It was a moment of grief for every Indian, irrespective of political affiliations. The huge sympathy wave catapulted the young Rajiv Gandhi to become the prime minister soon thereafter. Months later, Usha Bhagat disclosed to us that Indiraji had indeed seen our film and liked it, and would have taken steps to solve the censor issue within a day, if she had survived.

In about four months, the appellate tribunal directed the Censor Board to issue a certificate. It was a moral victory, but the government did not release it in India. As the MEA had distributed the film outside India, we received excellent feedback for objectivity from abroad.

In spite of her shortcomings, I remained an admirer of Indira Gandhi, but her charisma never converted me into a fan of her clan.

A day after she was assassinated, I got a call from Delhi that Doordarshan would telecast *Indus Valley to Indira Gandhi* again during the mourning period. The ministry requested whether it was possible to give a Hindi version of the whole four-hour film for telecast within those ten days. Such dubbing was an uphill task in such a short time. But I remembered that the great writer Khwaja Ahmed Abbas had sent me a telegram after the release of the English film showering praise on it. He had also insisted that if I dub it into Hindi, he would do the translation! I told him that I would deem it a privilege if he translated it, but I also told him that I might not be able to dub unless somebody financed the project. He nevertheless wanted a copy of the entire text of the commentary for his personal reading, which I gave him. Now, about seven years later, I called him and said we were planning to dub in Hindi as an urgent project. I was amazed when Abbas said that he had already translated it, since he had expected this to happen some day. He brushed up the script and sent me the entire four hours of narration the following day. Of course, for any film dubbing, such translation could not be used right away. We had to check the length of every sentence and synchronize it with the length of that visual in the English version; and it was a huge task. I requested Mohana to do this work. We rushed into dubbing within a couple of days. She was checking the Hindi dialogues in our editing room till midnight. During the day, Madhukar, an excellent Hindi voice artistee, narrated the commentary at a dubbing studio. We received them in another studio, where we mixed it with the original music track and got the final Hindi track ready. I took the print and delivered it in Delhi on the day it was to be telecast from Delhi.[25]

Coming in quick succession after the filming of the documentary on Punjab, this became an additional film-making experience for Mohana. She handled the work with remarkable speed, without compromising the creative flow of the film in its dubbed narration.

She had to take time off from her official position at the CSMDRI for this work. She was indeed getting disenchanted with the CSMDRI and this work helped her to get out of her depression. We realized that the politics of science in India was going from bad to worse. I suggested that she may try working part-time both at Krishnaswamy Associates and the CSMDRI to reduce her frustration.

We got involed in another interesting documentary project. It was well known that the Ganga was highly polluted. In 1985, the government initiated a mammoth project to clean the river. With the cooperation of the Ganga Action Plan, we produced two programmes in the style of TV reporting: one on the Ganga flowing from Rishikesh to Haridwar and the other on the river as

---

[25] A senior official in Doordarshan took the view that some scenes, which he considered as 'primarily entertaining' in the film would be 'inappropriate' to be telecast during the mourning period. So, they asked for a few scenes including a joyous song and Padma's dance sequence to be removed in the Hindi version. I thought that this was a problem for the Hindi version for a single telecast. But it did not work out that way. I have mentioned earlier about the irresponsible attitude of the film laboratory in Chennai in giving stepmotherly treatment to documentaries. In the intervening years, the ownership of the lab changed hands twice. The original negatives of my film were badly affected, and we had to depend on the Hindi print to reconstruct the English version. Sadly, the scenes which were removed for the Hindi version could not be restored at all.

it flows through Kanpur. The latter was the most polluted stretch of the river. Mohana anchored the Hindi version and I did it in English. The ease with which she anchored, nobody believed it was her first on-screen narration.

She resigned from the CSMDRI, but continued to be a part-time consultant there.

Indian Film, the book which I co-authored (first edition, 1963), was widely recognized as the first academic study of Indian cinema. Our chapter on Tamil cinema had an almost uncanny prediction that with the support of major film stars, the DMK may be on the road to capturing power in the state, which it did in 1967. In several of my articles since then, I had focused on the socio-political impact of Indian cinema. In this background, in 1986, the Washington Institute for Values, functioning under the Smithsonian umbrella in the US capital, invited me to present a

The author addressing the Washington Institute for Values, with Mangalam Srinivasan presiding

paper on 'Cinema as Political Phenomena'. When Mohana's career in science got affected by caste politics, I was triggered to study the history of the non-Brahmin movement. Hence, with due approval of the Washington Institute, I expanded the subject given to me as 'Culture as Political Phenomena' covering a much wider ground. Mangalam Srinivasan, a college professor in Washington, DC, who was associated with the Smithsonian Institution, presided over my lecture. It was a small and receptive audience, which included several academicians, senators and congressmen. Extracts from 'Culture as Political Phenomena' have been reproduced in the Annexure.

Gradually, Mohana was spending more time in our company. She got so vexed with the CSMDRI that after some time she bid farewell to it. She was already a director in our company and now I suggested that she should become the chairperson. It was by no means in the nature of offering something to someone

Mohana and the author working with a 35 mm Moviola film editing equipment

disappointed elsewhere, because I knew that she would fit in as the leader of a team to take our work to greater heights. She took over as producer of all our projects, including making TV serials.

One of her first creative initiatives in the company after becoming the chairperson was to make a documentary on the empowerment of women in Tamil Nadu. The Working Women's Forum founded by the activist Jaya Arunachalam, had several interesting case studies of how women could get out of their oppressive circumstances at the grassroots level. Mohana toured all over the state and directed the documentary *How They Left Hell Behind*. I was amazed at her grasp of not merely the subject, but the nuances of the film medium as displayed in her style of filming. The film won the first prize among all the films screened on the status of women at the Annual Convention of the International Federation of University Women at Helsinki. She has been firmly on her seat since then as head of a highly principled intentionally small media company.

On her taking over as chairperson of the company, she also streamlined some procedures for both revenue and expenditure. For instance, I had imported an Arriflex 35 mm high-speed camera for slow motion photography. It was the first of its kind available in Chennai and we were renting it out to feature-film-makers. It was in such high demand that it was working on hire for about twenty-five days a month. We also hired out other sophisticated film equipment of high professional quality. Under Mohana's direct supervision, these activities also flourished.

Mohana and I have never had differences in fundamentals that our work should be dedicated to ideological commitments and not escapist entertainment. Henry Ford is credited with the quote, 'If there are two people in business together and they agree with each other on every issue, one of them is redundant.' I am sure that neither of us was redundant, for our differences contributed to constructive dialogue and more often than not, wise decisions.

All In the Family

Over the last several pages, I have mostly dealt with the professional and creative challenges faced by Mohana and me up to about 1990. It is time that I reflect on our family story during those years.

My eldest child, Lata, was born in November 1969, when we were part of the joint family in my father's house. In 1971, we shifted as a unitary family to a house we had bought. Our second daughter, Gita, was born in 1971 and our son, Bharat, in 1973.

Mohana was a disciplinarian as a mother, while I unconsciously tried to compensate by being more lenient. I tried to impress on her that parents are really trustees of children—trusteeship assigned by God—and that we could pretend to be angry, but not really get angry at all with them. The pretention would keep us cool while conveying the intended message to the youngsters. She admired the idea as unique and valid; but had a complaint several years later. When she was reading Mahatma Gandhi's *My Experiments with Truth*, she told me, 'You have copied the concept of trusteeship from the Mahatma. I had an impression that it was your original thinking.'

I told her very sincerely, 'There may be several such other things in one's life. Whether your thoughts are influenced by hearing someone or reading a poem, once you have *internalized* the concept, it becomes your own.' Sometimes, we imbibe certain ideas—even a whole sentence—from somewhere, but years later, we forget the source and 'own' the concept. Today, psychologists call the phenomenon 'cryptomnesia'.

The five of us shared great moments of love for one another. Being of the same age group, the children often ganged up together and protected themselves from parental supervision.

Lata was a tomboy. When she was nine or ten, she would climb to the second floor open terrace, which had no parapet

Clockwise from top left: Gita and her father, Bharat and Lata with their mother, c.a. 1984

wall and celebrate her victory. Although less mischievous, Gita followed her example. Bharat was the timid one. Apparently, one day the girls encouraged their brother to walk up the ladder and play with them on the terrace, holding his hands as they climbed up. During these adventures of the 'three musketeers' in the afternoons, Mohana was away at work as a researcher with the CSMDRI and I was away in my office.

One day, Lata and Gita persuaded Bharat to climb up the ladder. After playing for a while, they discovered that they had a problem. The girls did not know how to bring their tiny brother down the ladder and suddenly realized the high risk they were taking. There was one more person in the house—Vedambal, of whom I have written earlier; the children were under her care when both of us were away. While she thought that the children were playing in the garden, she realized that they were actually on the terrace and at her age (about seventy years), she somehow managed herself to bring the children down and protected them from the ire of their parents for the mischief. But soon thereafter, the secret was out, as the little boy cried to his mother and said that the girls had taken him to the open terrace.

In every family, there are stories of childhood that are dear to every member and they do not tire of repeating them over the decades. Here are a few gems from my mental archives about our children.

◆

Lata had daily conversations with a cuckoo in our garden. She would clearly whistle her reply to every cuckoo call, and you could distinctly hear the bird responding. My mother, when she came on long visits to our house, was so touched by the fact that Lata sometimes insisted that she would grind flour for her idlis on a manual grinding stone. She also made chapattis for me with her tiny hands and was adamant that Vedambal should serve them to me. Although they were not the best chapattis of our kitchen, I was equally adamant on having them in my dinner plate even as Mohana and Vedambal sympathized with me.

◆

When Gita was in Class II, the school had declared an additional holiday (apparently for some local event, not mentioned in the school calendar).

Visitor to Gita: Why is it a holiday in your school?

Gita: You know, the President of India, Fakhruddin Ali Ahmed, died?

Visitor: But that was last week and you had a holiday for that?

Gita: Yes! And today, he came back alive. So, it is a holiday!

Apparently, she had heard the story of Jesus and his resurrection in the classroom only that week. She must have imagined it as a common occurrence among big people like the president of a country.

Gita was a voracious reader of children's literature. She rarely participated in the outdoor games played at Mohana's parents' house where several of her cousins assembled during holidays; Lata and Bharat were eager participants.

◆

Mohana accompanied Bharat for his admission in the reputed Sishya School in our neighbourhood, not sure whether they would take him in kindergarten. Interviewing the kid, the teacher asked him, 'Well, can you tell me the colour of the sari your mom is wearing?'

Bharat replied, 'She is wearing an orange sari with a yellow border, which has black dots.' He got admitted in Class I!

Visitor to Bharat (in Class III): When you grow up, which college do you wish to study in? What subjects?

Bharat: Oh, no! Only girls go to college. Boys go to office!

Yes! Mohana had registered for her PhD and I was going to office.

Bharat was in Class VII, and my mother was visiting us for a few weeks. Vedambal and my mother apparently had a loud argument about something. Although Vedambal had worked as a cook, nobody treated her as different from the family. Being of nearly equal age, my mother and she had friendly quarrels on issues relating to the household. One evening, when Mohana and I returned from work, Bharat called us to his room and said, 'Hear this conversation! And you will know how difficult it is to concentrate on studies in this house.' Yes! He had unobtrusively recorded the quarrel between his grandma and nanny in his cassette recorder! We couldn't stop laughing.

Although both Ramanu and I invited my mother to spend much of her time with either of us, our mother spent most of her time in Balu's house, visiting us for a few weeks only, once in a few months. I first thought that Balu's orthodoxy was most conducive for her. But she gave me two other reasons—one based on her 'duty' and the other on her 'right', as she perceived them—it was her duty to spend most of her time with her only unmarried daughter, Padma, to safeguard her interests; and it was her right to stay with Balu, to be taken care of in her old age, since he alone had benefited from her wealth.

The girls wanted to learn dance and we had organized their classes in Bharatanatyam with Vasanthalakshmi and Narasimhachari, the couple who became very dear to the students. Mohana wanted to revive her dance classes. That is how we fixed up Narasimhachari to teach her. When the girls got interested, Vasanthalakshmi began to coach them. These classes started in a thatched-roof shed on our terrace, which we later built as a proper hall for their dance practice.

The girls went to Rosary Matriculation School, while Bharat studied in Sishya. I realized that I became a disciplinarian with our son, while being lenient with our daughters, since Mohana tilted the balance the other way. There was need for me to be strict since Bharat sometimes became violent, attacking his sisters. Mohana's research lab was an hour's drive from our house, while I took less than five minutes to reach my office. I cannot forget little Bharat comparing the household to two political parties. He told his mother, 'You, belonging to *my party* go away very far during the day, while Dad who belongs to these *girls' party* is very near for them to approach whenever there is a quarrel between us.' We had a hearty laugh. By the time Bharat went to high school, there was an unmistakable sign of brilliance. After finishing Class X, he wanted to change his school and we shifted him to the famous Vidya Mandir, Mylapore, for Classes XI and XII. My cousin, Alamelu Gopalan, was the principal of that school and took a lot of personal interest in Bharat. She told me one day in a light-hearted manner, 'Your son is the most popular among the girls in the school.'

Lata and Gita got very involved in their dance and we organized their arangetram, first performance on stage, when Lata was nine and Gita seven. They became accomplished dancers and performed in every professional stage or sabhas as they are known in Chennai. As an accomplished dancer, Mohana could add a dimension, especially bhava, to what the girls were learning from their revered gurus.

Lata joined BSc at Stella Maris College followed by Gita joining BA (Corporate) at Ethiraj College.

Lata was finishing her graduation in 1989. That was my period of close association with the scholar-statesman Ma.Po. Sivagnanam, better known as Ma.Po.Si. One day, casually, he browsed through my English poems and fondly chided me for not writing in Tamil. He said, 'The poetic mind is not related to language. If you can write poems in a foreign language, you can very well write in your mother tongue.' I had occasionally written Tamil lyrics for our TV serials and Ma.Po.Si.'s words were like a tonic. As I was reading Sri Aurobindo's *Savitri*—the longest poem in the English language—the mystic nature of that esoteric classic hypnotized me.

Thus, when Lata and Gita insisted on my writing a dance-drama for them, I adapted extracts from Aurobindo, writing *Savitri* in Tamil in 1990. Shyam composed the music for *Savitri* and the dance-drama was born, choreographed and performed by Lata and Gita. Apart from the encomiums received for this dance-drama in India, BBC Tamilosai World Service Radio, London, commented, '*Savitri*, written by Krishnaswamy and choreographed by Lata and Gita, is on a new level of joyful experience for Tamil arts and culture.' In short, even when they were teenagers, Lata and Gita blossomed as creative artistees in their own right.

Watching them on the stage, parents of eligible young men began to approach us for possible matrimonial alliances.

Two of Lata's closest friends, including Padmaja who had been her classmate from kindergarten to graduation, got married soon after graduation. Mohana asked Lata if she was also ready for marriage. The innocent youngster replied, 'Yes, as long as you don't send me out of Chennai! I don't want to be away from you both and I am not interested in those grooms who promise heaven

Lata and Gita in the dance–drama Savitri

in America.' Mohana persuaded Lata to pursue MSc in biology. But she showed more interest in dance and in the production of TV serials and short films.

Among the shortlisted prospective suitors for Lata was Ashok Rajah, grandson of Rajah Iyer, erstwhile Advocate General of the state. While Rajah Iyer was no more, as art connoisseurs, his son, Krishnamurthy, and daughter-in-law, Kamala, parents of Ashok, said that they were admirers of Lata and Gita and that they would be fortunate if Lata would be their daughter-in-law. Ashok was a promising young advocate. The families agreed and so did the boy and the girl. Ashok was the youngest of three children and his two sisters had very impressive backgrounds and happy family lives—the elder settled in Canada, and the other in Chennai. We organized the wedding at one of the best wedding halls in 1989.

Lata became a director of our compay and gradually began to take many creative responsibilities. The Krishnamurthys lived in Harrington Road. Lata and Ashok were part of their joint family. Lata drove forty-five minutes each way to the office, shouldering many responsibilities at home and the office. Krishnamurthy and Kamala showered their affection on Lata. The two families were overjoyed when Lata's daughter, Kamini, was born in 1992.

When Gita completed her graduation, in 1991, she had already made up her mind to be part of Krishnaswamy Associates. She had, by then, performed as the heroine of our Hindi telefilm, *Thyagabhoomi*, with the veteran thespian Bharat Bhushan in the role of her father. My father's original Tamil *Thyagabhoomi* had been banned in 1939, in view of its propagating the ideals of the freedom struggle. We produced a remake as a Hindi telefilm to mark the golden jubilee of that ban and telecast it on Doordarshan in 1990. Gita also performed the lead role of 'Kannagi' in the first half of our Hindi serial *Upaasana*, in 1991, in which Lata performed the lead role as 'Manimekalai' in the second half of the twin epics. Both received encomiums from the press and public.

Gita, Bharat Bhushan and Kumari Sachu in Thyagabhoomi

We then made a TV version of *Savitri*, which won an award for 'Creative Excellence' at the US International Film and Video Festival.

Prompted by the success of *Savitri* on the stage and small

Lata and Gita receiving mementos from Abdul Kalam, President of India, after their dance recital at Rashtrapati Bhavan

screen, the girls wanted me to write another dance–drama. I wrote *Vaibhogame*, portraying four celestial weddings from mythology—the weddings of Rama and Sita, Krishna and Rukmini, Murugan and Valli, and Meenakshi and Sundareswara. With music by Shyam Joseph, this too was a runaway success on the stage.

The Hindu reviewed *Savitri* and *Vaibhogame* stating, 'Refreshing, well within tradition but in an innovative approach—*Vaibhogame* and *Savitri*. While the first is a celebration of life, the latter is defiance of death.'

Bharat, after finishing Class XII, got admission in the prestigious Birla Institute of Technology and Science (BITS), Pilani. This was a period when there was a complaint of brain-drain from India to the West, because the brightest students graduating out of these institutions were migrating to either America or elsewhere in the West. Their cost of education having been highly subsidized by the Indian government, there was much resentment about this brain-drain. The other side of the coin was that there were not many opportunities within the country for meritorious talents, partly also due to the politics of reservations (and of corruption) in government employment.

Although a private engineering college on the outskirts of Chennai was also willing to give a seat in the group of his choice for Bharat in return for some capitation fee, which we were willing to pay, Bharat refused to join this college since his heart was set on pursuing his studies in BITS, which had chosen him entirely on his merit. We admired his independence and judgement and both of us accompanied him for his admission in Pilani. Mohana was very upset to leave her child for the next five years in a hostel in Rajasthan. With her eyes wet, she asked me when we were returning in our taxi to Delhi, 'How could this boy be so quiet and walk away towards the college without showing any emotion?' I explained to her, 'If he shows any emotion, he will face severe ragging from the senior students.'

Courtroom Dramas On and Off Screen

While studying Indian history in depth from various sources, when I was making *Indus Valley to Indira Gandhi*, three subject areas in particular caught my imagination. First, I was fascinated by the fact that ancient India had a profound influence on the rest of Asia. Secondly, when India was at a low ebb in her culture and civilization, there was an intellectual and spiritual renaissance from about the mid-nineteenth century that lasted a century, the impact of which continues till today. Thirdly, I was intrigued, if not disturbed, by the fact that most of the national publications on India's freedom struggle mentioned very little about the contribution of Tamilians to that movement.

I dwelt in depth on these issues and made films on them at different periods of my professional work. The first was on the renaissance period, which I covered in a two-part documentary, of about twenty minutes each, titled *When the Waves Came!* I gave this proposal to the Films Division, which sponsored it in 1987, during the 40th anniversary of independence. It traces the story from Raja Ram Mohan Roy covering Sri Ramakrishna, Swami Vivekananda, the Arya Samaj, the Theosophical Society and the formation of the Indian National Congress, culminating in the period of Mahatma Gandhi. It covers the political and social churning of society at large during those decades.

My involvement with Southeast Asia could be translated into a series of films only much later, when I was nearing seventy. By that time, I had the able and active collaboration of Mohana, which added strength to my own pursuit since my earlier films on history had been lonely efforts.

On the question of ignoring the role of Tamil Nadu in India's freedom struggle, I began to dig out the background. Soon after independence, the Government of India appointed a committee to study the history of the freedom struggle and bring out an authentic report. S. Radhakrishnan, who later became President of India, was the chairman of the committee. After a couple of meetings of the unwieldy committee, he announced that it would be appropriate to postpone the work at the national level for about a decade, during which time every state should constitute state-level committees comprising academicians and freedom fighters, to bring out authentic reports of their respective regions. He further proposed that when all these state-level reports were published, they would constitute the raw material from which the national-level history should be written, perhaps twenty years from the time of independence.

While every state in India constituted such committees and came out with their books relating to their role in the freedom struggle, nothing of that sort happened in Tamil Nadu. We have to trace some history to understand this. In the whole subcontinent, the Justice Party (founded in 1917) had the dubious distinction of being the only political force that opposed Indian independence. This party had morphed into Dravida Kazhagam (DK) under E.V. Ramasamy Naicker alias Periyar. Soon after independence, a splinter group of the DK called DMK was formed. On a much later day, a splinter group of the DMK came into being called Anna DMK (later renamed All India Anna DMK or AIADMK). From 1967 onwards, Tamil Nadu was ruled by either the DMK or AIADMK.

These Dravidian parties tried their utmost to suppress this history and the fact that they had opposed the freedom struggle. This deliberate 'sweeping of facts under the carpet' by regional party leaders did not allow a history committee to surface in Tamil Nadu, resulting in the entire valiant participation of tens of thousands of Tamils in the freedom struggle being blacked out in the national narratives.

There are examples in the world where a political party may be embarrassed about certain aspects of its own history. For example, the Democratic Party in America was known for its racial prejudices in the nineteenth century—it had not even opposed slavery. It has come a very long way now by nominating an African-American—Obama—as its spectacularly successful presidential candidate.

A political party should have not only the maturity to adapt itself to new situations but also the courage to face the reality of its own past. Although the DMK, which had a separatist agenda till the early 1960s, began to owe allegiance to India's national unity more than a decade after independence, it lacked the courage to face its past.

Several years after the Congress party lost power in Tamil Nadu, there was one link between the ruling class and the freedom fighters—M.P. Sivagnanam (Ma.Po.Si.), chairman of the Legislative Council. An erudite scholar and freedom fighter—a follower of Rajaji—he had formed a new party after independence to promote Tamil culture. When I approached him for guidance to make a film on the role of Tamils in the freedom struggle, he had just finished his manuscript of a marathon book, *Viduthalai Poril Tamilagam* (The Role of Tamil Nadu in the Freedom Struggle), published soon thereafter.

Ma.Po.Si. gave me access to his manuscript and encouraged me to do additional research with other consultants for the film. All this resulted in our making a thirteen-episode Tamil docudrama[26] serial, *Ezhu Thalaimurai Ezhuchchi* (Seven Generations of Uprising), on the role of Tamils in the freedom struggle, telecast in 1988–89.

While I wrote the screenplay and commentary for the serial, besides being the on-screen anchor, I conceived a few scenes in the style of a docudrama and asked JK to write the dialogue for those scenes involving patriots like Subramania Bharati, V.O. Chidambaranar and Sathyamurthy.

A courtroom drama started in real life, when the fourth episode of this serial was telecast. K. Veeramani, head of the DK and successor to the legacy of E.V.R. Periyar, filed a writ petition in the Madras High Court challenging the authenticity of the serial. He claimed that it was one man's distorted interpretation of history and that it highlighted only the role of Brahmins in the freedom struggle and not that of the other communities in Tamil Nadu. The high court refused to give a stay order to continue the telecast, but took it up for hearing on a fast track. What apparently angered Veeramani was the fact that one of our researchers, the respected historian Pe Su Mani, had managed to get a 1944 headline of *Viduthalai*, DK's official organ. That news story gave emphasis to the resolution passed at the Salem conference of the DK, meaning effectively that 'in the unlikely and unfortunate event of India getting freedom from

---

[26] A docudrama is a documentary which has some dramatized scenes.

The author garlanding Ma.Po.Si.

the British rule, we in our state, would like to continue to be governed under the benevolent British rule and not be part of the newly independent nation'. This news was ignored by the English and Tamil newspapers perhaps because they treated it as an insignificant aberration of a fringe group. I had filmed the concerned 1944 headline from *Viduthalai* and included it in one of the later episodes of my serial. This obviously bothered Veeramani who came to know of it ahead of that episode being telecast and went to court. Justice Sivasubramanian not only dismissed the petition but also commented in the court, that 'The only good thing that the litigant has done to me is that I got an opportunity to see this authentic TV serial, which I may have otherwise missed in the midst of my preoccupations.'

In the casteist political atmosphere of Tamil Nadu, we were fortunate that this judgment was delivered by a non-Brahmin judge. We celebrated this victory by requesting Ma.Po.Si. (himself a non-Brahmin) to address a news conference.

Within two years of this court drama, the early 1990s compelled us to be in a courtroom again as respondents in another case. This case was an example of how regional, linguistic, chauvinism and casteism in India at every level, interfere unfairly in creative endeavours.

Silappadigaram and *Manimekalai* are Tamil epics, which are among the oldest extant literature in any Indian language other than Sanskrit. While the people of Tamil Nadu are familiar with the literature in northern languages to some extent, the citizens of the north are mostly ignorant of even the greatest works of Tamil literature and history. Consistent with my company's vision statement—'We film to build bridges of brotherhood. We shoot to destroy walls of prejudice!'—I thought of making a Hindi TV serial based on the Tamil twin classics *Silappadigaram* and *Manimekalai* to project them nationally.

Getting the permission to make this Hindi serial was an uphill task to start with, since Hindi-oriented cerebral lords in Delhi thought that there was no Tamil literature worthy of a Hindi serial.

The proposal met with opposition from various fronts. There had always been an element of truth in the allegation of the Dravidian movement that North India was ignoring the South, trying to dominate the rest of India. True to this, there was opposition in Doordarshan and in the MIB to make a Hindi version of Tamil classics. Remember, Doordarshan was the only TV channel in India in that period. However, with a sustained push, we succeeded in getting the authorities in Delhi to approve our project and sanction the budget for making such a Hindi serial. No sooner than we commenced shooting, a writ petition was filed in the Madras High Court by an anti-Brahmin lobby that this contract ought not to have been given to Krishnaswamy Associates, since Doordarshan had not floated a tender for awarding the production. It was a formidable combination of forces against us, including corrupt officials of Doordarshan, commercial rivals who would descend to any depths for getting business and the caste lobby that wanted to prevent a Brahmin organization from violating what they considered a non-Brahmin right over Tamil classics.

The records clearly supported us. The files showed that after much discussion the ministry had written to Ma.Po.Si. (as an authority on the *Silappadigaram*) for expert opinion about entrusting this production to my company. The statesman-scholar responded, 'They would be the best suited producers to take up the serial because of Krishnaswamy's intrinsic love for the subject and the Hindi expertise of Mohana, to produce such a serial.'

However, the litigants who had gone to court against us had a reason to rejoice when Justice Bhakthavatsala delivered a judgment in their favour. Among other things the judge said, 'Dr Krishnaswamy had lobbied at the highest levels of government for this project.'

Senior advocate Nalini Chidambaram, who was our lawyer, suggested our filing an appeal. From our perspective, it was not merely a question of getting a contract of a certain value but of re-establishing our integrity in public perception. A two-judge bench presided over by Justice P.S. Mishra observed that writing to a higher authority in the government does not amount to unethical pressure, and restored the validity of our contract with Doordarshan. The proposal had been given by us and there was no question of its being subjected to a tender, unless the proposal was given by an unqualified producer.

We resumed the filming of *Upaasana*, the title we had given to the Hindi serial, and worked more than whole-time. I wrote the screenplay; Valampuri Somanathan wrote the dialogue in Tamil, and Radha Janardan translated it in Hindi. As the director of the serial, I had a sense of satisfaction facing the challenge of creating the ambience of ancient Tamil Nadu with several elements of the supernatural into a serial that could appeal to the national audience, unfamiliar with the epics. From supervising the dialogue delivery to costume design, Mohana had several responsibilities.

It was telecast once almost every year in one of the networks of Doordarshan (DD National, DD Bharati and DD India). In a kind of reverse osmosis process, we dubbed this Hindi serial into Tamil also.

Upaasana featured Gita as 'Kannagi' (heroine of the first epic) and Lata as 'Manimekalai' (heroine of the second epic). The twin epics were written by two different authors in Tamil, but with some

Gita as Kannagi

Lata as Manimekalai

common characters from a historic past. While *Silappadigaram* is a reflection of the impact of Jainism, *Manimekalai* is that of Buddhism. Both are repositories of the culture of Tamil Nadu written about 2,000 years ago.

The uniqueness of these ancient epics is that unlike most literary works of that period around the world, they do not deal with royalty as their heroes and heroines. They portray the lives of common people and also reflect the glory of Tamil merchants, who sea traded with China at one end and Rome at the other.

Even as we were fighting a legal battle for *Upaasana*, there was one more regarding our Tamil TV serial *Oorarinda Rahasiyam* (Well-known Secret). We had acquired the TV rights of my friend JK's novel *Eswara Allah Tere Naam*, which had a theme of communal harmony with a Hindu–Muslim love story. In 1990, we gave the proposal to Doordarshan to make a sponsored serial based on this novel, and got an in-principle approval.

We continued the production when Doordarshan approved the pilot episode also.[27] And then we were shocked because Doordarshan withdrew the approval unilaterally. The officers orally explained that the approval was given before the Babri Masjid was demolished in Ayodhya and the concept had become controversial after that event. Although we tried our best to argue with them, they were not convinced. Doordarshan agreed to give us the time slot for a sponsored programme with a different title as per our choice. I wanted compensation for the value of work we had already done for *Eswara Allah Tere Naam*. Nambiar, a sensitive director of Doordarshan, in Chennai, said that there was no provision for financial compensation, but that instead of thirteen weeks for a sponsored slot[28] given to us for that title, Doordarshan would give a time slot for sixteen weeks, giving three additional slots as compensation.

When I explained to JK why Doordarshan had withdrawn their approval for *Eswara Allah Tere Naam*, he treated it as an affront to his reputation as a writer. This led to some unfortunate developments. As we had filmed one of his novels and about twenty-five of his short stories, some in Tamil and some in Hindi in the 1980s, as TV serials, there was a creative partnership

---

[27] It is common among TV channels to ask for one sample episode of a long serial to be produced before approving the proposal.

[28] A sponsored programme means that we buy a TV time slot, produce the material at our own cost and recover its cost as well as make any profit by selling a certain amount of advertisement time. In such instances, the TV channel merely sells the time slot, but the subject matter of what is telecast is to be approved by the channel.

between JK as writer and me as director. When we shot for his novel, *Parisukku Po* (Go to Paris), as a TV serial, *Nallthor Veenai* (A Good Veena), in 1984, he was so thrilled with the production that he made a statement quite uncharacteristic of him with legitimate pride as a writer. He declared on TV and in print that 'Krishnaswamy's screen adaptation of my novel is an improvement on my original'. The statement provoked a journalist to comment, 'Jayakanthan is a genius without doubt; however, humility is not one of his virtues. Hence, this tribute assumes special significance.'

From the time of his first feature film, *Unnai Pol Oruvan* in 1964, JK and I had remained intimate friends. But now, when I asked him to suggest a substitute to *Eswara Allah Tere Naam* from his own novels for the TV serial, he was reluctant to cooperate. I chose sixteen award-winning short stories by different Tamil writers and gave the serial the common title *Oorarinda Rahasiyam (Well-known Secrets)*. Doordarshan approved this. But a motivated gang, including elements from Doordarshan, instigated JK to go to court against Doordarshan allotting a time slot to Krishnaswamy Associates for a different writer's work, since originally JK's novel had been approved by Doordarshan.

Some friends tried to advise him that 'neither Krishnaswamy nor Doordarshan was against him'. But he became obstinate and filed a suit to say that Doordarshan giving time for any other story chosen by me was unethical and illegal.

Thus, even as we were facing the *Upaasana* battle, it was most unfortunate to confront a wonderful friend as an adversary. The court decreed that Doordarshan was at liberty to approve the proposal of Krishnaswamy Associates based on any other author's work as the time slot had been given to them on the basis of their professionalism, and so we could proceed with the

An Ambivalent Transition • 209

From left: Jayakanthan, the author and Mohana

production and telecast of *Oorarinda Rahasiyam*.[29] The motivated parties fighting the *Upaasana* battle impleaded themselves in this case, also stating that giving three weeks' extension (from thirteen proposed episodes of *Eswara Allah Tere Naam* to sixteen proposed episodes of *Oorarinda Rahasiyam*) was improper. Eventually, the court's verdict was in our favour.

Mohana was unhappy that I was in conflict with one of my closest friends and said, 'Whatever mistake that he has done, try to patch up.' I was not sure how JK would react because of his tempestuous temperament. I requested Nalini Chidambaram to talk to his lawyer. She settled, according to our formula, that we would pay JK the royalty agreed for his novel and hold the rights to produce it at any time in the future. I borrowed the money

---

[29]*Oorarinda Rahasiyam* received such a huge response that we extended it a few years later to a second season with thirty-four more episodes.

and settled it on the same day.

Just a few weeks after the court battles were over, JK dropped into my office as his normal self and apologized profusely, 'This was the single most terrible error of my life—going to court against you. I still don't know why I lost my balance.' We patched up without any malice on either side and remained friends till his last day. When he received the Gnanpith Award at Delhi, I was delighted with his initiative of screening for that audience two stories from a series of his short stories which Krishnaswamy Associates had produced in Hindi a decade earlier.

Think of it this way! Along with the common people of Punjab, we faced our own court drama and won the certificate of the Censor Board for the film on the army action in the Golden Temple. In the thousands of court dramas during the freedom struggle, our serial on the freedom struggle faced its own court scene in our real lives. We won that battle. If, as commoners, Kannagi and Manimekalai won their battles in their kings' courts, we had to win our own battles to bring their stories on the TV screen. We also won against caste and communal prejudices with the serial *Oorarinda Rahasiyam*.

While in all the above instances we were respondents in the court, occasionally, we were also litigants initiating cases in the high court. Two of these come to my mind. In 1972, we made an advertising film for Shaw Wallace to promote their product, 'Golconda brandy'.

Aesthetically, this film took very good shape. But the Censor Board and its appellate tribunal refused to give a certificate for public release. I moved the high court requesting V.P. Raman, a celebrated lawyer, to argue the case. My arguments were simple: 'While Prohibition was recommended in the Directive Principles of State Policy of our Constitution, such directive principles are not binding on individual citizens. They are intended for central and state governments to enact law for the prohibition of liquor. Since there was no prohibition in several states, advertising liquor should be allowed in such states. In all such states, the print and the outdoor media were allowed to advertise liquor. Hence, refusal of censor certificate for the film amounts to discrimination against the film medium.' The learned lawyer agreed to appear for us in the high court.

Those unfamiliar with the speed of the judicial process in India may be surprised to know that some four years later, the Madras High Court gave a judgment in our favour, directing the Government of India to issue a censor certificate. The government appealed to the Supreme Court. V.P. Raman had by then become the Advocate General and so he could not appear in a case against the government. In a way, it was a public interest litigation (PIL), since I was trying to argue that cinema should have the same level of freedom as other media. I did not pursue the case in the Supreme Court since senior lawyers advised me that the high court judgment was so strong that it was unlikely to be set aside by the Supreme Court. That is exactly what happened, albeit it meant a few more years of waiting.

I had filed another PIL in 2004 when a private TV channel had acquired the rights of telecasting India-Pakistan cricket matches. It was the first India–Pakistan match after several years and cricket fans would have felt deprived if Doordarshan did not telecast it. Private TV channels had limited viewership, while Doordarshan was the dominant channel, reaching the country due to its terrestrial distribution. I thought that the public at large should not be deprived of watching an important sports event and so, Krishnaswamy Associates filed a PIL in the high court. My friend and advocate N.L. Rajah appeared for us. The Consumer Action Group also filed a parallel writ petition with the same objective. We won the case hands down when the court heard the case in a fast track and gave the judgment that the private channel should give a link of the signal to DD National.

Later, Parliament enacted that TV coverage of such sports events should be accessible to Doordarshan in public interest.

In the Presence of Their Holinesses

Since the first property I bought had some vacant land with the building in one corner, we built a small shooting floor (studio) in 1989, which was the first air-conditioned studio in Chennai, outside Doordarshan. His Holiness Jayendra Saraswati, the Sankaracharya of the Kanchi Math, graciously inaugurated the studio with His Holiness Sankara Vijayendra Saraswati, Malcolm Adiseshiah, Ma.Po.Si. and JK participating. A few months later, we celebrated the silver jubilee of Krishnaswamy Associates with I.K. Gujral as the chief guest. He was then the external affairs minister. These two functions gave us a boost to carry on our mission of making the programmes of our choice

His Holiness Jayendra Saraswati Swamigal with the Krishnaswamys

As a shot in the arm, the Watumull Foundation, Hawaii, conferred on me its Honor Summus Award in December 1987, with the memorable words in the citation 'for his film-making with social commitment, combining technical skill with creative finesse'.

To disseminate the message of religious harmony, I conceived a film of about one hour with interviews of major religious leaders, including His Holiness the Dalai Lama, Mother Teresa, Poojya Swami Ranganathananda—then vice president, who later became the president of the Ramakrishna Math, Acharya Tulsi—head of one Jain sect, Dasturji, head priest of the Parsis. CS, (former union minister and Governor of Maharashtra, who was later conferred the highest civilian award of India, Bharat Ratna) then chairman of Bharatiya Vidya Bhavan, and S. Ramakrishnan, general secretary of the bhavan, extended their support for this project. The Bhavan also gave a subsidy for the production, partially covering the cost. Within a few weeks, we got appointments with the major personalities and started filming. However, Mother Teresa's diary was full and it looked as though we may not get time to include her in the film at all. But as luck would have it, an American producer, who had fixed up with her several months earlier, contacted me and asked for technical facility and collaboration in India to interview her. I was overjoyed by this offer and I hitchhiked with him and took Mother Teresa's permission for my interview also, at the same time. She spent almost one hour with us.

We had an appointment with the Dalai Lama at Dharamshala in the Himalayas. Unlike the short notice at which I flew to Kolkata to film the Mother with only two people in my film crew, this trip was planned well in advance and so Mohana, Lata, Gita and members of my crew took a flight with me to Delhi. Bharat, who was studying in Pilani, was keen to have a darshan of the monk, took a few days off and joined us in Delhi. Bharatiya

Vidya Bhavan's general secretary Ramakrishnan also landed in Delhi and we were in all a dozen people who took a flight to Dharamshala. After checking us in and collecting our luggage, the airlines announced cancellation of the flight due to technical reasons. There was no other way of reaching Dharamshala in time to meet the Dalai Lama. I frantically called his secretary asking whether the appointment could be postponed by one day. He expressed regret since the Dalai Lama was flying to Europe and was unlikely to find time for us. I asked whether it was possible to film the interview while he was in transit—in Delhi or Mumbai—and he said he would get back to me. There was a sense of disappointment for all of us. We returned to the India International Centre, where we were staying. What a delight it was to get a call confirming that we could film the interview

The author with St Teresa

with the monk in New Delhi. We filmed the interview at his hotel. I found him to be the personification of spirituality with simplicity. I suppose someone who is so holy will also be humble.

After the interview for the film, I took his permission to ask a few extra questions. 'Your Holiness, it is said that about 1,200 years ago, when Buddhism was the single most popular religion of India, Adi Sankara came on the scene and had the impact of reconverting most people to Hinduism. With that background, how did you think in terms of meeting His Holiness Chandrasekarendra Saraswati, the senior Sankaracharya of Kanchi, a year ago?'

The Dalai Lama laughed and replied with all simplicity. 'The differences are all only at the level of aspirants and rituals. The Sankaracharya and the Buddha followed their own path. I heard a great deal about the saint of Kanchi and I wanted to pay my respects to him. I found him a genuine monk who has chosen to live in poverty in a dark small room, while monks like me

The author with the Dalai Lama

live in luxury. I have great regard for him.' I perceived the Dalai Lama as a messenger of God.

Swami Ranganathananda was the vice president of the Ramakrishna Math at that time, heading the math at Hyderabad, where we had his darshan. I could use his words interspersed throughout my film, for he spoke of communal harmony most effectively with conviction. We also interviewed Justice Hidayatullah, former Vice President of India, to outline the message of peace in the Quran. The learned former judge of the Supreme Court came up with such a sparkling array of quotes from the Quran, establishing Islam as a religion of peace, in a manner of surpassing the chief qazi of a state, in expressing the depth of vision of the Prophet.

In short, making this film was a spiritually elevating experience. I had filmed a five-minute short story, which I screened to these religious leaders whenever time permitted, and

M.S. Subbalakshmi with the Krishnaswamys

if there was a time constraint, I narrated the story—which is a spoof on fake religious leaders. All the religious leaders smiled approvingly. But the one who enjoyed it most and endorsed the story was Acharya Tulsi in Rajasthan. In his message he confirms that all religions face this kind of danger and that religious leaders should be constantly vigilant.

Mohana wanted to add a few songs in this film. We requested the queen of Indian music, M.S. Subbalakshmi, to sing a few songs for us. Both MS and her husband, Sadasivam, enthusiastically agreed, and she sang a few songs to suit the theme of the film. We could not imagine anyone less than her in the film that had hallowed figures and it was a lyrical experience filming her in our studio. I titled the film *Reality Behind Religion*.[30]

Williams' Vision of Jesus

The ethnic conflict in Sri Lanka took an ugly turn in 1983, when the Tamils in northern Sri Lanka and in Colombo were persecuted by the majority Sinhalese in power. Several Tamils gave up their houses and belongings and shifted to Tamil Nadu. Such people, whose homes were looted and who had to run away from their motherland, included several qualified and affluent professionals in Colombo.

Among those who arrived in Chennai, two people became our close associates and family friends. First was V. Sundaralingam, a popular Tamil journalist, who had for long worked in the BBC Tamil Service in London, whom I had met during my brief visits to Sri Lanka. He commanded the respect of Tamils around the world by his genuine warmth. He joined our company as liaison officer, in addition to lending his voice as and when required for our TV programmes.

---

[30]*Reality Behind Religion* is available on *www.indianimprints.com*.

While Sri Lankan Tamils were being persecuted by the Sinhalese majority, they also suffered under the head of the Liberation Tigers of Tamil Eelam (LTTE)—Prabhakaran—described by some as the champion of the Tamils and by others as a terrorist. Rajiv Gandhi as Prime Minister of India took a historic decision to help Sri Lanka in managing the crisis and signed an accord with the Sri Lankan President Jayewardene by which India sent an army contingent to Sri Lanka as the Indian Peace Keeping Force (IPKF). Sundaralingam, who knew Sri Lankan politics inside out, had been urging me to make a film on the origin of the ethnic conflict. I thought this was an opportune time and I requested the cooperation of India's MEA.

The MEA came forward to sponsor our film, *A Paradise Regained,* expecting that Sri Lanka would regain its status as an island paradise within a short time, but history proved otherwise and the conflict extended to the early twenty-first century before finding 'hopefully' a final solution.

The making of this film was another unique experience. Besides Mohana and me, my crew included cameraman Mohan Sundaram, my nephew, and Sundaralingam and three helpers. The Indian Air Force (IAF) was flying several sorties from Chennai to Jaffna and accommodated us in one such, which carried rations for the IPKF, and gave us all the help we needed for the next four weeks of our sojourn in Sri Lanka. We spent more time in the Tamil northern province, filming the devastation caused by the Sinhalese army there, as well as the destruction caused by the LTTE. I interviewed some leaders in Colombo including a minister and the film star-turned-politician Kumaratunga, who had tried to work for peace between the ethnic groups. Incidentally, his wife, Chandrika, later emerged as the prime minister of Sri Lanka. Our tour within the island was primarily on IAF helicopters, whose pilots obliged us by allowing us to take aerial shots.

At that juncture, the local people enthusiastically welcomed the IPKF as a blessing that would bring peace to the island. The LTTE chief had not made up his mind whether or not to be supportive to the IPKF. His goal was to get Eelam as an independent country, seceding from Sri Lanka.

The IPKF functionaries facilitated our brief meeting with Prabhakaran at a highly guarded forest home. But he suggested that I should interview his deputy Mahatia for the film. Mahatia had armed guards around him and a pistol on his table for personal use, which he covered with a towel before the camera rolled.

When we returned after the rather tame and non-committal interview, Mohana was shocked to notice teenage boys wielding guns at the entrance to Mahatia's quarters. When we returned in our Indian Army vehicle, an LTTE car followed us until we got out of the forest area.

A sidelight of the trip was that only Mohana and I had passports. Nobody else in our crew had any travel documents. We travelled as guests of the IPKF to Sri Lanka and returned to

Mohana and the author with the IAF flight crew at Jaffna

Chennai with no stamp on arrival or departure anywhere. The mood of the Sri Lankan Tamils declared that their happy days lay ahead. Sundaralingam's presence was a great boon, since he had an insight into the intricacies of the conflict—having been a victim. He too perceived the Indian move as a great blessing for the people of Sri Lanka.

A Paradise Regained was distributed by the MEA globally on TV. Like our Punjab film, this film was also not screened within India at all.

The second Sri Lankan Tamil who was with us for maybe five years was the highly respected cinematographer Rajan Williams. He was our director of photography for most projects in the early 1990s.

When we screened our biopic of Ramana Maharshi at the Kanchi Math, I sought Paramacharya's (His Holiness Chandrasekarendra Saraswati was popularly referred to as Paramacharya) permission to make a film on him. Almost six years later I got word from his junior pontiff Jayendra Saraswati that he had granted permission on condition that it should be a documentary on the history of the Kanchi Sankara Math, and not just a biography of himself. Delighted and blessed, we worked on *Jaya Jaya Sankara* as our own project, to derive the satisfaction of making a humble contribution. Rajan Williams was our cameraman for this film, while we had two camera assistants, Mithilazzudin and Ibrahim Shaw—all three being our staff technicians. Some people in the lower level of the Math grumbled about my working with a Christian cameraman and two Muslim assistants I told them that Paramacharya was above these distinctions and I found no need to change my crew.

After filming several other scenes over a few weeks, including the interviews with Jayendra Saraswati and Vijayendra Saraswati, we were in the Kanchi Math waiting to film Paramacharya in a special event. I asked Williams to place his camera on the parapet wall of an open well. I had chosen that vantage point from which we would be able to see Paramacharya emerging from his room and walking to the meeting venue. Williams very rightly protested that it was a very dark passage and the camera would register nothing. We had been told to avoid using any glaring lights to film the revered nonagenarian monk and shoot only with natural available light. Williams insisted that he should be allowed either to use lights or change the angle to get a better view. Before we could resolve the dispute, the frail Paramacharya emerged from his room and started walking through the dark corridor. Williams was excited beyond words because he had an excellent exposure as though the monk was walking through a very well-lit corridor. I saw the shot in the monitor and turned to my cameraman. Williams was perspiring, elated and out of breath, as he whispered to me, 'I see Jesus Christ walking towards us down the corridor.' He left the camera with his assistants and walked down to prostrate himself in front of Paramacharya. I felt truly ecstatic and it took some time for Williams to return to normal from his sense of rapture.

Siblings, Parents and Memories

In 1980, A.R. Baji, retired chief of the Press Information Bureau of India, founded a not-for-profit initiative named Mass Media Foundation of India together with friends from the media. In the first meeting, I was elected chairman of the foundation, with Baji as director general. In 1984, I told Baji that 20 April that year would mark the eightieth birth anniversary of my father, whom we had lost more than a decade earlier. Out of great regard for my father, who he admired as a colossal media personality, Baji said that the foundation would celebrate his eightieth birth anniversary.

I invited Chief Minister MGR as the chief guest, since he considered my father as his father figure. When I had telephoned

MGR at the eightieth birth anniversary of K. Subrahmanyam

MGR and requested his presence, he spontaneously said, 'I will be delighted to participate, but there is a hitch; on 20 April, I am scheduled to be on tour.' So I said I would have it on a day convenient to him and he fixed 14 April (Tamil New Year). I told him we would organize a screening of my father's Thyagaboomi. He liked the idea.

Baji and I invited all my brothers and sisters. Padma said she would not be able to attend since she had a commitment for a performance on that day in Kerala. However, my mother and my other three sisters—Lalitha, Bama and Neela—participated in the event representing our family, along with several cousins.

MGR graciously turned up at the Gaiety Cinema which had a packed house for the screening of Thyaga*bhoomi*. Other guests included leaders of the Congress and the communist parties, and film industry stalwarts. MGR said that KS had been like his father and that he had consulted him on most occasions for advice,

Former President of India, R. Venkataraman, flanked by the author and his brother, Balu at the K Subrahmanyam Centenary Celebrations

except in politics.[31]

Thyagabhoomi was originally screened at the Gaiety Cinema in 1939, till it was banned. Based on advance information about the ban, my father threw open the doors of the cinema hall for free shows till the order arrived. We chose this historic place as the venue for the celebration.

In early 1987, we had to withstand two shocks on two consecutive days. I felt a deep loss when my stepmother, SDS, passed away suddenly on 16 January. The very next day, my mother passed away in her sleep in Balu's house. MGR was among the hundreds of people who called on both the houses to pay their last respects to the two women in my revered father's life.

---

[31] Extracts from MGR's speech are included in the English biopic of my father, which I made for the Public Service Broadcasting Trust; and in a Tamil biopic, *Thirai Ulaga Thanthai K. Subrahmanyam*. The latter can be viewed on *www.indianimprints.com*. Our Hindi telefilm *Thyagabhoomi* (1989) is also available on *www.indianimprints.com*.

Padma Subrahmanyam, Mohana and the author on an anniversary of Krishnaswamy Associates

The author with his brother S.V. Ramanan

From left: His Highness Nawab Mohammed Abdul Ali (the prince of Arcot); Jayakanthan; S. Krishnaswamy; Jaipal Reddy (union minister) releasing the Tamil biography of K. Subrahmanyam, the author of that book Valampuri Somanathan, N. Ram (Editor-in-Chief of The Hindu) *receiving the first copy, and Mohana, at the fortieth anniversary of Krishnaswamy Associates*

In 1991, we lost another emotionally and intellectually supportive parent—Mohana's mother, Mangalam, in her late eighties. A brave person, she had supported and blessed the marriage of her daughter, Lakshmi, with a person from a different caste and a different state, several years earlier, when many family members were frowning at Lakshmi. She had been a constant source of support to both Mohana and me.

After parting company from Krishnaswamy Associates in 1974 to pursue his independent path, Ramanu had started his own company and become a leading producer of ad films and radio commercials. Some years later, he also made the starstudded Tamil feature film *Uruvangal Maaralam*.

All of us siblings got together and celebrated my father's birth centenary in 2004 on a grand scale. R. Venkataraman, former

President of India; His Holiness Jayendra Saraswati and His Holiness Vijayendra Saraswati—Sankaracharyas of Kanchi; film stars—Kamal Hasan, Vijayakanth and Saroja Devi participated. The event became a springboard to bring unity among the brothers and sisters. In another event, the Department of Posts brought out a stamp to honour our father.

From left: Union Minister Arif Mohammed Khan, the Krishnaswamys and Congress General Secretary G.K. Moopanar, waiting for H.H. Jayendra Saraswathi at the entrance of Krishnaswamy Associates

Y2K[32]

The decade from 1995 to 2005 was—for Mohana, my children and me—one of joyful celebrations, creative satisfactions and smiles of triumph on the one hand; stressful challenges, emotional trauma and tears of agony on the other. When we made a corporate film for Bharat Electronics Limited (BEL) in 1984, we came in contact with P.K. Venkatasubramaniam (PKV), a pioneer of electronics, and he became our technical consultant soon after he retired from BEL. It is rare indeed to find a person of such high calibre combined with impeccable integrity. In the early years of his consultancy, we suggested his visiting Germany on behalf of our company to undergo a fortnight's training in maintenance and service of BOSCH TV equipment, which we had imported. We gave him the foreign exchange allowance permissible under government rules in those years of currency control. On his return after a fortnight, he promptly returned the entire foreign exchange that had been given to him saying that he had spent nothing because he stayed with his relative, who happened to live close to BOSCH factory, while old friends at the BOSCH picked him up and dropped him back all the time. This is just a sample of what kind of a man he is.

---

[32] The chapter heading is inspired by our film for Tata Consultancy Services portraying how they helped IT companies worldwide tackle the problem of change of century in computer programming.

While I was expanding my office building in 1989, PKV suggested our entrusting the air-conditioning contract to a new company founded by N. Ramamoorthy. Within a few years, Ramamoorthy became a good family friend. When Mohana and I started looking for a groom for Gita, the youngster said jokingly that she would not leave the pincode area of Chennai where we lived. In 1995, Bala Ramamoorthy told Mohana that she would like to explore the possibility of an alliance between their son, Krishnaraj, and our daughter. Things proceeded rather fast from that point. Krishnaraj, an engineer, was assisting his father in the business and Mohana was very impressed with the young man during her official interactions. He was also a gifted sportsman, who had played for Tamil Nadu in interstate cricket matches. Prompted by the parents, the boy and girl met a few times and gave their concurrence. We had a music performance by M.S. Subbalakshmi at their wedding reception, organized on a grand scale.

Some years later, Krishnaraj started another enterprise, setting up a chain of fitness centres. Since then, Gita has not only been a director of their venture 'Maverick', but has also trained herself abroad as a fitness trainer in her own right. She continues to be a part-time director at Krishnaswamy Associates and has directed some TV serials produced by the company. As I am writing this, Gita's daughter, Meenakshi, who has visited the US, Germany and Thailand, as an Indian student delegate to participate in international student conferences and debates, is studying for her master's degree at Cambridge University, UK.

In the late 1990s, Singapore-TV-12,[33] a Singapore government-owned Tamil TV channel, asked us to make a TV serial, predominantly based in Singapore but with several scenes in India, utilizing several actors in Singapore with lead artistees to

---

[33]The channel's name has subsequently been changed to Vasantham TV.

be recruited from Tamil Nadu. We chose a novel of Tamil writer Sujatha, *Chinna Kuyili*. It was 25 per cent based in Singapore and predominantly based in Tamil Nadu. With Sujatha's permission, I adapted it, making it predominantly based in Singapore. Ashish Dey, my close friend who had settled down in Singapore and had his own media company, became our co-producer in Singapore. We engaged popular Malayalam and Tamil film stars Rehman and Rekha to play the lead roles. Our whole crew camped in Singapore for a few months. With Mohana as the producer, Dey and his wife extended exemplary cooperation as co-producers, contributing significantly to the success of this serial directed by me.

Later, we produced for the same TV channel a twenty-part Tamil serial on Indian classical dances titled *Aadalenum Jeevanadhi* (Perennial River of Dance), directed by Lata and Gita, featuring some fifty star dancers from India, besides four major

The author interviewing the then Finance Minister Manmohan Singh, who later became the Prime Minister of India, for the documentary series,
INDIA 5555

In the first five decades from the time Krishnaswamy Associates was founded in 1963, the small company has produced about 325 documentaries, and industrial and corporate films; educational, training and motivational films; biopics, and historical and journalistic films; besides about two hundred advertising films

In 1985, Krishnaswamy Associates diversified into making entertainment TV serials. Over the next three decades, the company produced serials running cumulatively into 370 episodes in Tamil and Hindi

teaching institutions of Indian dance in Singapore. The English version of this serial, *When the Gods Dance*, won the Creative Excellence Award at the US International Film and Video Festival. Prompted by this success, we made thirteen more dance episodes, covering Bharatanatyam, Kuchipudi, Kathakali, Kathak and Manipuri styles, besides folk dances of India, featuring over a hundred dancers from across the country.

In the meantime, in 1997, the MEA approved our plan of making a documentary in four parts, thirty minutes each, titled *India 5555*, to mark the golden jubilee of independence. The title meant five millennia of civilizational values, five recent centuries of history, five decades of democracy and five years of a new economic policy.

When *India 5555* was completed, I.K. Gujral—whose association I always cherished—became the prime minister. I was happy to have him give the concluding remarks, wherein he expressed the hope that by 2020, India would be an Asian power, and that the development would be inclusive at all levels of the people.[34] R. Venkataraman, former President of India, and Gujral attended the premiere of this documentary. Through newspaper reports a year later, I was delighted to know that the film had been shown to the US President Bill Clinton as part of his orientation, before he visited India.

During Gujral's term, he emphasized India's 'Look East' policy of developing relationships with the countries east of India and not depending entirely on Western alliances. Although he is not often given due credit, his policy has influenced the Government of India's thinking over the years since then.

...A deeply felt personal loss to me was the passing away of Shyamala in 1997. She was sick for a few months, hospitalized

---

[34] The four parts of *India 5555* are available on *www.indianimprints.com*.

for a few weeks and then, she was gone. She had often risen above petty politics and tried to keep the tribe together. From the time of our conversations in the early 1960s, the next three decades and more, the special attachment between her and me never faded. She treated Mohana like a daughter, saying, 'If only I had married at a younger age, I would have had a daughter of her age.'

Mohana's father, Balachandra Iyer, missed his hundredth birthday by three months and met his end peacefully in 1998. Except that he had significant vision loss; he was not very sick for his age, and his mental faculties were strong and he had an amazing memory. The family celebrated his ninety-ninth birthday and he participated like a child with much enthusiasm. His sons and daughters were scattered, with one in London and the rest in different parts of India, and had chosen different avocations.

Mohana with her father in 1997

...In 1998, the International Documentary Association (IDA) invited me to address their conference in Hollywood. It was a wonderful opportunity to interact with like-minded people from around the world. It also gave me a chance to meet Erik Barnouw—who was about ninety years old—and that unfortunately proved to be my last meeting with him. Despite being physically weak, he remained mentally alert with a lot of zest when I met him and we even discussed the possibility of a third edition of *Indian Film* to be published early in the twenty-first century. But it did not materialize as the professor passed away soon thereafter. After the IDA conference, Mohana and I spent a couple of weeks with our son, Bharat, in Philadelphia.

At the turn of the century, I wrote the story and dialogue for a TV serial, *Visaalam,* on a family theme, stretching over a century. Mohana heard the script not only to get ready for logistics as producer, but also to give her critical inputs.

This fifty-two-episode serial, directed by Gita, portrays the social history of Tamil Nadu with special reference to the evolving status of women, depicting five generations of a matriarchal line from 1900 to 2000. A significant success with audience, it was repeated dozens of times on Doordarshan. Lata and Gita also performed lead roles of the fourth generation in the serial.

...In 1995, the Kanchi Sankaracharya Math sponsored the establishment of the Sri Jayendra Saraswati College of Ayurveda in the neighbourhood of Chennai. Knowing her background in Ayurvedic research, Jayendra Saraswati asked Mohana to get involved in the college, since it was to have a research wing too.

Retaining her position in our company as non-executive chairman, she joined as honorary deputy director of the college and worked hard to build it up. The research wing had to wait for a few years, since the college started at the undergraduate level. Some excellent Ayurvedic physicians joined as professors at the college and it had a very promising start. From the second year onwards, a large number of candidates applied for the limited number of seats. In the third year, there was even more demand. For unknown reasons, a real estate developer was taken into the selection committee for admissions. Neither an academician nor a physician, he perceived the college as a commercial institution. Several private educational institutions in the country as a whole and in Tamil Nadu, in particular, were charging exorbitant capitation fees for admission. Mohana expected the ethical standards of a college run by a nearly 2,000-year-old religious math to stand as an example to others. But gradually disappointment was setting in. For instance, when the academicians chose certain candidates for admission based on their qualification, aptitude and performance in the interview for admission, the real estate man, as a parallel power centre, chose candidates who could pay larger capitation fees. Mohana (and her colleagues) felt that some of the best candidates selected by them should positively be given admission, even if they were not in a position to pay the capitation fee fixed by an 'undeclared auction' and compete with richer candidates who were academically much poorer. They felt that it was a disservice to Ayurveda in the long run to accommodate second-grade candidates in return for their financial contributions at the cost of meritorious candidates, some of whom were denied seats. Agitated about this issue, Mohana told me that she was taking a drive seventy-five minutes each way only for deriving the satisfaction of working in a scientific atmosphere with academic excellence. She was willing to quit if this was not rectified. I told her that it would be better to discuss the issue with His Holiness as this kind of thing may be happening without his knowledge. When we met him, I remained an observer even as Mohana expressed her anguish to His Holiness about the developments. He said he would look into it soon. A few days later we were informed by a college official that the 'oral resignation given to His Holiness' had been accepted. We did not rush to any conclusion. But the whole episode left a bad taste.

...We were pleasantly surprised when Mohana received a letter that Shri Ramamohan Rao, Governor of Tamil Nadu, had nominated her as a member of the Madras University Senate. A very cordial and unassuming person, Rao had seen several of our films and in our conversations learnt how Mohana had combined in herself the role of a scientist while heading our small media company. When he had to nominate someone to the Madras University Senate, he thought of her. She enjoyed being a member of the senate during her term, taking active interest in university matters.

...And then came 1999—the most stressful year for us, more so for Lata. Although Lata's marriage initially had a happy phase, it had gradually deteriorated into one of frustrations for her from the time when her daughter Kamini had turned three. Showering of affection by her mother-in-law and father in-law was soothing for Lata, keeping the image of a happy marriage alive for everyone including her parents. In 1998, Lata's father-in-law passed away bringing great stress to my daughter. It is my surmise that Ashok's career never took off as a lawyer and that he was envious of his wife with a successful role in her parents' company and her emerging popularity as a dancer. For about one year, Mohana and I resisted Lata's idea of leaving Ashok, hoping that it woud be possible for them to patch up. But when we found that she had made up her mind, we helped Lata to apply for a divorce. She did not want any compensation or commitments from Ashok whatsoever. This she said despite the opinion of her lawyers, Bader Sayeed and Geetha Ramaseshan, that it was possible to collect a substantial alimony in view of the financial status of the man. Six months from the date of application, her divorce was granted by the court in 1999.[35]

Kamini remained confused for a short while. Then she realized what was going on, amazingly early. Ashok did not even ask the court for permission to visit his daughter and so he has never met her in the last more than sixteen years after his divorce.

Lata must be legitimately proud that as a single parent she has brought up her child since the age of seven. As Kamini grew up, she showed the flair to be involved in the entertainment film industry, aspiring to become a fourth-generation film director of the family. We sent her to the Film and TV School of the Academy of Performing Arts (FAMU)—a world-renowned institute at Prague, Czech Republic. On her return, she joined as assistant director to a well-known South Indian film director, and hopes to direct a film of her own soon.

When Bharat completed his master's degree at BITS, Pilani, he was keen to go abroad for further education. He was undecided about what avocation he wanted to pursue. He was deeply interested in cinema. While he was informally working in Krishnaswamy Associates for a few months, he asked me to help him to join Shyam Benegal to get trained in feature films. I spoke to my friend, Shyam, one of the most distinguished film-makers of India, for whom I have much admiration. Bharat worked with him for one feature film. Later he asked me if he could study film-making abroad. He got admission in the Temple University at Philadelphia. We financially supported his education for two years. On completing his film-making courses, and after working in Philadelphia for a couple of years, he had enough savings to pursue higher education. He got his MBA from the MIT Sloan

---

[35] Ashok married within a month of getting the divorce. About a year later, we were very sorry to learn that he did not even attend his mother's funeral due to the strained relations with his mother and sisters.

School of Management. He has worked for many large global corporates in senior capacities including IBM, McKinsey and Kaplan (a division of the *Washington Post*).

During his Philadelphia days, Bharat met Aarti—a student of Microbiology in Washington, DC, and daughter of Raja, a senior scientist and administrator in Indian Space Research Organization (ISRO), Bengaluru. Raja and his wife, Uma—a respected schoolteacher, met us and were keen to solemnize the marriage of Aarti with Bharat without delay. But the youngsters were not ready for it. Later, when Mohana and I were in Los Angeles for the IDA conference, we visited Bharat in Philadelphia and met Aarti in Washington. They took two more years before they were ready to tie the knot.

Raja organized their wedding in Bengaluru and we arranged a wedding reception at Chennai. Bharat and Aarti have joined the expanding tribe of American citizens of Indian origin. They have a handsome and brilliant thirteen-year-old son, Dhruv, and

Clockwise from top centre: Lata, Aarti, Bharat, Dhruv, Kamini, Krishnaswamy, Mohana, Meenakshi, Disha, Krishnaraj and Gita

a charming eight-year-old daughter, Disha, who has mischief written in her eyes. Aarti, with a Harward PhD in microbiology, is an associate professor in Nova Southeastern University in Florida.

Citizenly Thinking

In the 1960s, I co-founded Rasana, a film and art appreciation society, with D.N. Rao, director of the United States Education Foundation in India, and Jayakanthan, attracting people with a wide spectrum of interests. Besides screening of international award-winning films, we organized music concerts, dance recitals, art exhibitions and scholarly lectures. And then, Satyajit Ray nominated me as secretary (southern region) of the Federation of Film Societies of India. During that period, I was also secretary of the Advertising Club, Madras, and an active member of the Lions Club, Guindy, from where I roped in S.G. Ramachandran as the auditor of my company, and he remained so for five decades.

From 1963, when I had a room for a short stay at the Theosophical Society, I had always been interested in learning more about 'theosophy'. Mohana and I walked into the Theosophical Society in 1973 and met the international president John Coats, and enrolled ourselves as members. A very friendly English couple, Mrs and Mr Coats took a liking to us and we would meet often. The Theosophical Society functions through its several autonomous lodges across the world. The Adyar Lodge meetings are held at the Theosophical Society headquarters hall. We were fortunate to get many friends at the Theosophical Society, including Tudor Jayewardene—a cousin of the Sri Lankan President—and Russell Balfour Clarke—a non-agenarian, who could be seen on his bicycle criss-crossing the large expanse of the private campus. Balfour had personally known Annie Besant and Bishop Leadbeater when he migrated to India in the early 1900s.

At an annual general meeting, Balfour got up and said that as the oldest man in the group, he should have the first say. He dropped a surprise and proposed my name to be the next president of the lodge. As Balfour was treated with great respect, no other name was proposed, and I was unanimously elected president of the Adyar Lodge for two terms. With a lot of support from the society's international office bearers, I enjoyed those years getting to know a lot about theosophy and comparative religion. But I resigned all these positions when my attention shifted wholly to making *Indus Valley to Indira Gandhi*.

In 1996, Desikan reappeared on scene (we had met only occasionally in the previous decade) to renew our close association. He had become a social activist and president of the Federation of Consumer Organisations of Tamil Nadu. We both decided to do something together to help reform the electoral process without aligning ourselves with any political party. We met a small group of like-minded people, including B.S. Raghavan, senior IAS officer (retd), who had worked closely with Jawaharlal Nehru; Ravindran, Director General of Police (retd); S.P. Ambrose, senior IAS officer (retd); and N.L. Rajah, young but senior advocate, and decided to form a trust. The group liked my suggestion that since we aimed to be catalytic agents without entering party politics, we may call it the 'Catalyst Trust'. We launched a voters' awareness campaign in the print and electronic media, educating people to respect their power to vote, and be careful in selecting their representatives. Our campaign was also arguably India's first, urging the voter to vote for 'none of the above' by writing it in the register, since there was no such provision in the electronic voting machine. This was allowed a decade later by the Election Commission as NOTA (None Of The Above). Another retired IAS officer, A.K.

Venkatasubramanian, joined the trust and helped organize about a hundred citizen centres across Tamil Nadu.

I was convinced that without electoral and political reforms India would stagnate morally and ethically even if it achieved economic progress. It would be a tragedy for a civilization to decay in the sewerage of a defective system that encouraged corruption and moral turpitude. No model may be perfect, but we need mechanisms to keep the system as humane and equitable as possible. Our tolerance of imperfections will be suicidal. We see all around highly talented people compromising to achieve blatantly selfish ends.

The author with R. Desikan

In 2005, with Jayaprakash Narayan[36]—a brilliant IAS officer who had resigned from service to become a political activist—as the consultant, Krishnaswamy Associates produced *Who Loses When India Wins?*[37], a film funded by the Foundation for Democratic Reforms. It discusses, in detail, the alternatives to the 'First Past the Post' (FPTP) system of elections in India. After comparing several other models in the world, we suggested the Mixed-Member Proportional Representation (MMPR) system as most suitable for India.[38]

As a citizen, I sometimes protested against very powerful people. Except professional politicians, ordinary citizens normally did not dare to protest against Jayalalitha, chief minister of Tamil Nadu. Yet, with no allegiance to any political party, I wrote against the ugly demonstration of her wealth when she performed the wedding of her foster son. I sent a poem for favour of publication in the 'Letters to the Editor' column. However, *The Hindu* published it in the regular news columns on the day of the wedding, as reproduced on the following page.[39]

I got several reactions for and against the poem—not for or against the content, but for and against sticking my neck out: those who hailed my bravery and those who felt I was a Don Quixote.

What has given me strength in the midst of such isolation is the absence of self-interest. I would have fallen in my self-esteem if I had compromised on such issues. In all such situations, I cross-checked with my conscience-keeper, Mohana, and got her concurrence to publish.

---

[36]Jayaprakash Narayan later floated the political party Lok Satta, and is a member of legislative assembly of Andhra Pradesh.
[37]*Who Loses When India Wins?* is available on *www.indianimprints.com*.
[38]Extracts from my article in *The Indian Express* on electoral reforms is reproduced in the Annexure.
[39]Dr Chenna refers to Dr. Chenna Reddy, the then Governor of Tamil Nadu

Poetic protest

From Our Special Correspondent

MADRAS, Sept. 7.

Noted documentary and TV film producer, Dr. S. Krishnaswamy was provoked into writing this poem by the inconvenience the wedding of the Chief Minister's foster son at MRC Nagar on Santhome High Road caused to the people of the neighbourhood:

I emerged from a noble womb
In a great home in Santhome.
I live in an enchanting area,
Adyar — blessed with an aura
Of Annie Besant and Theosophy
Krishnajee and Rukmani Devi.
Alas! I am witness today
To vulgar shameful decay,
In this proud stretch of land,
A gaudy event posing as grand.
Demoniac is the mythical term
Devilish in religious realm
As History revives the medieval
Filthy wealth re-lives the feudal
Cine-Maya visits the unreal
Cee. Em. Jaya paints the sur-real
In Adyar we have a place
Where cancer patients get solace.
Dr. Channa ! Please save Chennai
From the tyranny of this 'Annai'.

Of Saints and Statesmen

Early in the new century, Mohana and I began to nurture a close association with two major national leaders—R. Venkataraman (RV), former President of India; and Bharat Ratna C. Subramaniam (CS), father of India's Green Revolution. Both of them knew me from my boyhood. During my student days in New York, RV was one of India's delegates to the UN. During his visits, in the midst of his busy schedules, he would call me to join him for lunch at the UN, and enquire about my welfare.

Around 1980, I had made three biographical documentaries—the first on C. Rajagopalachari (Rajaji), a doyen among the freedom fighters and the first Indian to be the head of state of independent India; the second on Kamaraj, who rose from the ranks to become the chief minister of Tamil Nadu in a period now proudly described as 'The Kamaraj Era' (he helped install Indira Gandhi as prime minister); and the third on Ramana Maharshi, who was accepted as a spiritual leader globally. These biographies gave me a great sense of satisfaction.

When RV was a minister in the central cabinet I requested him to be my consultant for my biopic on Kamaraj, since they had been very close to each other. He helped me by reading my script and watching the film as it was growing. Later, I requested his permission for making his biopic when he was the President of India. But his sense of propriety was so strong that he said, 'Yes, but only after I demit office, since my encouraging it now would amount to misuse of office.'

I reminded him about the same after his presidential term, and he agreed. About the same time, I requested CS also because I was his ardent admirer and often felt that the country did not adequately express gratitude to him for the yeoman service he had rendered. Well, when the film was almost ready, CS was honoured with the Bharat Ratna—the highest civilian award.

In the case of films of Rajaji, Kamaraj and Ramana Maharshi, I was dealing with personalities of earlier generations and obviously I had no opportunity to interview them. In the case of RV and CS, I had the advantage of talking to my heroes. Besides interviewing him on video for about twenty-eight hours in as many sessions, I also talked to RV at length behind the camera. Mohana had a personal rapport with his wife, Janaki Venkataraman. But although there were dramatic insights that we got from her, when the film was nearing completion the former President said, 'I want this to be just a political biography without any personal narratives.' And we respected that.

CS was nearing ninety when we were filming his biopic. Although RV was almost the same age, he was in better health. In the case of CS, we could add some personal details and feature a scene with his family too.

Our biopics on Rajaji, Kamaraj and Ramana Maharshi were sponsored by the Films Division. We produced a long film, *Chakravarti Rajagopalachari*[40] on Rajaji with a subsidy from Bharatiya Vidya Bhavan. Those on RV and CS were commissioned by Doordarshan.

Talking of biopics, we were most pleasantly surprised when in the 1980s I got a call from my journalist friend Manian that MGR would like me to make a short film about him and that it should be ready in one week! I visited MGR in his house at sunrise the next day for a briefing. Informal and friendly as ever, the charismatic leader said the film was for being shown at the Commonwealth Speakers Conference the following week. I politely told him that I could not treat this like a film for his fans since it was meant for an international audience, unfamiliar with him. He replied in one line, 'I am asking you to do this, since you are "The MGR of Documentaries". You would know how to

---

[40]*Chakravarti Rajagopalachari* is available on *www.indianimprints.com*.

The author with former President R. Venkataraman; Mohana is behind the President

present me to a worldwide audience.'

The production time factor was not the only challenge. Mohana was aware of my views that MGR was an outstanding political leader, but a mediocre actor, who had nevertheless become a matinee idol with a staggeringly incomparable fan following. She laughed saying that she was curious to see how I would treat the film. We completed the film in ten days in the style of a TV photo feature—*The MGR Phenomenon*.[41]

The essence of the short film comes out in my introductory narration. 'He was an actor by accident, but a seasoned politician by deliberate choice!' MGR visited my office for a late night preview; he liked the film immensely but suggested one small deletion—of an intimate scene between him and one of his heroines, who he

---

[41] *The MGR Phenomenon* is available on *www.indianimprints.com*.

M.S. Subbalakshmi, Janaki Venkataraman and Mohana

The author with C. Subramaniam during the filming of the latter's biopic

carries lustily in his arms. I deleted it to his satisfaction.

No doubt MGR was a phenomenon. Even in his personal interactions he remained a friendly, charismatic person, who did not carry ill-will in his genes. As I have narrated earlier, I had a very good rapport with him. And now, in spite of my critical reviews of him as an actor, in the *Illustrated Weekly*, he had magnanimously extended an invitation to me to make his short biopic meant for a high-profile global audience. His attitude was that of a true statesman.

Opportunity knocked at my door to make an inspirational film when, in 1979, Nambiar, retired chief engineer, Government of Tamil Nadu, visited me and conveyed his compliments for our film on Rajaji. This respectable stranger asked me what I knew about Ramana Maharshi. I honestly said, 'Not much, but my mother was his ardent devotee.'

He asked me whether I would be interested in making a documentary on Maharshi like the one on Rajaji. I said, 'I would be delighted to do that.' But he found that my answer was professional as a film-maker, not as one involved in the subject. He gave me a copy of Maharshi's biography by Colonel Osborne. It was such an inspiring book that I read it at one stretch. I called Nambiar the next morning and said, 'I am very keen indeed to make this film. Can you help raise some resources?'

Nambiar was hopeful of getting funds from Maharshi's devotees. But he didn't succeed. However, I accompanied him to Tiruvannamalai and spent a couple of days trying to understand the life and message of the Maharshi. Gradually, I became very passionate about making the film, but there was no resource in sight. Several months later, I got a call from Mushir Ahmed, chief producer of the Films Division, telling me, 'I have instructions from the ministry to get a film made on one Ramana Maharshi, who I learn lived in Tamil Nadu. Will you be interested in making it for us?' I could have jumped from my seat and I told him on the phone, 'Yes, of course. I am very interested. In fact, I have a script ready for a twenty-minute film.' Ahmed was very happy. But he cautioned, 'We have no time to call for a tender since we have to get something done urgently and this will have to be done at very low cost. Don't expect margins. We will fix a frugal compensation.'

Eventually, the budget sanctioned was almost the same as we had been looking for when we knocked at different doors, since I had not planned this as a project for profit. We made an inspirational film with a great deal of self-satisfaction. It was about a decade since my brother Ramanan had composed music for my films. I requested him to do the background score and he very gladly agreed. We completed the film within a few months and the Films Division released it in fourteen Indian languages, besides my original English version.

S.D. Sharma, Governor of Andhra Pradesh, seated between the Krishnaswamys, when he visited Krishnaswamy Associates to preview Ramana Maharshi. *Several years later, as President of India, he graciously hosted a preview of extracts from our TV serial* Upaasana *at the Rashtrapati Bhavan.*

Dr Karan Singh M.P., presents Vatavaran Award to Krishnaswamy at New Delhi

Union Minister G.K. Vasan handing over first copy of a DVD of Reality Behind Religion to Swami Gitasarananda of Sri Ramakrishna Mission

Mohana and Krishnaswamy receiving Dr Ma.Po.Si. Award from Union Minister Pon Radhakrishnan (Madhavi Bhaskaran of Ma.Po.Si. Trust is in the left

Film actor-turned-political leader Rajinikanth during a visit to Krishnaswamy Associates for the preview of A Different Pilgrimage

Sojourns in Search

I have mentioned earlier that my thirst to study the impact of ancient India on Southeast Asia began while studying Indian history for writing my script for *Indus Valley to Indira Gandhi*. However, I could quench this thirst by making films on that theme only when I was nearing seventy.

Mohana and the author while filming Angkor Wat in Cambodia

The author and his TV crew at work in Indonesia, Thailand, Cambodia, Laos and Vietnam

Although when we were making TV serials in Singapore in the 1990s we tried to make films on this area of interest, the ground situation in Cambodia was not conducive at all because of their civil war.

At the turn of the century, that situation changed and it became easier to film Angkor Wat and other sites—most of which had been cleared of the mines planted during the civil war. Mohana got equally involved in ancient India's connections with Southeast Asia, and we plunged into our research. But it was an uphill task again to raise resources for the films. We planned three projects. First, *A Different Pilgrimage* with a Hindu devotional orientation; second, *Indian Imprints* as a long, more informative TV serial; and third, *Tracking Indian Footmarks*, aimed at an international audience interested in Asian history. As a measure of economy, we decided to implement the three projects together.

When I was in hospital for a coronary bypass surgery in May 2005, the news that Doordarshan had agreed to commission *Indian Imprints* gave me energy to recover fast. Bashi, who operated on me, advised that I wait for six months before undertaking hectic tours for this. Mohana, my children and Ramanu were at the hospital for my surgery.

That a telephone call also greeted and cheered me up in the hospital would be an understatement. The US International Film and Video Festival, Los Angeles, conveyed the pleasant news that the festival had chosen me to receive their Lifetime Achievement Award. I became the ninth recipient in the forty-year history of their annual awards, and the first Afro-Asian to receive the honour. I was expected to take rest for two months, while the award was to be presented in a fortnight. When I profusely thanked Lee W. Gluckman, Jr., president of the Festival, and explained my position, he suggested that I nominate a friend to receive the award on my behalf. I requested Nirmala (Nimmu)—

my childhood friend, who was living in California—to receive the award. Nimmu and her husband, Vaidyanathan, graciously represented me and brought the award to India.

Within a few months I resumed our research on Southeast Asia. It was a great boon when Professor Lokesh Chandra, an erudite authority on the subject, agreed to be our consultant for the project. Over the next several months, Mohana and I made periodic visits to Delhi, to spend time in his fabulous library and in long discussions with him.

'Shooting' in Southeast Asia

We spent February and March 2006 in a whirlwind research tour of the five countries we planned to film—Indonesia, Thailand, Vietnam, Laos and Cambodia. We met several Indologists and local experts, who advised us on what to pursue, selected the locations to film in, established contacts with Indian embassies, spoke to the respective governments for permissions and recruited liaison officers in each country, who could also function as our interpreters.

Soon after our exploratory tour, we planned filming tours divided into two trips, taking into account the weather conditions; some events in the respective countries that we wanted to cover; and the need for a reasonable rest period for film crew between two long tours. The first tour was of Indonesia and Thailand. Including Mohana, me, Madhu Ambat (award-winning cinematographer) and two operative cameramen, we were seven people from India, recruiting local assistants in every country. Lata was my associate director for the first tour, covering Indonesia and Thailand, while Gita took that role in the second tour to Cambodia and Laos.

The filming of these three projects in Southeast Asia was indeed the most challenging and most satisfying of my whole career. The restrictions on my movement, mostly imposed by my family, since it was less than a year after a major surgery, had to be overcome only by my zestful involvement. It was also Mohana's most demanding work as Producer, assuming several responsibilities single-handedly.

We started shooting at Jakarta covering the National Museum and several important places in the city, including the world's largest sculpture of Krishna and Arjuna, in a busy road intersection—a contemporary sculpture installed by the Indonesian Government.

Our next flight was to Yogyakarta. After interviewing their minister for culture, Jero Wachik, we were proceeding to the airport in a chartered bus with our professional luggage of about 400 kg.

The very friendly, well-meaning minister had delayed us with his courtesies before we could pack up to the airport. Due to some procession on the way, it took us double the estimated time to reach the airport. We almost thought that we had missed the flight, but our local travel agent made the aircraft wait for us. We made a photo finish by sending the luggage from our bus to the aircraft.

I had run many an obstacle race all my professional and personal life and I took it in my stride as one more. But then, it was only the beginning of this one. We had a wonderful time for the first few days in Yogyakarta filming their puppet show on Indian mythology, the fantastic Prambanan temple of Brahma, Vishnu and Shiva which pre-dates any existing temple of that size in India, besides the Ramayana ballet performed with the Prambanan temple in the background.[42]

We kept our hotel room in Yogyakarta when we made a

---

[42]Our two-hour documentary, *A Different Pilgrimage*, which has snippets from the ballet, can be viewed on *www.indianimprints.com*.

side trip to Surakarta. After filming the whole day in Surakarta, we stayed in a hotel there, as planned, and we were to return to our hotel in Yogyakarta the next morning. It was 27 May 2006. When early in the morning we were all getting ready in the hotel rooms, suddenly our building trembled and all of us along with the other guests rushed out of the hotel to the open area. It was just a rumbling of the earth and the hotel staff advised us that it was nothing serious although there were cracks on the walls. We made bold to enter our rooms and brought the luggage to our cars. After about one hour on the highway, we saw an ocean of humanity rushing towards us from the opposite direction. We had no option but to stop. We realized that what we had felt in Surakarta as mild tremors was felt as a major earthquake of 6.5 magnitude on the Richter scale in Yogyakarta and that several buildings had collapsed. The people were running out of the city in all directions. In a situation like this, rumours spread faster than facts. People asked us to go back even as a man in the car coming in the opposite direction declared that the catastrophic earthquake had caused immense damage. As advised by the mob, we took a U-turn and depended on our guide and drivers to decide where to go. Our mobiles did not work because the towers had fallen down. Our drivers suggested that we should take a circuitous route around another mountain way and reach the safer side of the hill. In about five hours, we found a reasonably good hotel and camped there.

The next day we learnt that the earthquake had left 5,700 dead and 37,000 injured. Our guide and drivers were very worried about their families in Yogyakarta. Phone lines were working in our hotel and we talked to a hotel in Borobudur, where we planned to film one of the greatest Buddhist monuments. Although it was only about 50 miles from Yogyakarta, Borobudur was not affected by the earthquake. The hotel staff told us that they would give us rooms in the given circumstances. We spent a whole day travelling through a circuitous route around the mountain.

Somewhere on the way to Borobudur we got mobile connectivity. We spoke to our hotel in Yogyakarta and found it would remain closed for an indefinite period, but they promised to keep our luggage safe. We suddenly felt like nomads with no place to go to and cut off from the rest of the world. In the meantime, I got a call from H.K. Singh, Indian ambassador in Jakarta, not only to enquire about our safety but also to strongly advise us to cut short our tour and return to India in view of certain forecasts of seismic activity in the region. I told him that Yogyakarta airport was closed as the runway had been damaged. I promised to keep him informed of our next move. We reached Borobudur that night. Our guide and drivers left for Yogyakarta to look for their families, and did not return.

The staff of the hotel at the Borobudur monument was immensely cordial, understanding the trials we had faced in reaching there. Two days later, our hotel in Yogyakarta loaded our luggage in a small truck and got it delivered to us through a circuitous route.

We camped in Borobudur for about six days, filming the mammoth, magnificent spiritual edifice there, from sunrise to sunset and beyond. The monument's transcendent glory has to be felt by experiencing every inch of its multiple levels as one climbs the physical and ethereal planes, until one reaches the top of the pyramidal monument.

The tranquillity of the Pancha Pandava Chandis in the Dieang plateau made us forget that we were almost cut off from the rest of the world, as we filmed them and returned to our Borobudur hotel.

As per our original itinerary, we were to fly from Yogyakarta to Surabaya on the east coast of Java and we were way behind schedule. We were desperate to find a vehicle. The staff at the hotel managed to fix an old chartered bus. There was no way of taking a long journey at one stretch in that rickety vehicle, and we planned stopovers with a roadmap.

The bus driver knew only Bahasa, the language of Java. Mohana's linguistic talents came to our rescue in communicating with him. I decided to stop over on the way at Mojokerto the ancient capital of the Majapahit kingdom in East Java, where we filmed an exciting museum of ancient Hindu sculptures and a few Hindu temples. We had heard a lot about Mount Bromo, a hill station of sorts, and Lata was keen that we take a detour to Bromo for night stay. We decided to see what Bromo was like. Our rickety bus valiantly climbed quite a distance, but broke down a kilometre before reaching the top which had the only hotel. The driver said he would get the bus ready in an hour. And so we all walked the last kilometre up a steep road.

Seated: The author with Abdul Rahman Wahid, former President of Indonesia; Standing (from left): Ravi, officer of the Indian Embassy in Jakarta, Mohana, Lata and Madhu Ambat

It proved to be the highlight of our entire journey. The site was so enchanting with a mystic majesty of its own that I eventually decided to feature Bromo as the opening scene of *Indian Imprints*. Two volcanoes are visible at a short distance from that mountain—the shorter one is 'Bromo' meaning 'Brahma—the creator', while the taller is 'Sumeru', named after the mythical 'Meru' in the Himalayas. The Tengar people, who inhabit Bromo, are believed to be descendants of Majapahit kings, who ruled the area four centuries ago. We filmed the temple of the Hindu trinity in the foothills of Bromo, which is worshipped by the Tengars. Neither the books nor the tourist literature that I had read mentioned the importance of Bromo, and we were thrilled to be there—at the highest peak of Java.

Our bus broke down again, 10 km before Surabaya airport. We were afraid that we would miss our flight to Bali. Mohana spoke in broken Bahasa to the people in a small house nearby, who understood our problem and started stopping every other vehicle to see whether we could be shifted to other cars. Two vehicles volunteered to help us since no single vehicle could accommodate all of us and our luggage. We continued our voyage of discovery in two groups to Surabaya airport, making it just in time to catch our flight.

In situations like this you see the visible grace of the Omniscient in the most difficult times. The viewfinder of our camera started giving trouble when we were in Borobudur and it completely broke down by the time we reached Prambanan on the outskirts of Yogyakarta to see how the monument had withstood the earthquake. We had fortunately completed our filming there before the earthquake. We were again there due to curiosity. Thereafter, the entire filming in the sites of Majapahit and Bromo had to be done with the camera without the viewfinder. Madhu Ambat was framing the shots by looking at the monitor, which made camera movement very difficult. On the way in the bus from a point where mobile connectivity was available, I spoke to the Panasonic people in Hong Kong and they promised to order a replacement from Tokyo. Miraculously, the new viewfinder arrived in time, before we got our flight at Surabaya, thanks to the efficiency of the Japanese! Our friends Manoj Bhat and Sanjana Bhat collected the viewfinder and gave it to us at Surabaya.

As planned, Madhu Ambat's wife, Latha, joined us in Bali, arriving there straight from Chennai. We filmed some of the major Hindu temples as well as festivals celebrated in the island. On the whole, it was such a totally relaxing experience after ten days of turmoil between the earthquake in central Java and our reaching Bali. The presence of my daughters, Lata in Indonesia and Thailand, and Gita in Cambodia and Laos, proved to be important because of their creative contribution in addition to emotional support.

We flew from Bali to Bangkok. Despite our research, there were surprises when we reached some of the locations. The Shiva temple of Phanom Rung in northeast Thailand, 500 km from Bangkok, is an ancient temple built about 1,000 years ago on a hillock. There is no formal worship in this exceptionally beautiful temple, which is under the control of the archaeology department. However, we could hear chants from inside. Later, we came to know that the department gave permission to people to worship in the temple, but sparingly. The chants that we heard were praise for Shiva, sung by a woman whom we met.

Back in Bangkok, we had an interesting interview with the Rajguru of Thailand, Phra Vamadeva Muni, who told me that he was a descendant of a priest from Chidambaram, who had migrated to Thailand some seven hundred years ago. Since he practises a local form of Buddhism combined with Hinduism, he describes himself as a Buddhist Brahmin. It is his responsibility to perform the coronation of every new king according to Hindu

Vedic rights, although the king and his family are Buddhists. The royal family is keen to follow Hindu traditions and the princess herself is a Sanskrit scholar. Our first filming tour in Southeast Asia concluded in Bangkok.

After a gap of several weeks, we began our second tour, covering three countries—Cambodia, Laos and Vietnam. The vastness of the ancient capital of the Khmer Empire and the Angkor Wat Vishnu temple have to be seen to be believed. The satellite images show that the ancient Angkor city was larger than the present-day Manhattan. The Government of Cambodia has an elected parliament under a monarchy.

Mohana and I had met Buphadevi, Princess of Cambodia, during the research tour. She was a member of the senate and a former minister in the Cambodian government. We wanted to interview her for our film and she agreed readily. We were keeping in touch with her through her secretary. But when we were in Cambodia for filming, unfortunately the princess remained inaccessible. The officers confirmed that she would be available three weeks later. So we decided to return to Phnom Penh after we completed shooting elsewhere.

We flew to Siem Reap and spent an exciting fortnight in the Angkor Wat region. A Vishnu temple, Angkor Wat, is the largest stone temple on earth for any faith. Constructed by Khmer king Suryavarman II, a thousand years ago, this mammoth edifice is spread over 500 acres. Although converted into a Buddhist temple, it retains all its Hindu features including huge bas relief sculptures, depicting scenes from the Ramayana and Mahabharata. Apart from Angkor Wat, there are some two hundred Hindu temples in that area.

We started our shooting in Laos sailing in a small boat in the majestic perennial river Mekong at Champasak. Visible from the river is Lingaparvata, a hill where Shiva has been worshipped from time immemorial. Commencing from the foothills and culminating on top of the hills at different levels is Wat Phu, a Shiva temple converted into a Buddhist shrine some five hundred years ago. At the Laos National School of Dance, we filmed a rehearsal of a Palak Palang[43] ballet.

Very few people know about ancient India's impact on Cambodia, Thailand and Indonesia. It comes as a total surprise even to some historians that there are ancient Hindu temples in Vietnam and Laos. Very little academic work has been done on Vietnam, in particular. We had learnt from Professor Lokesh Chandra's library that there were Hindu temples in central Vietnam. These sites include the My-Son group of about seventy-five temples in ruins, besides several live temples with an unbroken tradition of daily worship over the centuries, such as Po Klong Garai and Po Nagar. Gita could not go to Vietnam with us since she had a commitment to be back in Chennai.

The Krishnaswamys with Bui Man Hai, the then Minister for Science and Technology, Vietnam

---

[43] Palak Palang is the Laos version of Ramayana.

From Vietnam we returned to Phnom Penh to interview Princess Buphadevi. However, on arrival in the Cambodian capital we were disappointed to learn that the princess was not able to allot time for our interview due to unavoidable preoccupations. We had no choice but to limit our filming for a day in the royal palace and catch our flight back to India. As we were 'shooting' in the palace, we heard orchestral music from an adjoining hall. We discovered that a group dance rehearsal was in progress in the apsara dance style of Cambodia. We asked for permission to film the same and got a positive response within minutes. As we started filming, Mohana found the teacher-trainer of the programme to be a familiar face. She wass none other than Buphadevi. Being an accomplished apsara dancer herself, she was training a group for a performance. Grabbing the opportunity, I walked up to her in a gap between two dance numbers and

The author interviewing Buphadevi, Princess of Cambodia

reminded her that she had promised us an interview for our documentary. She spontaneously agreed to give time—then and there—between two dance numbers, speaking eloquently about the ancient relationship between India and Cambodia. We took about six months for post-production and delivered eighteen episodes of *Indian Imprints* to Doordarshan, and they telecast it several times from 2007. The two-hour-long *A Different Pilgrimage* was screened in the Indian pavilion at the Cannes Film Festival and got released in limited cinema halls for school and college students.[44] As I am writing this, we are exploring a wider exposure for the four-part *Tracking Indian Footmarks*. On the whole, apart from our sojourns in Southeast Asia being the most challenging in my professional career, these films constitute one of our most important contributions as documentary-filmmakers.

When I was editing *Indian Imprints*, my brother, Balu, was keen to watch some scenes and I showed him extracts of about one-hour duration. He fell in love with it all. Incidentally, he also talked about an unusual experience of his meeting a soothsayer from Kerala, a few months earlier, who told him that one of our ancestors had committed suicide about a hundred years ago and that a curse of that soul had caused misunderstandings among the brothers. The soothsayer had also said that the period of the curse was nearly over and the family would be reunited again. Balu had enquired about the 'suicide story'. He found that my father's paternal uncle's wife had committed suicide early in the twentieth century. Should I believe in such a paranormal or occult story? I said to myself, 'Why not, if it proves a vehicle to heal wounds?'

A few months later, Balu passed away after a brief illness. I

---

[44]We carefully maintained different sets of video tapes for Indian Imprints' on the one hand and the other two documentary projects on the other to avoid any copyright issues.

only remembered that this brother, who was nine years elder to me, had been very loving in my childhood and my memories went back to the fact that, in a way, I found his bride for him and that he found mine for me. I couldn't help crying alone unconsolably.

Hindu-Buddhist Summit

Swami Dayananda Saraswati, who had branched off from the Chinmaya Mission several decades earlier, had seen extracts from our documentaries on Southeast Asia when he visited our studio. On his advice, the Global Peace Initiative of Women, New York, invited Mohana and me to screen some extracts from *A Different Pilgrimage*, in 2009, at a gathering of Hindu and Buddhist leaders in Phnom Penh. Gita, keen to visit Angkor Wat again, joined us. The invitation letter from Dena Merriam, Founder of the Global Peace Initiative, said:

> Much of the world's attention and that of religious communities have been focused on healing the divisions among the Abrahamic family—the Jewish, Christian and Islamic communities. This is essential if we are to create a more peaceful world. But the wisdom of the East can be a neutralizing or moderating influence and thus be an enormous asset in this effort. The resources of the Hindu and Buddhist communities have not yet been tapped. We must facilitate this process.
>
> 'Religions are being challenged today to move beyond the theologies of exclusivism and superiority and to evolve into a relationship of mutual respect and appreciation of the 'other'. Indeed, to a celebration of the many expressions of truth. This is where interreligious dialogue is now called to go, and the leadership for this must come from the East.

We were in sync with these objectives of the Hindu–Buddhist Summit, which was attended by several spiritual leaders from around the world. Most of the participants were monks, while only about a dozen of us were not. Presided over by Swami Dayananda Saraswati, the meet had the objective of giving a global voice to Eastern wisdom. Our film was very well received at the conference. Since there were monks and nuns from different Hindu and Buddhist sects, it was a fresh experience to interact with varied perceptions of 'Truth'.

In December 1976, A.R. Baji, then head of the Press Information Bureau, had told me informally that my name was under consideration for Padma Shri award—the fourth highest civilian award in India—to be announced on Republic Day in the following month. He also told me a week later that the competent authorities decided to postpone the award for me till the next year. By then, the government changed and the Janata Party government looked at *Indus Valley to Indira Gandhi* with jaundiced eyes—the myth of my having made a film on Indira Gandhi had taken root. When thirty-three years later the award was conferred on me in 2009, I received it with effervescent delight.

Over the last six decades: I have joined a prayer group in a synagogue in New York; worshipped in many heavenly cathedrals of Europe; not to mention the spiritually elevating sanctums of the Hindu pantheon in India. Mohana and I have paid obeisance to the Sun God in a mammoth temple on the banks of the Nile in Egypt and folded our hands in prayer before five hundred Buddhas in one temple in China. The experience in Southeast Asia included my identification with the Chams of Vietnam, who are struggling to keep their faith alive as a small minority worshipping Shiva, Bhagvati and other deities of the Sanatana Dharma. I could also easily identify myself with the jubilant Hindus of Bali, who worship the infinite without form. I could

The author receiving the Padma Shri award from Pratibha Patil, President of India, in 2009

empathize with a seemingly maverick-mystic woman in Phanom Rung, who was worshipping Shiva in a huge desolate temple. Mohana and I prayed in one of the world's largest mosques in

Jakarta. We have knelt down before many a giant Buddha in meditation in Thailand, besides the magnificent Pha That Luang stupa in Laos. Indeed, I could have been a horseman among the tribal groups of Bromo, worshipping the Tirumurtis near their volcano. We worshipped the mountain from where the Ten Commandments were delivered, and witnessed divinity filming in the snow-clad Himalayan peaks. Leave aside the declared places of worship, we experienced Kali in the brown shades of the awe-inspiring Grand Canyon, divine damsels in the fashion-parade walk of hundreds of penguins as they arrive from the sea on the southern shores of Australia, and the avatars of Vishnu in the Great Barrier Reef from the comfort of a glass-encased submarine, and while walking above the man-made wonder of the Great Wall of China. Incidentally, did you know that there are Sanskrit inscriptions on the northern gate of the Great Wall?

When a New Boat failed to Float

In 2001, Sushma Swaraj, Minister for Information and Broadcasting, inaugurated a Round Table on 'Broadcasting—Responsibilities and Rights' in Chennai. In the working paper given to the participants in advance, I wrote:

> In most of the TV channels today, which enjoy a mass audience, the telecast time is occupied at one extreme by exuberant advertising commercials and lifestyle programmes, which promise a fantasy of comforts, treating the audience as 'consumers', and not as 'citizens'; and on the other extreme by soul-depressing news, which is predominantly that of violence against humanity—war, terrorism, political intrigue and chicanery, fraudulent icons and their occasional fall—with nothing to justify the mood of celebration of the commercial spot! These

are sandwiched between soap-operatic melodrama of heartache, with ephemeral characters blown out of proportion to mimic epic standards, and the rehash of titillating movies that compete for their naivety.

In the psychic landscape of the individual viewer, this clash of conflicting undercurrents creates a virtual world of far-reaching consequences. America took some steps about twenty-five years ago to offset the negative impact of commercial TV by introducing Public Broadcasting Services. India has attempted to streamline Doordarshan to fulfil its original promise of being in the public interest, by forming the Prasar Bharati. But the problem with Doordarshan is that it started with a public broadcasting philosophy, which unceremoniously diluted this purpose with commercial broadcast protocol (but adopting managerially inefficient procedures unsuited to market objectives), and has later been fluctuating between the goals of commercial profit, goals of one-upmanship against private tinsel channels in capturing a mass audience with populist programmes, goals of competing with the best non-commercial public service broadcast channels of the world. These fluctuating priorities have made Doordarshan a blindfolded elephant of tremendous strength moving with no sense of direction, without a map, without a charter, without a compass and, indeed, without a road. The object of the Round Table is NOT to fix blame for this phenomenal failure of a few decades, but to chart a future for the medium.

Reflecting on the state of democracy in the world, Aldous Huxley remarked, 'Jeffersonian concepts of democracy are no longer applicable to twentieth century world. Thomas Jefferson and his colleagues could not have imagined a mass communication industry, which would be concerned in the main with neither the real nor the unreal, neither truth nor falsehood, neither beauty nor ugliness, but with the ephemeral—the more or less totally irrelevant.' Unfortunately for us, 'the more or less totally irrelevant' is taking on the posture of being guides to culture, guides to politics and to a way of life.

India has been a crucible for studying the influence of cinema on society. In many pockets of India, cinema has been negating the benefits of democracy. As a non-literate medium, it has held a hypnotic spell on the masses, which by and large, has been distorting their perception of the political processes and ideologies. The reason to mention cinema here is that private TV channels in India are satellite channels in another sense of the term—most of them are 'satellites' of the film industry. Productive use of TV has the power and potential to convert a population which is a 'burden' into an enlightened human 'resource'.

But the criteria of a free-market economy cannot apply to a cultural and communications product, such as a TV programme. The content of media being a product of culture and several millennia of our civilizational values, some of which are unique to India and some of which are common to mankind as a whole, the medium cannot be treated on par with other commodities of the market, whether they are material commodities or services. Hence, not all the rules that are applied for economic and market liberalization can be applied to media. Under the garb of a righteous and civilized attack on social obscurantism, TV cannot be allowed to become a demolition squad of perennial values—values of love, fidelity, motherhood and fatherhood.

In pursuance of my working paper, some participants came up

with the idea that an independent not-for-profit initiative should operate a TV channel with values of public broadcasting, to be funded by private industry. We all knew that it was an uphill task to achieve this. However, I drew up a plan to organize a TV channel with such a manifesto, which remained on paper over the years. Suddenly, one morning in 2008, my octogenarian neighbour Parthasarathy met me and said, 'The idea you mooted in that event should be put to action.'

He decided that he would contribute the seed capital to start such a TV channel, if it had a Hindu spiritual fervour. When I discussed it with a leading industrialist, he staunchly supported the idea, saying, 'If you do all the spadework and start

The author with Subramanian Swamy at the forty-eighth anniversary of Krishnaswamy Associates

the channel, I would chip in about ₹10 crore.' Encouraged by all this, we registered a not-for-profit entity and got a licence to operate a TV channel by name Krishna-TV.

In 2010, having made all the arrangements to launch the channel, we were disappointed when the industrialist backed out because of the global recession, and we thought that we would give up the idea. That's when the distinguished politician Subramanian Swamy, who was then the president of the Janata Party,[45] mentioned to me casually, in Delhi, that he would like to start a Hindu religious TV channel. I said I already had a licence to operate one and asked him if he would be interested. He jumped at the idea and soon a company he had founded agreed to extend the working capital of ₹20 crore. I think Swamy made this promise in good faith expecting financial support from one or more sources. Unfortunately, his expectations did not materialize. His support proved a mirage and my channel boat could not float for long on the waters of that mirage.

My nephew, K. Ramachandran (alias Kumar), has been a source of moral support for long—in spite of his busy schedules as a globetrotter in a senior managerial position in Larsen and Toubro. He had retired from that position by the time we launched Krishna-TV, in late 2011. When we incurred heavy losses, he helped us to

K. Ramachandran (alias Kumar)

---

[45]The Janata Party, which was the ruling party in 1977-79, merged with the BJP before Parliament elections of 2014.

wind up the operations in about two years from the start, to prevent our hard-earned resources going further down the drain. Even as a non-governmental public broadcasting channel awaits someone to build it successfully, in an attempt to implement this concept in the New Media, Krishnaswamy Associates launched *www.indianimprints.com*—a video-on-demand (VoD) Internet-based service in 2016, with Lata at its helm.

Walking in Hallowed Footsteps

Early in the new century, there was a philosophical yearning in me. Although I had read some of the major Hindu scriptures and philosophy as well as got a peek into comparative religion—both because of personal interest and due to professional opportunities—there were questions in the innermost recesses of my heart. As for Mohana, she could identify herself with the philosophy of Jiddu Krishnamurti (JK) and had become his ardent admirer. Indeed, JK disowned the idea that he was a guru and he proclaimed that each person has to find his answers directly. I had a link with the Ramakrishna Mission going back many decades. My mother had said in 1960, 'I learn there is a branch of the Ramakrishna Math in New York. Make sure you pay your obeisance to the Swamiji there.' Promptly, I had paid my respects to Swami Nikhilananda and Swami Buddhananda. On hearing that I was unwell, the latter had graciously visited me in the Columbia University infirmary. I had read some Vivekananda literature—primarily to be able to answer the questions on India and Hinduism in a foreign land.

The opportunity to revive that stream of thought knocked at my door when a young monk, Swami Gitasarananda, visited me in 2004, asking us to produce a documentary film to mark the centenary of the Ramakrishna Mission Students' Home in Chennai. When we made this film, my involvement with the Ramakrishna Math began to grow, with Swami Gitasarananda as a catalyst.

Historically, Tamil Nadu had a lot to do with Swami Vivekananda's mission in life, although he was born in West Bengal and had become a citizen of the world. It occurred to me that we should make a TV serial on the life and message of the great monk. Like several of our projects this also had a long gestation period. Mohana and I had the good fortune of meeting and interacting with several senior monks of the Ramakrishna order. Swami Gautamananda, Swami Atmaramananda and Swami Abhiramananda approved the idea of the math giving a subsidy to cover a part of the cost of producing our serial.

We commenced working on the project in 2009. It was broadcast weekly as a fifty-two-episode Tamil TV serial on Doordarshan in 2013–14, produced by Mohana with my screenplay and dialogues, and directed by Gita. Featuring about two hundred dialogue-speaking artistees, shot in many locations including Belur Math; Mayavati in the Himalayas; the International School of Wisdom, Bengaluru; Amir Mahal of the Prince of Arcot, His Highness Nawab Mohammed Abdul Ali, who in an exemplary act of interreligious cooperation permitted us to film in his palace; varied landscapes and forest areas of the headquarters of the Theosophical Society, with the cooperation of Radha Burnier, the Society's international president;[46] and our studio. The production was a paperwork sadhana for me, a challenge in logistics for Mohana to produce a glossy product on a TV-scale budget, besides her role in casting talented faces suitable to all the roles; a heightened creative experience for Gita, and indeed, a penance for all of us, including Lata who performed as Sister Nivedita—a principal disciple of Vivekananda.

Because of the nature of the subject, most TV and media

---

[46]Most of these locations like the Theosophical Society, Amir Mahal Palace, International School of Wisdom, and Advaita Ashram at Mayavati, besides the Belur Math, are usually not available for filming.

observers were sceptical about its appeal to a wide audience. But the serial proved them all wrong by securing the first rank in viewership among programmes in DD-Podhigai (Tamil regional DD network) over many weeks.

When I requested Swami Gautamanandaji Maharaj, Head of the Ramakrishna Math, Chennai, to give me deeksha (spiritual initiation), he very graciously asked if Mohana also would like to take deeksha along with me. We have both been most fortunate to get our spiritual initiation—a milestone in our journey together—from this enlightened torchbearer of the Ramakrishna–Vivekananda parampara (who is now international vice president of the Ramakrishna Math and Mission).

...In the 1970s we requested P.S. Srinivasa Rao, well-known singer of Hindustani bhajans, to teach Mohana. As a young man he had been a film actor, performing lead roles in Tamil films of the 1930s and had morphed into a wonderful music teacher.

Filming a scene for Swami Vivekananda

With Swami Gautamanandaji Maharaj at Krishnaswamy Associates

Years later, when he retired from teaching, Mohana had the good fortune to get Master Krishnanand, another reputed Hindustani music teacher of Chennai, as her guru. Another decade later, she started her classes again when Lalitha Sharma, a disciple of Pandit Jasraj began to teach in Chennai. In all three instances, the gurus visited us at home to teach Mohana. Although after so many years together I still don't follow much Hindi or Urdu, I enjoy the fact that Mohana is almost in a trance when she listens to bhajans and ghazals while cooking or working in our home garden. Sometimes, she explains the meaning of the songs. She firmly believes that the fifteenth-century queen Meera was the forerunner of feminism in the world.[47]

---

[47] Her article on Meera is reproduced in the Annexure.

My mind is in an elevated level as I hear Mohana sing Kabir, Surdas and Tulsidas, besides twentieth-century Hindi lyricists and translating them. She enjoys cooking every day for the two of us and says that culinary art is one of the sixty-four ancient Indian arts everyone should learn. It has been a practice for several decades now to clasp our hands while walking on the beach in the evenings like young lovers just engaged. Some friends call it zest, while some wink with jest. We have evolved over a period of years as each other's friend and guide. Our philosophy of life is common, but our strategies and outlook on some issues differ and so we still have our quarrels. Perhaps life will be boring if you agree on everything, without a chance to argue.

Early in my life I had a dream—something like a life-building architectural design—of how the decades ahead were to be shaped. This is not an afterthought of trying to interpret how one has lived, but an honest reflection of what values and objectives one has pursued, with what degree of success or otherwise. Rich or poor, educated or illiterate, every individual—partly consciously and mostly unconsciously—develops his/her philosophy of life. I pursued the goal of using film and TV as instruments to keep people well informed, build respect for their heritage, removing the superstitious layer of their traditions and learn more about not only the ancient past but of recent history and the great persons who moulded that history.

To raise resources for making such films, I indulged in making promotional and corporate-image-building films. I channelled the revenue from all this into making films of the kind that I wished to make. It may have been well-nigh impossible to pursue these goals if my life partner had had a different perspective of life. Between Mohana and me, our differences in attitude in subtle ways have become complementary because of our common philosophy, helping each other in our voyage. If she had influenced me to become a commercially oriented feature-film-maker, counting black money, I may have just become one. She could not pursue her dream of contributing to human welfare as a scientist because of the political landscape of India—with prejudices of caste and reverse discrimination. But she has used the opportunity to be the decisive head of our deliberately small organization to become my co-dreamer and not just my co-worker. This book is a very true, concise record of our joint dreams as we sail in a small raft in the real world.

If the Angel Returned

Our company's revenues from advertising films were subject to self-imposed conditions. To illustrate a few, we had a contract to make ad films for India's major cigarette manufacturer in the 1960s. By the end of that decade, the World Health Organization announced that smoking was injurious to health and urged the media not to glamorize smoking. *Reader's Digest* was one of the first to respond by refusing to take any more cigarette ads. This resulted in my unilaterally cancelling the contract I had with the

Imperial Tobacco Company (later renamed ITC Ltd).

My friends in advertising asked, 'If you don't make this film somebody else is going to make it. How will you prevent the spread of cancer?' I said, 'I have no such illusion. But I just don't want my mind or action to be carcinogenic.'

If my illusory angel of a week before my wedding returned decades later out of curiosity, she would have probably felt, thus.

> In them, I notice many a common trait—
> For one thing, both are very straight.
> They have neither malice nor avarice
> No trace of cowardice or prejudice,
> Their vision of the world in a panorama
> Echoing eternal values of Dharma!
> Every action born of love and compassion;
> Nothing done for fashion or compulsion!
> A few notches above perceptible probity,
> At a level higher than lawful integrity!
> His head in the clouds with mirth
> Yet, her feet firmly on planet earth!

In 1973 when Sundarlal Nahata made his infamous promise of financing my *Indus Valley to Indira Gandhi*, I went to the United States and Canada to explore interest abroad in the project, and spent two months there—staying with my brother Chandru in Toronto—travelling as and when required within the US and Canada. Before leaving on this tour, I went to a local hospital in Chennai for a master health check-up, just to carry medical records with me. I wanted Mohana also to get the check-up done, for which she found no necessity, since she was not travelling. Because of my insistence, she also got the checkup done. The cardiologist of the hospital (Let me call him PR.) cleared my reports and said that I could travel anywhere. But he gave us both a shock by saying that 'Non-specific T-wave changes in

Mohana's ECG are indicative of myocardial damage'. He gave this in writing and suggested that I admit her in the hospital for a fortnight for observation and treatment.

I first thought I would cancel my trip. But I decided to take a second opinion from C.R.R. Pillai, well-known cardiologist and a friend of my parents. Before looking at the ECG, he examined Mohana with his stethoscope, read her pulse and blood pressure and then he said, 'Let me now see the ECG.'

After looking at the ECG, he flared up in a manner most uncharacteristic of him since all of us knew him as a calm, kind and dignified professional. He said, 'You could have taken this fellow to court if you were in America because he has given you a baseless alarm. ECG is normal and Mohana is fine. You may confidently travel abroad.'

Along with my tremendous sense of relief, I must confess I developed a hatred for that vicious mercenary PR, which I have never been able to erase from my mind. PR had also done a protein-bound iodine test for Mohana. Being a biochemist, she asked the doctor, 'Are you equipped with a Geiger counter to do that test?' and the doctor replied, 'We have an understanding with the biochemistry department of the Madras University which has a Geiger counter.' What the doctor did not know was that the lady to whom he was talking was working for her PhD in that very department.

Having obtained the clearance from Pillai, we grew suspicious about PR's claim of using the equipment in the university lab. Mohana asked Professor E.R.B. Shanmugasundaram if there was any such understanding. The professor flared up calling the claim nonsense, and wrote a letter to the editor of a leading newspaper stating that people should not be misled by any hospital claiming to use the facilities of the university lab.

A decade later, when my company was in a position of leadership in making non-fiction films, PR, as 'promoter of a corporate hospital', visited me and requested us to make a film on the 'enterprise' he was promoting. I took a briefing, and asked for a few clarifications.

'Doctor PR! Major hospitals in this country have been either owned by the government or been charitable institutions like the Christian Medical College Hospital, Vellore. I have seen corporate hospitals as profit centres only in America. Are you planning to emulate that model?'

The doctor said, 'Yes, what I have in mind is an American model—of revenue from health insurance companies and from corporate clients who will pay the bills of their employees. Even as pharmaceutical companies are profit-making entities, why not hospitals?'

'You are making such heavy investments on your scanners, etc. Would you not be tempted to use them even on patients who don't need such tests—to pay dividends to your investors?' I asked and he said, 'Yes. That would be part of the business model.'

I politely regretted my inability to take up the project 'in view of other preoccupations', without continuing fruitless arguments of ethics with this Devil. Indeed, he went on to build a highly publicized hospital and recruited some admittedly good medical talents to work for him.

V.S. Padmanabhan, senior advertising professional, commented in a friendly chat, 'By adopting this policy that getting a promotional film made by your company is like securing an ISI mark for the quality of products you advertise, you are making it difficult for yourselves. I admire your ethics. But it is not a pragmatic approach.'

CELEBRATING EXCELLENCE

An advertisement in The Indian Express in 1984 is reproduced here.

A gigantic white lotus in the act of blossoming is sought to be wrought in concrete and marble. Talked about in the world of architecture as the single most significant and beautiful building being built since the construction of the Taj Mahal, this temple of the Bahai faith at New Delhi, yet to be consecrated, is constructed by ECC—a division of L&T.

The Tamilnad Newsprint and Papers Ltd. has become the first paper mill in the world to successfully produce 100 per cent, Bagasse-based Newsprint. Achieved with the technical consultancy of SPB, this technological breakthrough is watched with admiration and interest throughout the world.

Lubrizol (India) Ltd., Mumbai, is just one of the few companies in the world and the first among those of the developing countries, to acquire and develop highly sophisticated technology for the manufacture of chemical additives for lubricating oils, saving hundreds of millions in foreign exchange.

The period from Raja Ram Mohan Roy to Mahatma Gandhi produced an Indian renaissance of great vitality, dedicated leadership and spiritual presence—an influence which is perhaps yet to reach its zenith.

Bharat Electronics Ltd, with its units in Bengaluru, Ghaziabad, Pune and elsewhere, has come to be reckoned as one of the twelve largest Professional Electronics companies of the world, and has expertise that equal and rival the best in the world,

Canara Bank was the smallest of the fourteen major banks nationalized in 1969. It has not only risen, today, to the third rank among all the nationalized banks, but has also found itself listed as one of the fifty fastest-growing banks of the world.

The Thermal Power Station at Neyveli has often ranked above every other power station in India in terms of productivity while the super-power station to be inaugurated there is the single largest industrial enterprise of South India.

The Madras Refineries Ltd. has the highest record of productivity among all the refineries of India, and is poised for further growth with the recent dedication of its expansion project ahead of schedule.

Lucas-TVS maintain its position of leadership in the automobile- electrical-ancillaries industry, despite new formidable competition in this field.

The unique Tower Testing Centre on a hillock near the Madras Airport is reckoned by professionals to be the most advanced and sophisticated centre of its kind in the whole world. The Centre is under the umbrella of the CSIR.

The Kadamparai Hydroelectric Project is almost like a modern temple of Ellora. A powerhouse is being located in the belly of a hill, by scooping tunnels through the rock with precision and expertise by the engineers of the Tamilnadu Electricity Board.

With national awards and international recognition in their bags, Krishnaswamy Associates have either recently completed, or have under production, films to celebrate every one of these subjects of excellence. As quoted in *Indian Documentary* (written by Jag Mohan and published by the Publications Division, Government of India), an independent

> survey has found that Krishnaswamy Associates (P) Ltd., Chennai, has become Asia's largest non-governmental non-fiction film organization. Without diluting their commitment to non-fiction films, they now produce entertainment TV serials also. No wonder, their Tamil serial, *Nallathor Veenai*, being telecast on Fridays by Madras Doordarshan—has become the connoisseur's choice.

We have often thrived, and sometimes just survived, because of our policy of being a 'small organization with relatively large objectives'. Periodically, as explained earlier, we had invested wholly or partly in productions which may not have been commercially viable but gave tremendous sense of satisfaction. In 1989, we had made a five-minute cartoon just for fun—a sarcastic portrayal of the 'state of the nation'. Animator Srinivasan had volunteered to do the cell animation for a small professional fee. The result was *With Apologies to Tagore*.[48]

I suppose that for all of us there are some ideas in our mind which are consistent over a lifetime. There are others which do change. The pre-eminent American philosopher John Dewey, when accused by some of being repetitive in his books, and by others of contradicting himself over the years, said, 'It shows that over eighty years, I have been consistent but not quite stagnant at the same time.' Let me give an example from my own thinking. In 2010, I wrote and anchored the film *5,000 Years in 50 Minutes*, edited and directed by my daughter Lata, for the Films Division. Nearly at the end of the film, I make the following statement on screen:

> Drawing a societal balance sheet of the last six decades since India became a republic, some fundamentally strong institutional frameworks stand out with calibre and

---

[48] *With Apologies to Tagore* is available on *www.indianimprints.com*.

credibility—such as the Election Commission, which has autonomous powers and functions; the Comptroller and Auditor General of India, who sometimes questions the financial propriety of governmental costs; a completely independent judiciary, which has a tradition of upholding the rule of law. A fair system of checks and balances has been built in between the legislature, the executive and the judiciary in such a manner that fault lines in any one of them can be found by another and corrected. In addition to these constitutional mechanisms, the proactive print and electronic media enjoy and enforce their freedom, acting as watchdogs in the interests of the people. Well, nothing in the world is perfect—sometimes there are charges of corruption against politicians and civil servants, cash-for-vote scam against candidates and voters, not-so-often charges of impropriety against the judiciary, occasionally of 'paid news' against the media. And action against all these moral violations is painfully slow. But Democracy is slow-acting and it is part of the price for freedom. The people of India have chosen to pay that price to remain free.

I am not sure today if those words are merely the expression of wishful thinking of a naive patriot. Sri Aurobindo said many decades ago, 'The parliamentary system of democracy may not be suitable to India since it is basically a European concept. An Indian system of governance has to be formulated from the native genius of India.

If I apply that idea of Sri Aurobindo to our contemporary context in India, some things are glaring. In recent decades, elections were often financed by illicit profits made by illegitimate means, deceiving an illiterate electorate in any which way you can think of. Headlines talk about Rajya Sabha seats being sold for ₹100 crore. The crony capitalist bubble, in which the nation is

Justice Ramasubramanian (Hon'ble Judge, Madras High Court) with the Krishnaswamys at the golden jubilee celebrations of Krishnaswamy Associates in 2014

caught up, is bound to explode sooner or later by a revolution in the new generation. It is disheartening to find that democracies elsewhere in the world generally considered more mature are in no better shape—with election funding becoming part of an illicit global trade with crap values of capitalist competition in Germany, France and the USA.[49]

However, one of the factors of my 'citizenly thinking' at the turn of the century was that we cannot shy away from the reality of the political scene and that perhaps we should identify ourselves with the party nearest to our ideology. With those limitations, I was getting drawn to the BJP as being the closest to my thinking.

The idea got strengthened when a follower of Swami Vivekananda (Narendra Modi) was projected by the BJP to take the leadership. Actually, this thinking process of supporting the

---

[49]Refer to 'Campaign Funding Goes Global' by Jane Bussey in the spring issue of *Foreign Policy* of 2000.

K. Rosaiah, Governor of Tamil Nadu (standing) and Swami Abhiramananda of Sri Ramakrishna Mission (sitting) at the golden jubilee celebrations with the Krishnaswamys.

BJP had started in my mind when Atal Bihari Vajpayee was the prime minister for just thirteen days in 1996. On the initiative of a friend, some of us signed an appeal to the MPs to support the Vajpayee government by giving the new regime a fair chance. It was reported in *The Hindu* dated 26 May 1996 (reproduced herein).

Prominent citizens' plea to MPs

From Our Special Correspondent

MADRAS, May 25.

Eight prominent citizens in Madras have appealed to the elected Members of Parliament to support the present Government at the Centre as a sign of respect for the people's mandate, for the office of the President of India and for the norms of democracy.

In a joint statement issued here on Saturday, they said: "The results of the elections to the 11th Lok Sabha mark a watershed in this country's history. No party has received the decisive mandate of the people. In these circumstances, the President, in keeping with well-established precedents has called upon the BJP as the single largest party to form the Government."

"The BJP, with its allies, is also the single largest group which had formed a pre-poll alliance. We cannot emphasise enough the absolute necessity for any country to have a Government capable of taking decisions on the basis of well-defined policies. The need of the hour is cohesive Government which can withstand and overcome the pressures of inimical forces within and without the country and which pose a threat to the country's integrity and wellbeing."

"It, therefore, behoves all elected Members of Parliament to support the present Government as a sign of respect for the people's mandate, for the office of the President of India and for the norms of democracy. We, therefore, request all parties to keep the nation's interests in sight and in mind. The strength of a nation lies in its ability to come together spontaneously at the time of national crisis. Failure to do so can weaken the fabric that holds us together."

"We, therefore, appeal to the newly elected Members of Parliament to strengthen the country and in the process strengthen our democracy by upholding the will of the people," the statement said. The signatories to the statement were Dr. M. S. Udayamurthy (Makkal Sakthi Iyakkam), Dr. S. Krishnaswamy (T. V. and Documentary film producer), Mr. K. Ravindran (former DGP), Mr. S. V. S. Raghavan (former Chairman, BHEL and MMTC), Mr. Srinivas Acharya (Corporate Executive), Mr. I. Mahadevan, IAS (Retd) (Former Editor, 'Dina Mani'), Mr. K. A. Panchapakesan (Senior Advocate) and Mr. R. Desikan (Consumer Activist).

The Hindu/26-05-1996/4

Both Mohana and I had till then decided not to join any political party. We don't subscribe to the idea of secularism as interpreted by most political parties, because some of them equate secularism with atheism or agnosticism, and the majority of them make compromises with the minority vote banks.

When we were discussing this issue between ourselves, a respected friend from the BJP, L. Ganesan, former president of the Tamil Nadu BJP unit, invited us to a 'Meeting of Friends of BJP', in Chennai, a few weeks before the 2014 parliamentary elections.

We were deeply impressed with the speeches of Venkaiah Naidu (a former national president of the BJP —now as this book goes to print, the vice president of India) and Ganesan (now an MP). Shortly thereafter, Ganesan visited our house and convinced us that we should join his party. We gladly agreed and became formal members of the BJP.

Can a new ordinary member of a political party give unsolicited opinions to the national leadership of such a party? Yes, I believe that is the essence of democracy. At seventy-nine, as I am writing this, I have no axe to grind or position to seek, but as one who has been deeply involved in grasping the civilizational values of his motherland for seven decades; as one who has taken passionate voyages of exploring history and culture through the documentary medium; as a citizen exposed to the world; as one who sincerely feels the need for harmony among all the religious, linguistic and other groups of India, I ardently appeal to the leaders of the BJP to consider this:

> At the time of writing this, there is no alternative political force which can achieve the same commanding position as our party. If we believe truly in Hindutva, we cannot hate those of any other religion—as over the centuries, we have received followers of religions persecuted abroad such as

the Zoroastrians and given them a new home to prosper. In humanitarian and philosophical terms, India should take leadership of the world in fostering universal brotherhood. Let us try to be the party that represents the whole of India, not just a section of it. It is possible if we are truly Hindu.

Moving from the philosophical to the pragmatic level, there is no way India can prosper unless it achieves communal harmony and unity among all its linguistic and other groups. There are extremists in all religions. But let us not allow them to take hold of this party—more so when it is the only ray of hope for India in the foreseeable future.

In the past decades, India has suffered from the absence of a strong idealistic opposition to the Congress party. As a consequence, the Congress has degenerated into a party governed by a coterie. The BJP should learn this from history and not allow itself to become one ruled by another kind of coterie, although, thank God, there is no family coterie.

Swami Vivekananda warned a century ago that the 'survival of the fittest' theory extrapolated from Darwin's observations should not be applied to human beings—as they are a higher species. Darwin never propounded it as a value, but only recorded it as an observation in his theory of evolution. But the cannibalistic competitive crony capitalist culture is reducing man to the level of a beast, with no values of egalitarianism, environmental concern and social responsibility. .

It has become a unipolar world with America at the epicentre. Looking back into the millennia of human civilization, history has shown us that several nations have had their rise and fall. We see on the horizon a post-American world in which other nations like Brazil, Russia, India and China are emerging into important positions of leadership. But there are also new avatars of the 'devil' like the Islamic State. Even if we can

Sushma Swaraj, the then Minister for Information and Broadcasting, as the chief guest at the 37th anniversary of Krishnaswamy Associates (2001) with the author and with Mohana; at the time of writing this book, she is the Minister for External Affairs.

avoid conventional wars as we have known them, terrorism—the new war on humanism and humanity—has cropped up all over. The basis of capitalism, communism, democracy and totalitarianism—in the forms in which they are practised in the world today—are all founded on dialectic materialism. Almost all religions are derived from non-dialectic beliefs. The deeper spiritual dimensions of every religion are also beyond the intellect—at the level of consciousness.

Religions got discounted with the advancement of science in recent centuries. Unfortunately, values of humanism, sympathy, compassion and love for the fraternity of man were sacrificed by post-religious, materialistic societies, along with superstitions and irrationality on the surface of religious beliefs. Like 'throwing the baby along with the bathwater', the spiritual foundations of religions were being thrown away both in capitalist and communist societies.

UNESCO is founded with the laudable conviction that 'Since wars begin in the minds of men, the fortresses of peace will have to be built in the minds of men'. We are facing a grim reality and have to find the means to build those fortresses of peace. Economic progress, democracy and alternative forms of government within the framework of what are in existence in the world today seem incapable of building these fortresses. It is essential to strike a balance between economic and scientific progress on the one hand and the development of those ethereal and meditative qualities of the spiritual plane on the other. As the iconic man of Science, Albert Einstein said, 'Science without religion is lame; religion without science is blind.'

It has been argued that nationalism and religious beliefs have been the root causes of wars in the world. Primordial man developed into a socially conscious man by identifying himself with small groups such as family, tribe or territory or presiding deities of such groups. Unfortunately, while man's power to produce goods including weapons of destruction has grown to astronomical proportions, he still remains primitive in terms of his wisdom and love for fellow men. The balancing force of spirituality has to be reintroduced since religion has been discounted by the spread of rationalism.

The reason why Indogenic religions (Hinduism, Buddhism, Jainism, Sikhism) can be looked upon as sources of support for giving this balancing factor to the future of man is that these religions look inward for divinity. This spiritual inheritance has to be rekindled in modern man—whether it is the Christian 'Love thy neighbour' or the Hindu 'Sarve janah sukhino bhavanthu' (Let there be prosperity for the whole of humanity). A sobering influence has to envelop the world through the spiritual path. There is no clash between pure science and the world view of the deeper aspects of Hinduism—forget the ritualistic aspects as relics of the past. Without chauvinistic pride, I believe, it puts India in a special position to influence the future of man. Enlightened Western thinkers in recent centuries have assigned this unique role to India.

In 1813, Sir Thomas Munro, Governor of Madras, wrote to the Directors of the East India Company in London, 'If civilization was to become an article of trade between Britain and India, I am convinced that Britain will benefit from the import cargo.'

Romain Rolland (1866-1944), in his Foreword to *The Dance of Shiva* by Ananda K. Coomaraswamy, writes, 'The Western world, abandoning itself utterly to its search of individual and social happiness, maims and disfigures life by the very frenzy of its haste, and kills in the shell, the happiness which it pursues. Like a runaway horse who from between his blinkers sees only the blinding road before him, the average European cannot see beyond the boundaries of his individual life, or of the life of his class, or his country, or his party. In the great philosophy of Brahma, such violent turns of the scale are quite unknown. It embraces vast stretches of time, cycles of human ages, whose successive lives gravitate in concentric circles, and travel ever slowly towards the centre...

Arnold Toynbee (1889–1975) wrote, 'It is already becoming clear that a chapter which had a Western beginning will have to have an Indian ending if it is not to end in self-destruction of the human race. At this supremely dangerous moment in human history, the only way of salvation is the ancient Hindu way. Here we have the attitude and spirit that can make it possible for the human race to grow together into a single family.' Later, in 1952, he observed, 'In fifty years, the world would be under the hegemony of the US, but in the twenty-first century, as religion captures the place of technology, it is possible that India, the conquered, will conquer its conquerors.'

Will Durant (1885–1981) said, 'Perhaps in return for conquest, arrogance and spoliation, India will teach us the tolerance and gentleness of the mature mind, the quiet content of the unacquisitive soul, the calm of the understanding spirit, and a unifying—a pacifying—love for all living things.'

Even as these great thinkers conceived of modern man's future evolving from India's ancient wisdom—a future of universal brotherhood, peace and harmony, a glorious aeon wedded to truth—I am witness to India's reality of hatred, unbridled selfishness, and misguided valour pedalling petty politics.

Is it possible to globalize the economy without an imported globalized materialistic culture which comes with it as a 'Free Gift', in advertising language? It has influenced the Indian spiritual scene too; for in the midst of many worshipful religious leaders, there are also pseudo-sacred vampires building their own empires, sucking the blood of their damned devotees.

India, you have been hailed as the mother of civilization—

as one who would guide the future of humanity! Against this expectation, will you let down the world and life on this planet? Beyond my lifetime in this birth, you may become a major economic and political power, as some economists are forecasting. But will you remember your tryst with the infinite that you will stand up as the guardian of wisdom and truth; as the custodian of Dharma; as the conscience keeper of the gods of the Universe; as the inheritor of the light and insight of the rishis; the Buddha and Mahavira; Sankara and Ramanuja; Sri Ramakrishna and Vivekananda?

(From the top, clockwise, Meenakshi, Dhruv, Kamini and Disha)

I hope and pray you do, for it is nothing less than your destiny. The spirit of India, I plead with you to take the non-dialectic leadership of this troubled world by imbibing the sane spiritual values of your millennia with zeal; and let's work towards universal peace and harmony, honesty and humanism—shaping a world fit for all of us...for our four grandchildren, Mohana and I love so intensely, and for the millions of their descendants in the future aeons.

Annexures

Extracts from select lectures and articles of S. Krishnaswamy and Mohana Krishnaswamy

Annexure-1: Culture as political phenomena	300
Annexure-2: In the cerebral circuit	316
Annexure-2A: A roadmap to reforming elections	321
Annexure-3: Reviews of the first edition of Indian Film	326
Annexure-4: Ayurveda's answer to the challenge of cancer?	328
Annexure-5: Report and recommendations based on my visit to IMPLAD and other institutions connected with traditional medicine in China	332
Annexure-6: Status of research in ayurveda	339
Annexure-7: Will ayurveda be hijacked	344
Annexure-8: Meera: An advocate of feminism	349

ANNEXURE-1
CULTURE AS POLITICAL PHENOMENA

Abridged from a paper presented by S. Krishnaswamy at the Washington Institute for Values on 10 September 1986

The Eskimo has some twenty words to denote snow, while the Arab has no word for snow in his language. The Eskimo can distinguish between fresh and well-settled snow and between different grades of snow with one word to denote each, because his geography demands that subtlety. Language reflects not only the demands of physical geography but also of the collective psychic geography of a people.

In my mother tongue, Tamil, when a person is sick, he says *'Enakku udambu sari illai'*, which when literally translated would mean 'My body is unwell'. Commonly, this sentence is translated into English as 'I am unwell'. While this translation is consistent with accepted English, it is not faithful to the innate cultural nuance of the original, which says 'My body is unwell'. When the same person is convalescing, a friend would ask him *'Udambu thevalaya?'* or *'Udambu sugama?'*, literally meaning 'Is your body better?' or 'Is your body healthy now?' There is an irreparable cultural loss in the English translation 'Are you better?' A man's state of ill-health in other Indian languages would read exactly in the same fashion. For instance, in Hindi you would say *'Meri tabiyat theek nahin hai'*, in Telugu *'Na ontla baga ledu'*, in Marathi *'Maji tabiat theek nahin aahe'*, all of which mean 'My body is unwell'.

The primordial cultural root of the Indian makes him distinguish even in everyday language and habit between the body and the soul. 'I' refers to the soul, not the body. Literate or illiterate, wealthy or poor, irrespective of caste and other traditional or modern status, the individual subconsciously believes that he or she is different from the body. In a vast majority, this subconscious feeling is dormant, while in others it is conscious 'awareness'. This awareness is one of degree. While rarely one may have it as a continuous awareness, several others in normal occupations often reach this state of awareness, whether they sustain it or not. It is said that languages of North India have common linguistic roots in Sanskrit, while the languages of the South belong to an independent linguistic group of Dravidian roots. But in terms of basic cultural expression, the languages of India belong to a common socio-philosophical stream.

A crucial aspect of the Indian world view is that the individual soul is an integral part of the infinite soul. The Hindus call it Brahman—'the imperishable and causeless universal soul', filling all space, and projecting itself as the living and the non-living. If the Hindu hymn of 3000 BC declares *'Aham Brahmasmi'* (I am the infinite), the celebrated modern Indian philosopher J. Krishnamurti declares, 'You are the world and the world is yourself. When you realize this you will find that reforming the world is easy. Just reform yourself, and the world will be reformed.' The hundreds of gods and goddesses of the Hindu pantheon are recognized in a spiritual sense to be manifestations of the one and only divinity which is already present in man. If man sheds ignorance and ego, he realizes his innate divine nature within himself.

Indian performing arts symbolize god as Nataraja—the dancing Shiva. This is India's ultimate cultural expression. It signifies that the creator and the creation are one and the same. The painter is different from the painting, the poem from the poet, the sculpture from the sculptor. But dance is created from out of the body of the dancer. There is no external matter. When the writer creates a novel, it acquires an independent identity once he has finished his creation. However, the dancer and her dance are indivisible. The creator and the creation are one and the same. The phenomenal universe is a reflection as well as a part of the ultimate reality. The whole creation is the cosmic dance of Shiva.

Thus, the two basic premises of Indian culture are these: the body is different from the soul; and the individual soul is identical with the infinite soul and that the whole of humanity is thereby integrated. The microcosm and the macrocosm are one and the same. Hindu metaphysics inspire man to search for god within him—not outside.

Although India was not a single nation-state in historic periods, it shared not only a common culture, but also common codes of civil and criminal law and justice. The political treatises of the Mauryan period indicate the presence of highly organized government departments, five centuries before Christ. The two centuries just before and after Christ also saw the codification of Indian law. Generally, kings were not expected to legislate but only follow codes of law, enunciated by lawgivers like Manu.[50] The code of conduct was followed within the kingdoms of the subcontinent, as well as in terms of international relations and during wars between kings.

In any system, there is an inevitable gap between the cultural ideal and the social reality. India was no exception, but this gap widened during the later centuries and became an anachronism by the eighteenth century. A society that spoke of the universal soul being identical with the individual soul, practised untouchability and inflicted indignity on vast masses of people; women were oppressed; in some areas, widows were burnt on the funeral pyre of their husbands, while in others, they were enslaved by primitive orthodoxy.

In the words of the philosopher-statesman former President Sarvepalli Radhakrishnan, '[Hinduism was] at once

---

[50]There were ancient rishis or seers who codified laws governing citizens, families, and all classes of society including the royalty. The most prominent among them was Manu (c.a. First Century B.C. or A D).

saintly and savage; beautifully wise and dangerously silly; generous beyond measure and mean beyond all example.' The political situation in India in the eighteenth century was equally chaotic. Self-centred autocratic rajas and nawabs presided over petty kingdoms that committed atrocities by a combination of indolence, inaction and vanity. There was, no doubt, some oasis in this political desert-land.

How did valiant and astute people of wisdom as described in the ancient mythical Rama Rajya (conceptually more grand than Utopia) descend to this level? How did the ancient people—who wrote the first major grammatical work of any language in the world; who invented 'zero' and contributed to mathematics and algebra; whose theoretical abstractions of the universe and the understanding of astronomy astound the modern thinker; whose sculpture and painting, poetry and music, dance and crafts, politics and government, law and justice, had reached an exemplary degree of development—descend and degenerate to what India was in the eighteenth century?

According to the Hindu view, man has three gunas or mental qualities, and his actions are determined by the guna that dominates him. Sattva guna is a positive, non-aggressive, tender, compassionate, egalitarian, tolerant and contemplative plane of action, which radiates happiness and peace; rajo guna is an assertive, competitive, ambitious, egocentric and achievement-oriented positive plane of action, which spreads material prosperity; tamo guna is an indolent, lazy, gross and pleasure-oriented plane of inaction.

The dividing line between active contemplation and lazy inaction can be very thin. Both are free from anxiety and tension. I suspect that at a time when decisive action was required, Indians in the middle ages meekly descended to lazy inaction under the garb of contemplation.

Thus, during the early nineteenth century, Indian maharajas and nawabs were enjoying themselves, even as time was running out against them in political terms. It is this India of anachronism—profound thought and banal practice, burdened with dead weights and superstitions—which came in contact with Western thoughts and traditions during the British colonization of India. This produced illegitimate offspring of British feudal society with the caste hierarchy of India, such as the zamindari system. A new relationship developed between the British overlords and Indian royalty, serving their mutual interest in exploiting the people.

Simultaneously, Western liberal thought made a significant impact on India, acting as a catalytic agent for awakening the dormant energy of India. This positive interaction between contemporary Western thought and ancient Indian wisdom produced a colourful and interesting mosaic in the form of different social, religious and political movements, which together contributed to what is now described as the Indian renaissance of the nineteenth century.

This renaissance blossomed—as a cultural movement, as a movement of social reform and religious transformation—and worked for women's emancipation, widow remarriage, abolition of the caste system and untouchability, spread of education, attempting to cleanse the accretions to the Indian cultural ethos. The Brahmo Samaj, the Arya Samaj and the Ramakrishna Mission under the leadership of Swami Vivekananda, among others, became part of this renaissance. Another cultural trend of the period was that even as India was importing a Western intellectual model, several Westerners were attracted to the mystique of India. Max Mueller of Germany began to interpret Indian philosophy to Indians themselves. The Russian mystic Madam Blavatsky, and Colonel Henry Olcott, a friend of Abraham Lincoln, co-founded the Theosophical Society in New York and shifted their headquarters to Chennai. These spiritual and social organizations had a profound influence on new generations, preaching universal brotherhood beyond caste, creed, sex, race and religion.

The different threads of nationalist activity involved in social and religious reforms were brought together in 1885, in the formation of the Indian National Congress, which became a political party eventually instrumental in liberating India from colonial rule. The freedom movement was deeply rooted in Indian moral, ethical and spiritual foundations. Indeed, the relationship between culture and politics during the freedom struggle was intense under the leadership of Mahatma Gandhi. The leaders of the freedom movement were concerned about what model of government would suit independent India.

Man has over the centuries made different attempts to evolve political systems, in terms of his basic metaphysical and philosophical belief. These metaphysical presuppositions can be broadly classified into the dialectical and the non-dialectical.

The political impact of dialectical metaphysics meant probably one of three forms of government. First, a government based on the dualism of the elite and the masses, allowing a natural aristocracy to govern a country; second, a government based on democracy, which allows for a full play of individualism with minimum restraint on individuals for social, cultural and commercial activity; third, a dictatorship/totalitarian system.

On the other hand, a political system based on a non-dialectical model would treat the government not primarily as an agency of power but as one associated with wisdom—as an agency of coordination bringing together the interests of all the citizens and harmonizing them into one unified whole.

If we look back, in ancient Hindu India we see examples of the non-dialectical system of politics in action.

The codes of Hindu law emphasized duties, more than rights. Freedom was understood not as freedom to acquire and possess, but as freedom to renounce. The emphasis was on internal freedom as a prerequisite for external freedom. One may be externally free in that he is not prohibited from moving about physically. But at the same time his mind or psyche may be enslaved.

Several nationalists believed that a reorientation of India's socio-political system to suit modernization and economic progress was required. They were keen to adopt the Western democratic processes with individuals as the prime entities of society. However, there were many who did not agree with this view. Some groups rejected everything that was foreign in nature. Others were keen to relinquish everything that was Indian on the basis that the indigenous culture had failed.

The best minds during the freedom struggle and thereafter have followed a middle path, trying to reconcile between different cultural systems, evolving a socio-political system suited to modern India.

Indian polity in the middle ages had been entrenched in elitism of its own brand, with some castes prohibited from even learning religious texts. The major reform movements combined cultural and political objectives. The Arya Samaj wanted to teach English as well as the Vedic religion to all Indians regardless of their caste or creed. Mahatma Gandhi's objective of Indian freedom was not merely political freedom for India, but freedom for every individual, freedom for the untouchable from oppression by higher castes, freedom for women from enslavement by men, freedom of the labour force from exploitation by feudal lords. Gandhiji's concept of freedom was unmistakably non-dialectic in character.

Despite all the arguments during the freedom struggle, when India adopted a Constitution, it was one largely based on dialectical Western models. Since independence, we find national policies based on non-dialectical Indian culture, translated into political terms, functioning within the framework of a dialectical Constitution. What do I mean by non-dialectical policies? India's commitment to treat followers of all religions as equals is a product of the perennial current of Hindu philosophy. Sri Ramakrishna experientially attained the ultimate ecstasy through the paths of Hinduism, Islam and Christianity. Mahatma Gandhi gave it a political significance to that experience. When you believe that the individual soul is the same as the universal soul, how can the souls of individuals professing religions other than your own be different? The idea of human equality and universal brotherhood is deeply steeped in Indian tradition. Our Constitution guarantees freedom from discrimination based on religion. This is a political product of India's cultural will.

However, in the functioning of Indian democracy, the cultural impact on day-to-day politics has not always been influenced by ancient Indian culture, but has meant also the cultural influence of escapist entertainment media.[51]

---

[51] UNESCO evolved a measure of the penetration of cinema by the number of cinema halls in relation to the population of a country. This showed the proportion to be very low in India compared to the western world. I realised that the formula is inappropriate for a large country like India, and applied the formula state-wise since I thought that the states have to be dealt with separately to understand the penetration. I found that Tamil Nadu had the deepest penetration of the film medium and Uttar Pradesh the most-shallow penetration. My analyses showed that the penetration of cinema next only to Tamil Nadu was in Andhra Pradesh, Kerala, Maharashtra, Karnataka and West Bengal, in that order. The rest of India had low penetration.

Culture nevertheless influences political reality; aspects of culture is another question. For instance, if you treat the institution of caste as an aberration of Indian culture, it has certainly manifested itself as a political phenomena. Caste has changed from a vertical institution of higher and lower social groups involved in insular crafts and professions to horizontal groups with primordial attachments competing in commercial and political activity. Caste-based political parties have become common.

While examples can be quoted from different parts of India, let me briefly take one specific example—that of the Dravidian movement in Tamil Nadu. To combat the Brahmin hegemony perpetrating caste superiority, combined with comparative affluence and acquisition of modern status due to Western education, certain sections among the non-Brahmin Hindu community in Tamil Nadu fancied themselves, on sketchy and extended hypothesis, to be the direct descendants of the original Dravidian racial stock who populated these regions before the invasion of India by the Aryan tribes from Central Asia. By another fancy of their imagination, they also believed that the Brahmins were direct descendants of the Aryan tribes alleged to have migrated from Central Asia some 3,000 years before Christ.

Contemporary researchers believe that there was no such 'invasion' by Aryans at all. As part of their 'divide and rule' strategy, the British had created this myth of the Aryan invasion. Such a concept was not known till the end of the nineteenth century. The non-Brahmins of the Madras Presidency, who had a genuine cause to fight against the discriminatory practices of the Brahmin community, grabbed the Aryan invasion theory and fantasized themselves as direct descendants of the Dravidians.

In this background, the South Indian People's Association was formed in 1916, which later came to be known as the Justice

Party, representing the interests of a section of non-Brahmins. The non-Brahmin manifesto issued by them proclaimed, 'We are deeply devoted and loyally attached to British rule.' Afraid of Brahmin domination in an independent India, they staunchly supported British rule and were opposed to the freedom struggle, even at the height of the independence movement, in later years. A complex and colourful leader of the Congress party, E.V. Ramasamy Naicker, who later came to be known as Periyar (great man), broke away from the Congress party, accusing it of Brahmin domination, joined the Justice Party on his own conditions, in the mid-1930s, and later reorganized that party as the DRAVIDA KAZHAGAM (DK). Periyar, sometimes an agnostic, sometimes an atheist, was in any case a militant protagonist who declared publicly, 'If you see a Brahmin and a cobra, kill the Brahmin first.'

Periyar and his followers boycotted the independence Day celebrations of India, in 1947. Within two years, Periyar's lieutenant, Annadurai, broke away from his mentor, taking with him a band of young leaders, and organized the DMK—Dravidian Progressive Party. The growth of this movement—its ascendency to political power in the state of Tamil Nadu—is the most glaring example of cultural phenomena as political phenomena. It is appropriate at this stage, to examine the role of Indian media in the cultural and political growth of the country.

But for a very short period during the Emergency in the mid-1970s, the Indian press has been unfettered and as free as it can be in any country of the world, ventilating political and economic grievances. The Indian press is unsparing in exposing political bigotry. However, it had its limitations, because hardly 16 per cent of India's population was literate at the time of independence. This figure has grown to 45 per cent in recent times. A film was screened in India within months of the Lumiere Brothers demonstrating their cinematographe in Paris in 1895. The first Indian feature film was made in 1913. Although the number of cinemas (the national average) has not been very high, cinema has had a profound influence on Indian attitudes and worldview. When movies became talkies, Indian cinema acquired a natural protection from competing imported films.

The first Hindi film was made in 1931. Within a short time, film production started in Bengali, Tamil, Telugu, and a few years thereafter, in other languages of India. Indian films inherited two traditions: first, the tradition of silent cinema representing a new international non-verbal visual style of presentation; second, the style of the ancient Sanskrit theatre going back to a tradition of over 2,000 years. The Sanskrit theatre was an amalgam of music, dance and drama, all rolled into one. Ancient Sanskrit theatre, which flourished under court patronage, dwindled in importance after the Islamic invasion. The Islamic theological tradition was against performing arts, and hence there was no patronage of dance or drama during Mughal rule in India.

During these centuries when Sanskrit theatre was eclipsed, its formula of dance–music–dialogue permeated into folk theatre, known by different names in different part of India, that carried on the traditions of Indian theatre with regional variations.

When a new Indian theatre was born between the late nineeenth and early twentieth centuries, it was highly influenced by the folk tradition, which in turn had its roots in ancient Sanskrit theatre. When Indian films acquired sound, they naturally inherited the style of the contemporary Indian theatre. Hence, cinema acquired two characteristics: first, the subject matter of a large percentage of films was drawn from Indian mythology; second, a cinematic style became unique to India in the sense of being a combination of opera, ballet and drama fused with a new technology. Indian films became stylistically distinct from the rest of the world.

I strongly believe that Indian films became a political tool by just being Indian. The strict political censorship of the British administration could only prevent direct propaganda on the Indian screen, because Indian films as a whole had a subliminal value, projecting Indian mythology, glorifying ancient Indian themes, resurrecting in the native memory of a people their glorious past and tradition. In addition to these films based on mythology, there were some films that portrayed contemporary Indian life, a few of which began to tackle problems including caste, untouchability and women's emancipation, presenting a new cosmopolitan environment and encouraging individual liberty. Occasionally, despite strict censorship, film-makers indulged in introducing political imagery. Some film-makers went several steps ahead and introduced direct political ideas in their films. Anyone interested in this subject may like to see my short film—*Through a Different Lens*—based on the politically significant films of India before independence.[52]

After independence, the circumstances resulted in a special relationship between cinema and politics in Tamil Nadu, because of the penetration of cinema in that state, more than anywhere else. In the 1960s, Tamil Nadu had one cinema house for 30,000 people, as against Uttar Pradesh at the other end of the numbers, which had one cinema house for over 2,00,000 people.

If we look at the motivations of all the communicators in all the media, there were not many interested in communicating with rural India. Most people in the print media were least interested in the rural man, because of the high rate of illiteracy in these areas. Hence, journalism became almost exclusively urban oriented. The advertising man was not interested in the rural man, because in the first three decades after independence, the Indian farmer had no purchasing power. TV was nascent. There were only three kinds of communicators who were interested in the rural man. First, the radio broadcaster—his time, however, was more devoted to music and to developmental communication—any political

---

[52] *Through a Different Lens* is available on *www.indianimprints.com*.

message was inhibited by the fact that radio was a government-owned medium. Second, the politicians—the rural citizen was a prospective consumer, because he had a vote in his hand. Third, the film-maker—the rural man was an important client for his profits came from rural cinemas. Thus, the only two kinds of communicators for whom the rural man became important in the first three decades of independence were politicians and feature-film-makers. This combination became more valid in Tamil Nadu than elsewhere, because of the deep penetration of cinema in that state. An unintended social engineering began to take place, with far-reaching political consequences. In fact, the relationship between cinema and politics in Tamil Nadu has been such that it is difficult to discuss the history of either without bringing in the relationship between the two. Annadurai, the founder of the DMK, was himself a dramatist, who began to write screenplays in Tamil more or less from the time he founded his party in 1949. He attracted a few other writers and a large number of actors to the fold of the DMK. Several symbols of the DMK movement, such as its party colours and its party election symbol, as well as dialogue either directly or obliquely referring to the domination of the North over the South, besides the domination by Brahmins, were all introduced in feature films, which were otherwise mediocre, ordinary formula films with no specific political themes. Throughout these years, film actors played a role in party rallies.

In a subsequent era, the star who dominated the whole movement was M.G. Ramachandran. MGR, as he came to be worshipped by his fans, began to specialize in stunt roles in the Douglas Fairbanks tradition. He appeared as folk hero, battling royal usurpers and their henchmen, fighting against incredible odds. In fact, he had begun to perform one archetype role in all his films. In the nearly two hundred films in which he played the hero, he met with death only in one film, in the 1950s. In all the other films, he was the indomitable and indefatigable hero. The dream image that he built for himself in the subconscious mind of his audience is unique. In simple terms, the character which he always performed combined the strength of a Hercules, with the love and compassion of a Jesus Christ and the modernity of a James Bond. Girls always fell in love with him in every film and it was up to him to respond. Yet his character could be identified with the morality of none less than Rama. He did not touch liquor or smoke a cigarette on the screen through most of his film career.

Even while building up a conscious screen image, in his real life MGR took an active part in the politics of the DMK evolving an unprecedented public relations organization. MGR fan clubs all over Tamil Nadu became active units of the political party, with much publicized charities from his personal income for relief after flood and other natural calamities.

Gradually, a stage was reached when the on-screen and off-screen image of the man merged, creating a fusion of dream and reality, fact and fiction, transcending the elements of entertainment and culture, to perform major political roles in real life. Looking at the DMK popularity based on fan rallies of film stars, Kamaraj, a respected Congress leader and former chief minister of Tamil Nadu, asked in the late 1950s, 'How can there be a government by mountebanks?' The contempt rallied the screen world to the DMK. Indian film tradition has been closely meshed with a hero–villain pantheon. Most of MGR's films had villains and prominent among them was M.R. Radha. Shortly before the 1967 Tamil Nadu state elections, Radha visited MGR, who was a DMK candidate for the state assembly. Radha shot MGR and shot himself too. It was an extraordinary event, when common film situations were re-enacted in real life.

Radha was convicted and sentenced to jail. MGR was critically wounded and hospitalized. As millions of fans prayed for him all over Tamil Nadu, and thousands of them arrived in the hospital compound, the 'hero' survived, reaffirming his demigod image, as he had survived any number of attacks of the same 'villian' in any number of films.

The DMK used posters of MGR in bandages, as part of the election campaign. The elections to state legislatures all over India came up with a confused political picture, with no party obtaining clear majorities in several states. In sharp contrast, the DMK swept to power in Tamil Nadu, defeating the Congress party. Annadurai was sworn in as chief minister. After his passing away, within a few years the party broke up. MGR founded his own party called Anna DMK, which he later renamed All India Anna DMK to remove the parochial stigma. He proclaimed 'Annaism' as his doctrine in the memory of C.N. Annadurai and defined it as 'the best of capitalism combined with the best of communism'. The large electorate was in any case not interested in the subtle details of ideology. They could back their hero. In 1977, MGR became the chief minister.

Among other cultural elements which have influenced the course of politics in India in recent times is 'language'. The national policy provides for the propagation of Hindi as a link language. This has contributed to tensions in some non-Hindi-speaking areas, notably in the south. One of the sources of emotional identification of the Tamil people with the DMK has been opposition to Hindi.

In general, Indian politics has been very substantially personality oriented. This has been more so after independence. Every major political party depends on the charisma and public image of its individual leaders rather than economic and political philosophy or an ideology. It is elementary that 'persona' is built by visibility. The hero–villain mesh of Indian cinema ideally fits in with the cult-dominated Indian politics to promote such personalities. Thus, the style of popular commercial Indian cinema is immensely suited to the style of functioning of Indian political party, with common trappings, converting 'stars' to 'tsars'.

Philosophers of the East as well as the West, from ancient times to the current day, have been concerned with man's elevation from a perception of the mere phenomenal world, to an understanding of the reality behind phenomena, to transcend fact in order to understand the truth. The media today, in most parts of the world, is functioning as an instrument of descent. Increasingly, we seem to be more concerned with images than with phenomena. If the media can be transformed into instrument of ascent in a cultural sense—ascent not necessarily from phenomena to reality, but at least from illusion and images to phenomenal fact—the manifestation of culture as a political phenomenon will take mankind to new levels of perception, harmony and achievement.

ANNEXURE-2

IN THE CEREBRAL CIRCUIT

From the 1960s, S. Krishnaswamy has delivered about a hundred lectures in various forums and participated in some seminars/conferences in India and abroad. Here are glimpses from some them.

1977—Woodrow Wilson Centre for International Scholars

Woodrow Wilson Centre for International Scholars, Washington, DC, invited me in April 1977 to deliver a guest lecture on 'Cinema—A Mirror of Society'. I was delighted to address an erudite audience of about fifty resident scholars of the Centre, from different countries, pursuing their own varied channels of research.

1978—International Documentary Seminar, Alma Ata

When the Soviet authorities invited me to spend a few days in Alma Ata, capital of Kazakhstan, to address an international seminar on documentary films, although it was extempore and I don't have a copy, I do remember what I said, tongue in cheek, 'I suppose it is difficult to be a documentary-film-maker in the Soviet Union, because after all your country has no more social or human problems. Everything has been solved! The communist utopia that has been achieved is unlikely to be dramatic enough in the absence of social conflict to make a film on any current issue!' I also paid tributes to what the Soviet state had achieved. But I expressed my apprehension by citing this example.

A husband-and-wife team from East Germany had made a six-hour documentary titled *The Russian Miracle* on the birth of the Soviet Union, documenting the condition of Russia under the czar and the changes that had taken place bringing the story to the 1960s. I saw this whole film with great interest and I asked at the end of the show whether the film-makers had not heard at all of a man called Joseph Stalin. Stalin had been blacked out in the whole narrative of the film as per the new policy of the Soviet regime.

1981—IIC, Strasbourg Conference

The International Institute of Communications of London had organized a conference in 1981 at the European Parliament Building in Strasbourg, France. We were only four Indians participating in the conference—I.K. Gujral (soon after demitting his office as ambassador to the USSR), Parthasarathy, a media man from Bengaluru, Mohana and me. There were about five hundred delegates from around the world. Mohana and I arrived there after she had addressed a Nutrition Congress at San Diego.

When my turn came and I had just begun my address, unexpectedly I.K. Gujral got up from the front row and got the permission of the chairperson to say a few words. Very graciously, he said, 'I want to add to the introduction given about my colleague from India since what the announcer said was just formal.' He went on to make a brief but impressive introduction mentioning *Indus Valley to Indira Gandhi,* a few of my short films and my book *Indian Film.*

Later, when I thanked him for this very beautiful gesture, Gujral said, 'Very often Indians suffer from their egos to introduce their distinguished friends from their own country. It looks as though Indians always compete with one another for attention in international forums. I wanted to ensure that you get the best audience attention by intervening with those words because promoting a deserving fellow Indian is promoting India.' It was a truthful statement since I have noticed in many other places that Indians suffer from complexes that prevent them from giving due importance to their colleagues.

After I completed my speech of about fifteen minutes, in the interactive session someone asked, 'Is it true that film stars enjoy high political status in India?' and I replied, 'Well, I am glad Walt Disney was not born in India, although, surely I am an admirer of that genius. My reservation is that if he had been born in India, Mickey Mouse would have become one of our tallest political leaders.' There was roaring laughter in the audience, because only a few months earlier, Ronald Reagan had been elected President of America and most of the audience (unfamiliar with the Indian scene) thought that I was digging at him.

1983—Mass Media Foundation, Chennai

In 1983, the Mass Media Foundation organized a national seminar on documentary films at Krishnaswamy Associates in Chennai, which was attended by a few delegates from Germany and others from around the country, including non-fiction film pioneers such as Fali Bilimoria, Clement Baptista and Hari Dasgupta, besides Sai Paranjpye, Aravindan and Aruna Vasudev; I.K. Gujral not only inaugurated the seminar, but also attended all the sessions of the four-day seminar. Max Mueller Bhavan, Chennai, extended their cooperation by hosting all the delegates and getting Christine Grote of West German Television as a guest speaker. Films of the participants were also screened. Although I was the chairman of the Mass Media Foundation, organizing such a seminar was really A.R. Baji's brainchild. It was possibly the first time that such a meeting was held by a non-governmental organization in India, seeking greater recognition for non-fiction films. The participants resolved at the end of the seminar that an international documentary festival should be hosted by India and that the Films Division should take that responsibility. Those of us who moved this idea were gratified when the Government of India supported the idea of the Films Division organizing international festival of documentary films every alternate year in Mumbai, soon thereafter.

1983—AMIC

The Asian Mass Communication Research Institute (AMIC), Singapore, invited me to chair the session on 'Film as Communication' in their international seminar at the University of Chiang Mai. Coming soon after our round-the-world trip, Mohana felt like spending time with the children and did not travel with me. In that first visit to Thailand, I spent a few days in the beautiful hill resort of Chiang Mai. While I thoroughly enjoyed the academic atmosphere at the seminar, I also came to see the other side of the coin. Although exposed to the nightclubs at Paris and New York, the utterly repulsive commoditization of the female body in Chiang Mai came as a disgusting shock. I was told that it was only an extension of the call girl culture of Bangkok—fine-tuned in the holiday resort. A professor at the university escorted all of us—international delegates—to introduce us to this aspect of Thailand in a hotel of sorts. Several very scantily dressed and some totally nude girls were seated in voluptuous postures in a gallery with price tags. Clients booked the product(s) of their choice and took them to their rooms. Apparently because of the local professor's presence, our group was allowed in as spectators of the show.

1995—IAMHIST at Gutenberg

In 1995, the International Association for Audiovisual Media in Historical Research (IAMHIST) organized a seminar and screening of some newsreels and documentaries at Gutenberg in Germany. Mohana and I screened a few of our films including *Through a Different Lens* (1987) on the role of Indian cinema in the freedom struggle and *Unknown Freedom Fighters* (1976). The major theme of the conference was how cinema contributed to political perceptions in the years before and during the Second World War. Some documentaries like my film explained the role of cinema in politics while others were themselves examples of how governments and political parties have used cinema as major tools of subliminal propaganda—very often portraying half-truths or just lies. Several such newsreels and documentaries of the Second World War Era were screened which created hatred against the enemy country—films made by the Allies against Germany and those made by the Germans against the Allies. The seminar strengthened my views that cinema—fiction or non-fiction—was generally not truthful to history—save with great exceptions.

After the seminar, Mohana and I took a train for a visit to Denmark for a few days before we reached Paris to attend another informative and enjoyable IQ conference.

1998—International Documentary Symposium, Hollywood

The International Documentary Association (IDA) which has its headquarters in Los Angeles invited me to address their International Documentary Symposium in 1998, in the historic auditorium where Oscars are presented. My cartoon *With Apologies to Tagore* was also screened there.

ANNEXURE-2A

A ROADMAP TO REFORMING ELECTIONS[53]

In India, politics breaks the law of gravity—for it leaks more from the top than from the bottom. The cancer of corruption is eroding the country. We need significant systemic changes to control it. A fundamental change required is in the electoral system.

It is a public secret that the amount of money spent in elections by any candidate is many times in excess of the legal ceiling. Since political parties have their own vote banks, elections are decided by the marginal voters, whose votes are purchased, vitiating the entire electoral process. To raise the resources required for this, the candidates need to have either accumulated unaccounted wealth or get the support of people who can fund elections out of their illicit money. Thus, the role of black money to win elections is the dominant cause for corruption.

Having inherited the British model, we have also adopted their 'First Past the Post' (FPTP) electoral system in which the 'winner takes all' and the opposing candidates get nothing even if they lose by very small margins. Hypothetically, if there are hundred voters in your constituency and on an average if sixty people turn out to vote, often a candidate for whom twenty-three out of these sixty people have voted gets elected since the balance thirty-seven are split between more than one opposition candidate. This would mean that the elected representative really represents only 23 per cent of the total electorate. The balance 77 per cent have no voice to represent them in the next five years. In typical results from an FPTP election there is a serious mismatch between the vote share and the seat share of all the parties.

Several democratic countries have adopted 'proportional

---

[53] Abridged version of S. Krishnaswamy's article in *The Indian Express*, September 2011

representation' (PR). Briefly, under the PR system, if there are four parties contesting and they get 40, 30, 20 and 10 per cent of votes polled throughout a state, respectively, their parties will get proportionately 40, 30, 20 and 10 seats in an assembly of a hundred seats in the proportion in which they have polled the popular votes. This means that every voter is represented in the assembly and not merely those whose candidate wins as in the FPTP system.

Among the democratic countries, sixty-eight nations have the FPTP system, while ninety-three follow one form or another of PR. In the FPTP system, a large percentage of voters feel that their votes are wasted on losing candidates. Thus, there is no motivation for the voter to go to the polling booth and exercise his franchise. On the other hand, in the PR system everybody's vote counts in electing a representative, and there is motivation to exercise his/her franchise.

In the Swedish Parliament (elected by PR), women get 40–45 per cent of the seats. Indeed PR will give better representation to all kinds of scattered minority groups across the country, since they will get a cumulative strength based on the votes polled in various constituencies across the country or across a state. In South Africa they have differences on the basis of race besides strong tribal loyalties. Due to PR, South Africans belonging to many tribes are happily forced to work together on issues that divided them during the century of apartheid. All their tribes have the satisfaction of being represented in Parliament.

In the PR system, since politics becomes 'issue based', there will be no need for expenses on an exorbitant scale to win elections. It will be impractical to buy the whole country or buy a whole state in favour of a party. Thus, circulation of black money will reduce.

If there is a party which does not command a majority in a pocket, but has a widespread following throughout the country or a region, in the FPTP system it does not get represented at all in Parliament or assembly. On the contrary, in the PR system such minorities will find their voice heard in the halls of the Parliament and legislatures. In short, the FPTP system penalizes parties with broad but scattered public support and favours locally powerful candidates, whose strength may be derived typically on the basis of caste, family clout, or money and muscle power. It results in parties being forced to nominate locally powerful candidates with criminal or corrupt records

However, there is an inherent weakness in PR, for it will eliminate the direct relationship of voters with their elected representatives. This defect is avoided in the 'Mixed-Member Proportional Representation' (MMPR), which works in a manner wherein half the number of the elected representatives will be elected in the conventional FPTP system. Hypothetically, if there are hundred seats in a legislative assembly in the old system, these hundred constituencies will be subject to delimitation by which there will be fifty constituencies merging two old constituencies into one.

These fifty larger constituencies will elect fifty MLAs by the FPTP system. Each voter will have two votes: one vote for the candidate in his individual name and the other vote for a party without any individual name. Thus, a voter will have the choice to vote for a particular candidate, irrespective of the party to which she or he belongs. The same voter may vote either for the same party or for a different party while exercising the franchise for the 'party vote'.

After accommodating the fifty candidates who have won directly on the FPTP model, the balance fifty seats will be allotted on the basis of PR by compensatory allocation of seats. So if one crore people vote for a hundred-member assembly, the results would be thus.

Party A may have won twenty-seven seats out of the fifty

for which individual candidates have contested. But it may have won forty lakh votes in the name of the party, which is 40 per cent of the total votes polled, and hence the party is entitled to forty seats. Since the party candidates have won twenty-seven seats, the balance thirteen will be given as compensatory PR seats. These thirteen are to be chosen from the list of candidates given by the party, published by it in advance. Thus, for getting 40 per cent of the votes polled, Party A will get forty seats—twenty-seven directly elected and the balance thirteen under PR. Party B, with a widespread presence in all the constituencies, may have won only fifteen seats, although with a popular vote of thirty lakh. This will entitle the party to have thirty seats. Hence, fifteen additional seats will be given to the party based on the party list. When no party obtains a legislative majority on its own, coalitions are the only way to form a government. In the FPTP system, a coalition government may not at all represent the majority of the voters. But a coalition government formed on the MMPR will surely have the electoral mandate, as otherwise they would not be able to form the government.

In 1999, the Law Commission stated that 'a combination of present FPTP with a List System may best meet our needs'. By list system, the Law Commission meant the PR system with a list of party candidates. Indeed, the CPI(M) committed itself to electoral reforms including PR with partial list system in its 1999 election manifesto. At the other end of the political spectrum, in 1996, Vajpayee himself reflected BJP support when he said, 'The present FPTP system weakens the representative character of elective bodies. This anomaly needs to be corrected by introducing PR in at least 50 per cent of the total number of seats in the Lok Sabha.'

However, to get the advantage of the MMPR proposal, the democratic functioning of parties themselves becomes imperative. These parties need to be governed on principles of internal democracy. For this, we need legislation on the lines of the Political Parties Act in Germany. The law should govern matters related to membership; regular election of office bearers by secret ballot; and fair and democratic choice of candidates of the party list for PR purposes.

Incidentally, changing to the MMPR system requires no constitutional amendment. Just a change in the Representation of Peoples Act by a simple majority in Parliament can revolutionize the entire political process, improve governance and substantially diminish the use of black money in elections.

ANNEXURE-3

REVIEWS OF THE FIRST EDITION

Indian Film
By Erik Barnouw and S. Krishnaswamy

Immensely readable; a richly alive and instructive book.
—Washington Post

The book should have a lasting usefulness as a handy reference volume. The growing numbers of students who study the cinema as a medium of international communication must find this rewarding stuff. Certainly among the more cerebral denizens of our own US production complexes, many will read Indian Film *with fascination and respect.*
—Variety

Since it is without a peer, it is the book about moving pictures in India.
—AV Communication Review

As regional and national cultures interpenetrate in the emergence of a global community, we shall be fortunate if we have more clear solid books like this.
—Annals of the American Academy of Political and Social Science

Recommended for all film history collections.
—The Library Journal

India's gigantic film industry has been considerably neglected as a field of study and research and the public will be grateful for this analytical yet highly readable survey.

—The Hindu

The story of the industry's development, including its relationship to historic and social currents is fascinatingly told in this informative volume.

—The Hollywood Reporter

ANNEXURE-4

AYURVEDA'S ANSWER TO THE CHALLENGE OF CANCER?

Lecture delivered by
Mohana Krishnaswamy
At the Central Council of Ayurveda and Siddha (CCRAS)
New Delhi, 1985

As every aspect of traditional culture, arts and crafts suffered during the two centuries of colonial exploitation, Indian systems of medicine, including Ayurveda and Siddha, suffered a terrible blow. Western medicine had to its credit a contemporary scientific approach as well as economic and political patronage. The Western systems overshadowed the Indian systems of medicine not merely by a new level of efficacy, but also by a substantial support of glamour and propaganda. During the freedom struggle (and more so after independence) a movement strengthened for the revival of Ayurveda and its widespread practise in a modern form.

Textual references are there that the Ayurvedic system within itself is not a complete solution or remedy for all the diseases encountered and recognized by society. Diseases including tuberculosis, diabetes, leprosy, etc., are some of the fatal diseases (maharogas) for which even the best votaries of the Ayurvedic system could not assure a radical cure. A society which believed in reincarnation consoled itself that these maharogas are incurable and are the direct result of one's actions in previous lives (karma-phala). This belief retarded further progress in the treatment in these areas.

Rejoicing in our glorious past, we have remained dormant for many centuries. With the advent of modern drug therapy in the allopathic system of medicine for radical cure of diseases, which were considered incurable in Ayurveda, there is a gradual awareness regarding the scope for further improvement both in methodology and drug therapy. The most conservative amongst the traditional systems of medicines also admit this.

The renaissance in the traditional systems of medicine has flared up after the world was thrilled by the isolation of reputed chemotherapeutic agents, such as reserpine, berberine, khellin, podophyllotoxin, maytansine, etc., from popular drugs used in the traditional systems of medicine.

Three primary goals of research have been identified in this context: first, established Ayurvedic drugs have to be subjected to tests on modern parameters to ensure their efficacy for the diseases for which they have been traditionally prescribed; second, because the systems of practice in Ayurveda and Siddha have been shrouded in mystery and secrecy in different parts of the country and the methods of drug production have varied from place to place, it has become essential to standardize the ingredients and the proportions in which they are utilized in the manufacture of every given Ayurvedic drug; third, and a very important area, it is recognized that like any other science, Ayurveda has to have expanding horizons.

No science can stagnate based on ancient research and work done; Ayurveda cannot confine itself merely to the drugs and formulations discovered centuries ago. It is essential to develop new ones and find new applications for existing Ayurvedic drugs. For example, while Vinca rosea has been traditionally prescribed in Ayurvedic literature as a curative for diabetes, the alkaloids derived from this plant are now used as chemotherapeutic agents in the treatment of certain types of cancer.

In spite of the fact that modern systems of medicine have taken advantage of the latest technological innovations, cancer is even today an unsolved problem and a very painful disease. The present modalities of treatment are surgery, radiation therapy, immunotherapy and chemotherapy.

The first two modalities of treatment cannot be applied where the disease has spread throughout the body. Immunotherapy is still in its infancy. The present chemotherapeutic agents have been developed on the theory that the cytotoxicity of a compound is the reason for its success in the treatment of cancer. This is because cancer itself is defined as an uncontrolled mitosis of the cells. A cytotoxic compound naturally will have very dangerous side effects which is the weak point in the present chemotherapy of cancer. Most of these compounds are synthetics. At the Captain Srinivasamurthy Drug Research Institute at Chennai we have been screening a wide variety of plants for potential anticancer activity. The active principle includes both alkaloids and non-alkaloids. Among the large number of plants screened in our experience we found a few which have shown promise in their anticancer activity. The alkaloids so tested include Echitamine chloride from Alstonia scholaris and STG from Solanum trilobatum. The non-alkaloids include plumbagin from Plumbacio zeylanica and arbotristoside from Nyctanthis arbotristotis. After successfully completing preclinical research which is at par with international standards, the next logical step is to put these chosen promising anticancer drugs to clinical trial.

In this process of graduating to clinical trial, we should keep these factors in mind: first, to formulate clinical trials which will give truthful, credible results acceptable to the international scientific community; second, to ensure the drug remains Indian and Ayurvedic by the specificity of its formulation, consistent with age-old accepted Ayurvedic tradition, such as vehicle for the delivery of the drug; third, the clinical trial should be completed in a reasonable time so that the successful drug can be launched to alleviate suffering patients as early as practicable. To achieve this, it is essential that Ayurvedic physicians with a modern bent of mind and paramedical specialists in pure science with intrinsic respect for Ayurveda should work in cooperation to achieve results.

An important legal aspect also deserves to be discussed in this context. According to the present law, an Ayurvedic formulation can be manufactured and marketed only if it is a crude extract and only when it is supported by textual reference. As I mentioned earlier, no science can afford to stagnate based on ancient texts alone. The moment we accept research in Ayurveda, it is a logical corollary that we accept the modern scientific papers published by our generation as acceptable textual reference. Hence, the scope of textual reference acceptable for legal purposes to define an Ayurvedic drug should include all the publications of the CCRAS and comparable organizations of national stature in medical research. The idea that crude extract alone is to be accepted as an Ayurvedic drug needs re-examination. For instance, a pure chemical extract hypothetically may prove effective with Ayurvedic vehicles traditionally recommended.

Thus, to help expand the horizons of Ayurveda it is necessary that we change the obscurantist legal definitions. If we fail to do so, the results of contemporary research in Ayurveda may end up as allopathic drugs without due credit to the native genius of the Ayurvedic systems.

ANNEXURE-5

REPORT AND RECOMMENDATIONS* BASED ON MY VISIT TO IMPLAD AND OTHER INSTITUTIONS CONNECTED WITH TRADITIONAL MEDICINE IN CHINA

Presented by Mohana Krishnaswamy to the Secretary Ministry of Health, Government of India, April—May, 1985

During a discussion with her at Beijing, Sarala Grewal, the Secretary, Ministry of Health, suggested my giving her a report of specific recommendations emanating from my China visit.

I received an invitation from the Institute of Medicinal Plant Development (IMPLAD), Beijing, to visit China for three weeks as their guest. My interests were generally to understand:

- the levels of efficacy of the traditional Chinese medicine.
- the methodology used by the Chinese to test and utilize their traditional systems.
- the level of research and the direction of research in these sciences.

Naturally, I was more specifically concerned to observe any ongoing research they had in anticancer drugs and antifertility drugs, since I am personally involved in these specific fields of research. I collected much scientific material related to these fields.

I visited these institutions related to my field of interest in three cities (Beijing, Nanjing and Guangdong) and their neighbourhood.

- IMPLAD, Chinese Academy of Medical Sciences, Beijing
- Institute of Materia Medica, Beijing
- Institute of Medicine Control, Beijing

- College of Pharmacy, Nanjing
- Jinangsu Institute of Botany, Nanjing
- Institute of Materia Medica, Nanjing
- Botanical Garden
- Medical Pharmaceutical College, Guangdong
- Municipal Drug Control Institute of Guangdong
- College of Traditional Chinese Medicine, Guangdong
- South China Botanical Garden
- Baiyunshan Pharmaceutical Plant
- South China Botanical Institute

I delivered two formal lectures at the IMPLAD, Beijing, and at the Institute of Materia Medica, Nanjing.

My first impressions are that health care in China is based on a well-knit clear-cut policy. The national policy of including Chinese traditional medicine with Western allopathic systems is reflected all round, right from medical education to delivery of medicare. Although there are independent graduate courses for traditional medicine and modern medicine, students of either system are supposed to know the rudiments of the other and respect the systems and values of all the systems. The national health policy is designed in such a fashion that the traditional and modern systems of medicine are made use of in specific fields without distinguishing between them in terms of status. The facilities for research given for either system are equal in terms of resources of finance and manpower. The graduates of modern medicine go through a refresher course in traditional medicine, and vice versa. Both the systems of medicine are practised in the major hospitals all over China. The patient is admitted for treatment under one system or the other based on the common experience of the hospital in terms of the system which is likely to have more efficacy for the concerned ailment.

We find a cordial relationship between the scientists and doctors practising the different systems of medicine.

In choosing the drugs and therapy based on ancient Chinese systems, the government has largely gone by the experience of the system without trying to put every drug or every method of therapy to test on the parameters of modern test systems. However, in terms of research, it is recognized that traditional medicine is not a static system. It requires innovation and research directed of:

- standardizing drugs;
- evolution of new drugs;
- discovering new methodologies of manufacture; and
- popularizing the system beyond the national borders of China.

Both research and marketing of traditional drugs are taken up in an aggressive manner. Since there is no discrimination between laboratories based on Western systems and those based on traditional Chinese systems, the infrastructural facilities given to research organizations of both the systems are comparable and on par with similar institutions around the world. This has resulted in the involvement of modern scientists with no inhibition to work for research in the traditional systems.

Although it is not my intention to compare with our own conditions, it becomes essential to make such a comparison; not with any intention to complain or with any attitude to be hypercritical, but to present certain facts that inhibit research in traditional medicine in our conditions. As much research in modern medicine is to be carried out by a team of specialists in pure science with the involvement of practising physicians—limited to that of clinical trials—it is essential that research in traditional systems of medicine is also carried out by a team of scientists with the involvement of practising indigenous physicians—at the time of clinical trial. Modern medicine and drugs are formulated in the laboratories of pharmaceutical organizations and universities where the involvement of practising physicians is minimal and incidental. In the Chinese situation, the same model has been adopted for research in Chinese traditional medicine as well. However, in our conditions in India, councils meant for research in Ayurveda and Siddha and other traditional medical systems are guided by practising physicians of the traditional systems. The specialists in pure science have been relegated to a secondary position. To practitioners of the traditional system, medicine is as much a faith as a science. Obviously, scientific research cannot fructify in such an atmosphere, since the spirit of science may at times question the faith—analyse and not necessarily accept.

The major lesson to be learnt from the Chinese experience is to place our own research institutions related to traditional medicine on par with the institutions involved in research in modern medicine.

The Botanical Gardens in China have specialized sections devoted to medicinal plants. The IMPLAD itself has got a vast area of about 200 acres of a medicinal plant farm where a variety of medicinal plants are grown. China has not only identified but has access to over 5,000 medicinal plants. The Chinese have published an exhaustive book of pharmacopoeia with detailed descriptions and illustrations. The interdisciplinary work carried out in some of the institutions I visited is truly remarkable. The facilities created for such interdisciplinary research at these institutions is far superior to the facilities available in any unit of the CCRAS. The Chinese facilities for research in traditional medicine are of the same standard as in the ICMR, CSIR and the national laboratories of India.

The Chinese institutions concentrate on these.

1. Standardization of drugs that are already in vogue in the

traditional systems. In this context, probably the work being done in India is already in the right direction.
2. The Chinese institutions have developed facilities for several technologies to be involved in research. For instance, there are exhaustive facilities for tissue culture of concerned plants. We have no comparable facility in any unit of the CCRAS.

For example, hypothetically, if we find that the root of particular plant is of medicinal significance it is now possible in a tissue culture laboratory to grow the cells of the roots alone in large proportion. This facilitates:

a. Research with abundant quantity of a specific material without going through the whole process of cultivating plants, harvesting and utilizing the roots alone.
b. In the case of a sensitive plant product, it is possible to grow it in a tissue culture laboratory on a commercial scale, irrespective of the origin of the plant and geographical factors, such as climate, season, soil, etc.

In other words, medicinal plants of tropical and subtropical origin, desert origin as well as Himalayan origin can not only be tested but commercially produced in well-equipped tissue culture laboratories in any part of the world. The institutions of research involved in Chinese traditional medicine have given due importance to this aspect. Isolated academic and research institutes in India have these facilities too. However, since they are not integrated or oriented to the specific objectives of research in Indian indigenous medicine, there is a lacuna.

Assuming that we discover a very important plant product of international medical significance, the absence of tissue culture facilities will inhibit our producing the material indigenously. A more advanced country will be able to import a small quantity from an Indian source and subsequently be able to not only experiment but commercially produce the relevant plant tissue by the tissue culture method. Hence, it is imperative that we develop this facility of our own. The most ideal unit of the CCRAS in India to develop this infrastructure is the CSMDRI, Chennai.

Clinical trial facilities: The Chinese have evolved and perfected a chain system of inbuilt facilities for research under one umbrella. For instance, a drug which is found effective in preclinical trials, such as animal experiments, is put through clinical trial without any loss of time, since the same apex body controls such hospital facilities. The moment it is found to be effective in animal models, it is put through clinical trial under modern parameters. A few drugs of this nature are already in the domestic market. Unfortunately, in our conditions, there is a long gap between various stages of research due to a lack of coordination between different disciplines and organizations that should collaborate. Let me take the liberty of citing an example. I have been involved in research in tumour biology at the CSMDRI for about seven years now. I have tested over forty plant products and extracts in animal experiments. Two such drugs are very promising in results obtained so far in animal systems— Plumbagin derived from Plumbago zeylanica and Echitamine Chloride extracted from Alstonia scholaris. Since the regression in induced tumour in the animals was impressive at our institute, we continued and carried on with other pharmacological work, including toxicity studies. The time arrived for the drug to be put through clinical trials more than two years ago. However, since no system exists of handing over, from one stage to the next in a systematic manner, clinical trials have *not* been undertaken till now. In the absence of facilities for this within the institute or related organizations, a dialogue was started with the Amla Cancer Hospital, a private Christian missionary hospital in Trichur, Kerala. The hospital authorities agreed to put our drug through clinical trial, subject to their getting a small grant per patient from the CCRAS. Administrative financial sanction has not so far arrived from the CCRAS for this.

May I take this opportunity to appeal that the concerned sanction may please be expedited to enable the much-delayed clinical trials to start? Without meaning any offence, may I say I am doing what an individual scientist can do to pursue a research goal, under a difficult environment. Even my travel to Trichur to negotiate and organize a clinical trial has been at my own cost, since I am only an honorary consultant and the CCRAS did not agree to pay my first-class train fare.

In running from pillar to post for getting clinical trials done, these weaknesses are unavoidable.

We locate a hospital which may or may not be as involved as our own organizations in the project we assign. When a clinical trial takes place in a hospital attached to the Research Institution, constant coordination between the physicians and the scientists is much more practical than when the clinical trial takes place in a distant hospital.

However, until such time that a more satisfactory arrangement is made for such clinical trials, it is essential to go ahead with what is possible, without loss of time.

ANNEXURE-6

STATUS OF RESEARCH IN AYURVEDA[54]
by Mohana Krishnaswamy

As every aspect of traditional culture, arts and crafts suffered during the two centuries of colonial exploitation, Indian systems of medicine such as Ayurveda and Siddha suffered a terrible blow. Western medicine had to its credit a contemporary scientific approach as well as economic and political patronage. The Western systems overshadowed the Indian systems of medicine not merely by a new level of efficacy, but also by a substantial support of glamour and propaganda. During the freedom struggle (and more so after independence), a movement strengthened for the revival of Ayurveda, and its widespread practice in a modern form.

Recognizing the need for modern scientific research in this discipline, the Government of India created the CCRAS. The Council has got more than two hundred units involved in research and development in different parts of India.

Three primary goals of research have been identified in this context: first, established Ayurvedic drugs have to be subjected to tests on modern parameters to ensure their efficacy for the diseases for which they have been traditionally prescribed; second, because the systems of practice in Ayurveda and Siddha have been shrouded in mystery and secrecy in different parts of the country and the methods of drug production have varied from place to place, it has become essential to standardize the ingredients and in what proportions are they utilized in the manufacture of every given Ayurvedic drug; third, in a very important area, it is recognized that like any other science,

---

[54]Published in *The Hindu* on Sunday, 14 December 1986

Ayurveda has to have expanding horizons.

No science can stagnate based on ancient research and work done. Ayurveda cannot confine itself merely to the drugs and formulations discovered centuries ago. It is essential to develop new ones and find new applications for existing Ayurvedic drugs. For example, while Vinca rosea has been traditionally prescribed in Ayurvedic literature as a curative for diabetes, the alkaloids derived from this plant are now used as chemotherapeutic agents in the treatment of certain types of cancer. Similarly, in the personal research work of this author, she has found that a chemical extract from the plant Plumbago zeylanica (agni in Sanskrit and chitramoloom in Tamil) is now found to be a promising cure for certain types of cancer, although Ayurvedic and Siddha literature prescribes this drug for leprosy and as an abortifacient agent.

There is hardly any recognition of the importance of the research that is being done in these fields of medicine. If research shows that a traditional drug is effective, the Ayurvedic physician says that there is nothing new in the research since this has been known for centuries. If, on the other hand, the research shows that the drug is not efficacious, then the result is often unacceptable to the traditional physician who considers it sacrosanct, since the ancient literature is considered sacred. Despite the revival of interest in Indian arts and Indian cultural environment, unfortunately there has not been adequate revival of interest in Indian medicine—an important branch of Indian culture. The glamour attached to the modern medical profession takes away the best of students to learn allopathic systems of medicine, not attracting the best of talents to learn traditional Ayurvedic systems of medicine.

Although we have heard for over half a century that the spirit of India lies in our villages, that 80 per cent of our people live in the villages, and although we know that a very substantial percentage of our population is even today treated effectively with our traditional medicines, these realities are not reflected in the budgets allotted for research in Ayurveda. The quantum of allocations for research in Ayurveda is disproportionately small compared to the allocations made for research in allopathic systems of medicine in our country. For instance, the facilities enjoyed by the Indian Council of Medical Research (ICMR) are enviable compared to the meagre facilities that are given to the various research institutions under the CCRAS.

This author found during a visit to the People's Republic of China that the Chinese have well-developed traditional systems of medicine and that there is much greater respect for these systems and a greater empathy between the practitioners of modern medicine and those of traditional Chinese medicine. The facilities provided for research in traditional medicine are comparable not merely with those provided in the Chinese institutions of modern medicine, but also those available in the institutions of modern medical research in any part of the world. The scientist under the CCRAS in India has to go from pillar to post to find meagre funds to pursue follow-up action for clinical trials of drugs which have proved efficacious in the pre-clinical trials. In similar circumstances, the laboratories involved in research in Chinese traditional medicine are streamlined in such a manner that in any assembly line kind of operation it is possible to try out a chemical which is potentially interesting, proceeding from stage one to stage two, to stage three, within one campus, so that an effective drug can be produced and brought to the market within a reasonable time.

The prejudices and compartmentalization of science is so extreme in our context that the facilities of the ICMR and CSIR are not available to the scientists of the CCRAS. Even if our budgetary constraints are such that duplication of such facilities is not always practical, at least an atmosphere must be nurtured by which these scientists can exchange and share facilities.

Not that our country is lacking either in scientific talent or in worthwhile scientific research at the fundamental level, but that in the absence of a holistic approach to scientific research we are in a sense subsidizing a new colonial exploitation of research in our traditional medicine. To cite an instance, a researcher at a national laboratory isolated a chemical from an Ayurvedic plant during the early 1960s. His work was properly published in scientific journals. In a more developed country, such a result would have immediately been taken up for further work, such as establishing a proper procedure to maximize the extraction of the chemical from the plant source and obtaining a commercial patent so that the material can be brought to profitable utilization. However, the scientists of the national laboratory concerned did not have the environment to do this. As a result, a multinational company operating in India took over the procedure, developed it in its own laboratory and has perfected the technique of obtaining maximum yield of the chemical from the plant. Giving it a commercial name, the company has been able to export large quantities of this chemical of purely Indian plant origin. But the original extraction of this chemical is made by an Indian scientist in an Indian laboratory. However, the commercial exploitation of this has been taken up by a multinational company. There is nothing illegal about what the multinational is doing, because it is entirely the lacuna in the Indian scientific environment by which we let go opportunities of this kind. Hence, what is potentially a profitable research venture slides into an unproductive exercise owing to the lack of follow-up; facilities in the research institutions; and political and bureaucratic will and understanding to support research all the way to its logical conclusion.

A review of the total situation relating to research in Indian medical systems has to be taken up at the highest levels of government with experts being called in to advise and formulate a new set of policies which redirect the entire functioning of these institutions in a more productive and scientific manner for the benefit of India and for the benefit of mankind. At the moment, these institutions are adolescent. We needed these four decades after independence to stabilize our position and become mature. But at some point in time it is necessary to become mature; and it is better that it is done sooner than later.

ANNEXURE-7

WILL AYURVEDA BE HIJACKED?[55]

The science of Ayurveda rests on the wealth of India's biological diversity. Many fear that the developing countries will lose control over their genetic material if intellectual property rights become a force. These fears are unfounded but makes a case for protecting a nation's traditional knowledge.

The signing of the agreement of intellectual property rights has raised several questions in the field of Ayurveda and other holistic systems of Indian medicine. A wide range of wild fears has been expressed, including multinationals may copy the formula of effective Indian indigenous drugs and patent them as their own; plant formulations may be patented in an unscrupulous manner by transnational pharmaceutical companies; a situation may arise by which Indians may have to pay royalty to a foreign organization to manufacture and use native medicines.

A renowned scientist even went to the extent of stating last year, 'It may be essential to document the DNA fingerprints of major medicinal herbs of Indian origin and protect them by claiming copyright on them—perhaps by assigning such copyrights to a charitable Indian organization to protect the Indian medical legacy.'

A study of the provisions of the intellectual property rights under the Uruguay Round Agreement reveals that the fears about Ayurvedic drugs being hijacked by foreign vested interests are unfounded. However, it is equally true that a balanced approach to the problem is essential to safeguard Indian national interests.

Intellectual property consists mainly of two branches, namely, industrial property generally in respect of technological

---

[55]Published in *The Hindu* on Sunday, 26 January 1997

inventions, industrial designs, and scientific formulations; and copyright mainly in literary, music and other artisteic endeavours.

The principal objective in protecting intellectual property is to encourage creative activity by giving due recognition to the creators, and by providing them a suitable monetary reward for their innovations, thereby preventing others from using such products without compensating the creators of such technical or aesthetic products.

None of the medications traditionally mentioned in our ancient literature can be patented by anybody now claiming proprietary rights over any of them as long as such a medicine is manufactured according to the tradition-bound systems and formula of manufacture. However, any improvement or variation of an existing formula entitles the author of such change to apply for a patent. The exclusive rights conferred by a patent relate to the commercial exploitation of an invention. Such rights are granted on a technical and not on a market-need basis.

The problem with Ayurvedic pharmacopoeia is that ancient literature uses terminology that is sometimes shrouded in mystery giving rise to more than one interpretation.

The identification of the plant recommended in the literature becomes difficult under such circumstances. The traditional nomenclature for plants sometimes indicates a group of plants with comparable medicinal properties, but which may otherwise be very different from one another: by local custom and experience, the correct plants are identified by vaidyas.

Organizations such as the CCRAS have been labouring for a few decades with the problem of standardizing these drugs. The DNA-fingerprinting of medicinal herbs acquires importance in the context of identification of different plants for medicinal use—the traditional Sanskrit or Tamil terminology with the corresponding Latin nomenclature for the same plant. The question of DNA-fingerprinting for the purpose of establishing a patent will arise only in the case of creating a new plant species in the laboratory by a recombinant DNA technology and by establishing the medicinal use of such a new laboratory-produced species.

Given these circumstances, Indian scientists and traditional Ayurvedic physicians can have no quarrel with modern scientific organizations, whether in India or abroad, extending the horizons of traditional medicines by inventing new formulations of greater efficacy for established diseases; finding new applications of drugs, known earlier for diseases unspecified in ancient literature; improving presentation in the context of modern lifestyles; and patenting such new formulations that are improvements upon and modifications of even well-known drugs.

What is important is that the Indian pharmaceutical industry, practitioners of Indian medicine and scientists associated with indigenous medicine should ensure that such vibrant developments take place within India to capitalize on and be proud of our heritage. If we lose this initiative to foreign scientific organizations and pharmaceutical companies we cannot obviously blame them. For instance, we know of Italian, French and other pharmaceutical companies which approach well-established practitioners of Indian medicine and buy for a pittance formulas of Ayurvedic drugs. A proper coordination of such specialists is needed to ensure that such traditional knowledge is not sold for meagre commercial considerations.

Secondly, the research fraternity should take up work in right earnest within the country in government-owned laboratories and private sector pharmaceutical industry (particularly those specializing in traditional Indian drug manufacture) to ensure that they are competitively competent to produce goods consistent with market needs not only in terms of presentation, but also in terms of quality control, authentic research and the needs of society. If multinationals come forward to improve what is originally an indigenous Indian medicinal preparation by adding or otherwise modifying ingredients and improving efficacy, they cannot be blamed, because ultimately medical science is to work for combating ailments.

National pride will be justified if Indian institutions produce results which can have a global market because India has easier access to information on formulations, a ready force of practitioners and their practical wisdom in relation to traditional medicine, ease of identification of the herbs and their availability combined with better knowledge of methods of cultivation, and trained scientists to update and upgrade the formulation. The question is, whether or not the Indian pharmaceutical industry will rise to the challenge.

Tradition must be understood as an expanding circle. The spirit of enquiry cannot be confined in terms of ancient texts alone. Constant innovation and adaptation to societal needs will keep Ayurveda not merely alive but also vibrant and active. It is important to protect Indian plant species by obtaining a legal ownership patent on their 'genes'. It is equally important to obtain a patent on what may be described as 'ethnic traditional knowledge'.

The convention of biodiversity negotiated at the Earth Summit at Rio de Janeiro recognized for the first time the right of communities 'to free and equitable sharing of benefits arising out of utilization of their genetic resource', as a kind of compensation for the preservation, cultivation and conservation of genetic material over the centuries.

In addition to the intrinsic proprietorial rights of a community over the plant species of its natural habitat, another proprietary right should be deemed attached to the society concerned in respect of the cumulative knowledge of pharmacopoeia, and the practical application of such knowledge in the treatment of ailments, gathered by many generations over several centuries.

One obstacle to this is that the World Trade Organization does not accept a 'community' as a legal entity.

As much as the contemporary international community would like to safeguard the ownership of 'intellectual property', it becomes ethical to safeguard traditional knowledge and plant species as part of the wealth of a nation. A nation's traditional knowledge should be deemed as 'intellectual property' and its plant species and all genetic derivatives of native origin as its 'inherited national property'.

The third world is endowed with such biodiversity. However, it is the prosperous 'Northern' countries which have the scientific know-how to exploit this biodiversity. India is in a unique position, since in terms of its scientific community it is far ahead of several other third world countries.

It is India's duty to protect and preserve the rights of its citizens to own without hindrance the nation's wealth of biodiversity and to enjoy the knowledge handed down over the centuries on the basis of 'possession'.

Mexico has already taken the first step in this direction by entering into an agreement with multinational enterprises (MNEs) recognizing that country's right over genetic resources which may be commercially used by the said MNEs.

Thus, the tropical countries could allow MNEs to work on the genetic material of their countries and identify the useful genes and even help develop a gene bank, on the condition that the country can use the genes and also have a share in their commercial exploitation. The relative values to be allotted in such a situation for criteria such as 'value of genetic resources', 'the value of traditional knowledge to build on', and 'the value of new technical inputs for modern application' are to be carefully weighed, for which a new law should provide the basis. India has to play a crucial and historic role in this.

ANNEXURE-8

MEERA: AN ADVOCATE OF FEMINISM[56]
By Mohana Krishnaswamy

There is, in general, confusion in the Indian mind between history, mythology and religion, relating even to saints and events of recent centuries. In this context, it is the moral responsibility of religious preachers to ensure that they preach positive aspects of their own religion and not descend to mudslinging other religions. It is equally important to ensure the historic authenticity of their narratives.

Being an ardent admirer of the devotional lyrics of Meerabai, I recently attended a Tamil musical discourse (*Kathakalakshepam*) on Meera by a well-known artiste. I was deeply perturbed by the gross misrepresentation of Meera's philosophy as well as misinformation about her in the details of her biography. I perceive Meera as the first advocate of feminism, who stood for bhakti not only as a path of spiritual liberation, but also as a path of liberation from male chauvinism, which was dominant in the Rajput kingdoms of her times. The narrator reduced her stature by treating her as just another stereotype of an 'obedient wife', and gave many unauthentic details of her life, based on hearsay. According to the generally accepted narrative of her biography (despite uncertainties about dates and details), the most dramatic and striking feature of Meera was that she was a widow who did not burn on the funeral pyre of her husband despite it being lit as per the contemporary custom of Rajasthani royal households, and that she continued to write poems of love for her beloved god, Krishna, replete with bhakti and shringara rasas.

---

[56]Published in *The Hindu* on Sunday, 28 December 2008

A Poet and Saint

She could sing not only erotic poems in the midst of an extremely obscurantist atmosphere of male domination, but also become a worshipful saint who has stood the test of time. A musical discourse depicting King Rana Khumba as Meera's husband had provoked me. The artistee eulogized him as one who had admired Meera's bhakti and built a temple for Krishna, for her to worship. The generally accepted version is that the husband (whose name is given as Bhoj Raj) was a Shaivite, who objected to Meera worshipping a Vaishnavite god—Krishna. There is a longing, a pain of separation, combined with surrender to the Lord, in Meera's poetry.

The exponent went on to say that Emperor Akbar, having heard of the reputation of the great poet-queen, went in disguise to her temple to hear her sing. It is believed that Akbar and Meera were contemporaries, and so it is quite possible that the great emperor, who was known for his habit of travelling in disguise, for his attitude of inter-religious harmony and for his love of music, visited her.

Although there is some uncertainty about the exact date of Meera's birth, historians believe that she was about forty years older than Emperor Akbar. The narrator of the evening relied on some obscure sources to say that Meera's husband developed suspicions about Meera's relationship with Akbar. While Akbar, out of his devotion, respect and love for music, may have appeared in disguise in her temple, there is nothing at all to suggest that her husband (who was by then dead according to most versions) suspected her of having a relationship with the Mughal emperor, who was forty years younger to her. The narrator added 'insult to injury' by constantly describing Emperor Akbar as a 'Mlecha'.

Such a derogatory reference to a pan-Indian ruler who contributed a great deal towards inter-religious harmony is condemnable. The narrator, gifted with an excellent voice to render the musical portions of her discourse, has a fluent command over language as well as traditional style of the Harikatha. But it is disturbing to note that such a religious preacher of the younger generation should propagate such intolerant views about other religions, which goes against the grain of Hindu Dharma.

Acknowledgements

I owe a debt of gratitude to the architect of India's Green Revolution; the professor acclaimed by *Time* magazine as one of the twenty most influential Asians of the twentieth century (among them only three from India, the other two being Mahatma Gandhi and Rabindranath Tagore); recipient of seventy-three honorary doctorate degrees from universities around the world besides Padma Vibhushan (India's second highest civilian award); the Ramon Magsaysay Award; Mahatma Gandhi Prize of UNESCO; Albert Einstein's World Science Award and so on—the living legend, Professor M.S. Swaminathan, who has given an exciting Foreword to this book.

I am indeed grateful to my wife, Mohana—the *raison d'etre* of this book—for her suggestions and constructive criticism in finalizing the book.

I thank my secretary, Akila, for patiently taking down my dictation of the first draft of this book in instalments over a period of eighteen months, feeding them into the computer; enabling me to work on the second draft; and for giving a few sensitive reactions, in the midst of her normal reticence—using the opportunity of being the first reader of this book.

I thank *The Hindu* for their gracious permission to reproduce a photograph (of Smt. Sushma Swaraj and me) from *The Business Line* issue of 2001, and to reproduce two paper cuttings from *The Hindu*. I thank Kumar Rajendran of MGR

Janaki College for permission to use the photograph of MGR at Madras airport, giving me a send-off to the USA as a student.

I thank my respected friends N.L. Rajah and Geetha Ramaseshan (senior lawyers) and journalist A.R. Krishnan for reading the draft and giving me valuable feedback.

I am grateful to Dibakar Ghosh (Editorial Director) and Ananya Sharma (Editor) of Rupa Publications for their creative inputs, giving this book its final shape.

S. Krishnaswamy